In Loving Memory of
Dr. Mohan Singhal

Journey of the Soul

Our Websites

www.purebhakti.com
for news, updates, and free downloads of books and lectures

www.harikatha.com
to receive, by email, the lectures and videos of
Śrīla Bhaktivedānta Nārāyaṇa Gosvāmī Mahārāja on his world tours

www.purebhakti.tv
to watch and hear, or to download, classes online

For More Information

If you are interested to know more about the books,
lectures, audios, videos, teachings, and international society of
Śrīla Bhaktivedānta Nārāyaṇa Gosvāmī Mahārāja,
please contact the secretary, Vasanti dāsī, at
connectwithussoon@gmail.com

Contributors

There were many contributors to the completion of Journey of the Soul, in the form of translators, editors and Sanskrit editors, proofreaders, artists, designers, typists and typesetters, and their names are listed here:
Śrīpāda Bhāgavata Mahārāja, Śrīpāda Mādhava Mahārāja; Acyuta dāsa, Ānitā dāsī, Bhakti-latā dāsī, Brajanāth dāsa, Devānanda dāsa, Govinda-priya dāsī, Haladara dāsa, Haridāsa dāsa, Hari-vallabha dāsī, Īśa dāsa, Jāhnavā dāsī, Jaya-gopāla dāsa, Jānakī dāsī, Kṛṣṇa-bhakti dāsī, Kṛṣṇa-kāminī dāsī, Kṛṣṇa-kāruṇya dāsa, Kṛṣṇa-vallabha dāsī, Kumudinī dāsī, Lalitā dāsī, Mana-mohana dāsa, Nārāyaṇī dāsī, Prema-prayojana dāsa, Premavatī dāsī, Rādhikā dāsī, Raghunātha-bhaṭṭa dāsa, Sītā dāsī, Sucitrā dāsī, Sudevī dāsī, Śukada dāsī, Sumaṅgala dāsī, Svāti dāsī, Śyāmarāṇī dāsī, Vaijayantī-māla dāsī, Vasanta dāsa, Vasanti dāsī, Vijaya-kṛṣṇa dāsa, Vṛndāvaneśvari dāsī.

Journey of the Soul

Śrī Śrīmad Bhaktivedānta Nārāyaṇa Gosvāmī Mahārāja

with supportive evidence from
Śrīla Bhaktivinoda Ṭhakūra's
Jaiva-dharma

and the works of
Śrī Śrīmad Bhaktivedānta Svāmī Mahārāja

Graphic design and layout: Haladara dāsa and Kṛṣṇa-kāruṇya dāsa
Paintings on pages 42 and 26 © Śyāmarāṇī dāsī. Used with permission.
Paintings on pages 12, 14, 16, 23, 31, 37, 38, 39, 58, 100, and 101 by Śyāmarāṇī dāsī © BBT International. Used with permission.
Drawings on pages 72, 80, 87, and 192 courtesy Sucitrā dāsī. Used with permission.
Drawings on pages 36 and 55 courtesy Jaya-gopāla dāsa. Used with permission.
Photograph of Śrīla Prabhupāda Bhaktivedānta Svāmī Mahārāja © Bhaktivedanta Book Trust International. Used with permission. www.krishna.com

Journey of the Soul
by Śrī Śrīmad Bhaktivedānta Nārāyaṇa Gosvāmī Mahārāja

First Edition: March 2010 (10,000 copies)
Second Edition: December 2011 (5,000 copies)
Second Edition, Second Printing: September 2015 (5,000 copies)
Printed by: Spectrum Printing Press Pvt. Ltd., New Delhi (India)

ISBN 978-1-935428-19-0

Library of Congress Control Number 2011961330

Cataloging in Publication Data--DK
Courtesy: D.K. Agencies (P) Ltd. <docinfo@dkagencies.com>

Bhaktivedānta Nārāyaṇa 1921-
Journey of the soul / Bhaktivedānta Nārāyaṇa Gosvāmī Mahārāja.
p. cm.
Reprint.
Includes bibliographical references (p.).
ISBN 9781935428190

1. Soul--Hinduism. I. Title.

DDC 294.5 23

Śrī Śrīmad
Bhaktivedānta Nārāyaṇa Gosvāmī Mahārāja

Śrī Śrīmad
Bhaktivedānta Vāmana Gosvāmī Mahārāja

Śrī Śrīmad
Bhaktivedānta Svāmī Mahārāja

Śrī Śrīmad
Bhakti Prajñāna Keśava Gosvāmī Mahārāja

Śrī Śrīmad
Bhaktisiddhānta Sarasvatī Ṭhākura Prabhupāda

Saccidānanda
Śrīla Bhaktivinoda Ṭhākura

TABLE OF CONTENTS

FOREWORD

A NOTE FROM THE EDITORS

"Who am I?"

"Where have I come from?"

"How can I be free from the suffering and limitations imposed upon me by this world?"

"Is there a way for me to attain knowledge of my hidden spiritual self that is beyond the chains of matter?"

"What is my ultimate destination and how do I reach it?"

These questions have been asked by sincere seekers of truth for millennia. According to India's ancient Vedic wisdom, the answers to these timeless questions live in the hearts of great, self-realized spiritual masters. The sages of India have realized these answers through a perfect deductive process, by the transcendental unbroken chain of disciplic succession.

In this connection, consider the analogy of a mango tree. On the top of the mango tree there is a very ripe and delicious fruit. If someone were to drop a fruit from the top of the tree, it would be destroyed. Therefore it is passed from one person on the tree to another, and in this way the mango comes down intact.

The ripe and delicious fruit at the top of the tree is analogous to the Vedic process of divine knowledge, which is descending through transcendental authority, person to person, so that each soul can receive this knowledge gently and with its most powerful effect. *Journey of the Soul* has come in the disciplic line of an ancient succession of spiritual teachers, a spiritual succession whose goal is to assist the soul in his journey to the supreme destination.

About the Author

Śrīla Bhaktivedānta Nārāyaṇa Gosvāmī Mahārāja is recognized by prominent spiritual leaders and hundreds of thousands of spiritual seekers as a realized soul in this unbroken succession of pure spiritual preceptors. He is the foremost disciple of his spiritual master, Śrīla Bhakti Prajñāna Keśava Gosvāmī Mahārāja, and has also received profound instruction from the world-famous preacher of Kṛṣṇa-consciousness and *bhakti-yoga*, Śrīla Bhaktivedānta Svāmī Mahārāja.

Śrīla Bhaktivedānta Nārāyaṇa Gosvāmī Mahārāja is the author's full, respected name, and his honorific title is even longer: Tridaṇḍisvāmī Śrī Śrīmad Bhaktivedānta Nārāyaṇa Gosvāmī Mahārāja. Because we have written his name so many times throughout this book, for ease and accessibility to our readers, we will generally refer to him as Śrīla Nārāyaṇa Gosvāmī Mahārāja.

A scholar of resilient erudition in the field of Vedic wisdom, Śrīla Nārāyaṇa Gosvāmī Mahārāja has been inspiring seekers of spiritual and philosophical truth for over sixty years. He has published dozens of devotional literatures on the timeless science of *bhakti-yoga*, in both Hindi and English, which in turn have been translated into most of the major world languages. At present ninety years old, he continues to lecture around the globe, giving spiritual shelter and guidance to sincere souls. To date he has completed his thirtieth world-preaching tour.

In response to the yearning questions of numerous spiritual aspirants, Śrīla Nārāyaṇa Gosvāmī Mahārāja requested some of his editors to compile a book of his lectures and informal talks on the subject of the eternal soul (*jīva-tattva*) and the individual soul's relationship with the Supreme Soul. In his compassion, he desired that all people become eligible to enter the Lord's kingdom of eternal life in unending bliss and unfathomable knowledge. He wanted to inspire in people's hearts a strong faith in that spiritual kingdom and devotional greed to enter it.

Like other pure masters in his transcendental lineage, Śrīla Nārāyaṇa Gosvāmī Mahārāja wanted to share with his spiritual daughters and sons this understanding: we are not these mortal bodies and this world is not our real home. As eternal parts and parcels of the Lord, who is known throughout the Vedic literature as Śrī Kṛṣṇa, we have manifested from a region between the pure spiritual world and this material netherworld. By proper education we can enter the Lord's abode, our real home, which we have not yet experienced and which is beyond the limit of our imagination.

The Divisions of this Book

Journey of the Soul is divided into three parts. Part One, the main body of the book, consists of selected lectures, interviews, and informal meetings with Śrīla Nārāyaṇa Gosvāmī Mahārāja on the topic of *jīva-tattva*, which were given by him over a span of about twelve years.

As editors, we had two choices in regard to the presentation of the subject matter. We could keep his lectures and discussions, with his points in the order that he spoke them; or we could write our own adaptation, based on his words. Keeping his discussions intact would mean much repetition of ideas. This is because each lecture presented the entire theme of *jīva-tattva*. The lectures were not a development from a previous lecture or interview on the same subject. Also, his words were spoken to live audiences or to individuals, and therefore his language was conversational rather than literary.

If we had chosen the adaptation, we would have made a fully step-by-step development of ideas throughout the book, without repetition of ideas. But then it would be a book written by conditioned souls; it would not have the full potency that this important literature needs in order to inspire and imbue the reader with true spiritual understanding.

We therefore opted to keep Śrīla Nārāyaṇa Gosvāmī Mahārāja's discussions intact, for in that way the potency of the pure devotee is present on each page. We have not presented these lectures and interviews chronologically, but in a manner that best develops the book's theme. With Śrīla Nārāyaṇa Gosvāmī Mahārāja's authorization and guidance we have edited his spoken words for grammatical precision, as English is not his mother tongue. We have also edited them for flow of language, because of the fact that the lectures and interviews were spoken for audiences, not written for pages. Even though you will find repetition of the same theme, we pray that this repetition will serve to clarify the profound message and help you to more easily imbibe the sacred truths herein.

Part Two is an excerpt of three chapters from Śrīla Bhaktivinoda Ṭhākura's book, *Jaiva-dharma*, which elaborates on the subject of *jīva-tattva*, a Sanskrit term that literally means 'the fundamental truth of the eternal spirit soul.' In his own discourses Śrīla Nārāyaṇa Gosvāmī Mahārāja glorifies *Jaiva-dharma*. During one such discourse he said, "If you want to advance in Kṛṣṇa consciousness, try to read this book again and again with very strong faith. In this book you can very easily experience the essence of all Vedic literature; that is, the Vedas, the Upaniṣads, the *Śrīmad-Bhāgavatam*, and the *Śrī Caitanya-caritāmṛta*. Śrīla Bhaktivinoda Ṭhākura has written *Jaiva-dharma* in the form of a dialogue, with questions and profound answers. If you go deep in your reading, so many new spiritual understandings and realizations will come to you. I have personally read *Jaiva-dharma* no less than 108 times."

Part Three of *Journey of the Soul* consists of quotes from the books, lectures, and letters of another divine representative in the Supreme Lord Śrī Kṛṣṇa's personal succession of realized masters, Śrīla Bhaktivedānta Svāmī Mahārāja, who is renowned throughout the world as Śrīla Prabhupāda. Śrīla Prabhupāda's inspired and authoritative statements illuminate the conclusive truths on the origin, nature, and fully excellent destination of the spirit soul. Although acclaimed internationally for his establishment of a worldwide confederation of almost one hundred *āśramas*, schools, temples, institutes, and farm communities, he always considered his treasure of devotional literature to be his most significant contribution to the world. In fact, the Bhaktivedānta Book Trust, established in 1972 to exclusively publish his works, is known as the world's largest publisher of books in the field of Indian religion and philosophy. All of the quotes that cite his books, lectures, discussions, and letters in Part Three, as well as all the quotes in Part One, are sourced from his Vedabase folio, the digital compilation of all of his original written and spoken words.

In Part One, Śrīla Nārāyaṇa Gosvāmī Mahārāja draws extensively from the ancient Vedic texts, and he often refers to Śrīla Prabhupāda's translations and commentaries. We have also cited Śrīla Prabhupāda's quotes in the form of footnotes, and unless otherwise mentioned, all the pull-quotes in the colored pull-quote boxes placed throughout the text were taken from his Vedabase-folio. The pull-quote boxes that have statements from *Bhakti-rasāyana*, *Going Beyond Vaikuṇṭha*, *Veṇu-gīta* and *Jaiva-dharma* are from the lectures and translations of Śrīla Nārāyaṇa Gosvāmī Mahārāja.

We have attempted to keep the language of the book very straightforward and easy to understand. Nevertheless, Śrīla Nārāyaṇa Gosvāmī Mahārāja uses many Sanskrit terms in his discourses, and we have kept them in the text in order to preserve the mood and precision of the meaning. For the benefit of the readers, these terms are always explained in English, either in the text itself or in the footnotes. When you find the explanation in the text or footnote insufficient, you are invited to turn to the glossary at the back of the book.

Following the tradition of our spiritual preceptors, we use standard diacritical markings to indicate the pronunciation of the Sanskrit words. Pronounce *ā* like a in father, *ī* like ea in neat, *ū* like oo in root, *ṛ* like ri in rip, *ṁ* and *ṅ* like ng in hung, *ś* and *ṣ* like sh in shy, and *c* like ch in chap.

We pray that you, our respected readers, receive new light regarding this most profound journey of the spirit soul, whose pure being is more brilliant than millions of suns, and who has the potency to become a personal associate of God Himself.

Welcome to *Journey of the Soul*, the window to your own journey. Please excuse any errors on our part in presenting this compilation.

The Editorial Team
Gaura-Purnima: February, 2010

Part One

DISCOURSES

INTRODUCTION

WHOM CAN YOU TRUST?

We trust various persons of authority to inform us about material subject matters, but whom shall we trust in regard to transcendental subject matters and the transcendental world? We cannot experience transcendence with any of our material senses. How then, can we have an idea of that pure reality? We can see the body, but not the soul. How can we verify that there is a soul beyond matter?

Though God is everywhere, we don't see Him. How then, can we determine who is God? Although it is evident that we cannot control the world, how can we trust that there is a God from whom this creation has come, and how can we be confident that it is He who controls it? Millions of people are born daily, and millions also die. Who controls this overwhelming tide of birth and death? Sea waves come on schedule, the sun appears on schedule, and new days come with continuous regularity. We do not control those rhythms, yet somehow, everything is maintained.

Our senses are imperfect, and therefore it may not be possible to trust the information given by them. Our eyes cannot even see the underside of the eyelids, the closest thing to them, what to speak of seeing inside our body, and more significantly, the soul within the body. Our material senses of seeing, hearing, and touching have some abilities, but they are extremely limited. Therefore, especially regarding transcendental subject matters, we can trust neither the imperfect senses nor the authorities who rely on those senses to formulate their conclusions.

Pragmatists say that we can trust only what we can see, but factually there are many instances wherein we trust as reality that which is beyond our own vision. For example, once I was on a train with my Gurudeva, and a railway officer approached him.

"Do you believe in God?" he asked.

Gurudeva replied, "Yes."

The officer said, "I don't believe in God, because I can't see Him. I only trust what my eyes can see."

Gurudeva replied, "This is not true. You believe many things you have not seen. Can you say who your father is?"

The officer said, "Yes," and told him the name of his father.

Gurudeva asked, "How do you know he is your father? Do you have any proof?"

Realizing that he had no proof, the officer felt uncomfortable and became somewhat restless. His mother had told him, "Here is your father," and on this 'evidence' he would say, "He is my father." If our mother is lying, we have no other recourse; we trust that our mother will not deceive us.

The officer then asked him, "Who is God?"

Gurudeva replied, "Kṛṣṇa is the Supreme Personality of Godhead."

The officer asked, "Why do you say that? In what way is He God?"

Gurudeva replied, "Some persons say that God has no form, attributes, or qualities, but the Vedic scriptures tell us that He has a form and many qualities. If He has no form, then from where did this world manifest? The world is replete with an endless diversity of forms. 'Something' cannot come from 'nothing.' Therefore, God must have a form, and His form must be the most beautiful. There is no one as beautiful or full of worthy qualities as He. For example, He can generate, regulate, and destroy the entire material world in a moment. He can create millions of worlds, suns, and moons within a second, and it is thus certain that He is all-powerful; we cannot do as He does. Moreover, He is extremely merciful. Otherwise, how can He know our difficulties, sorrows, and sufferings, and how can He help us? He is the embodiment of love and affection. If He were not so, if He were not able to love us and help us in our miseries, what would be the need of that God?"

Perfect Words

According to the great sages and saints of India, only transcendental words can be trusted. Such words can reveal the real path; what they describe is immaculate. Transcendental matters are discussed in the Vedas, the Upaniṣads, and especially the *Śrīmad-Bhāgavatam*, the most ancient of all revealed scriptures.

The words of the Vedas are more trustworthy than those of our mother, father, or anyone else in this world. A mother may tell a lie, but transcendental words carry no defect. According to sages, the Vedas are

Ancient Vedic Wisdom

"The Vedas are not compilations of human knowledge. Vedic knowledge comes from the spiritual world, from Lord Kṛṣṇa...The Vedas are considered to be the mother, and Brahmā (the creator of this Universe) is called the grandfather, the forefather, because he was the first to be instructed in the Vedic knowledge. In the beginning (of creation), the first living creature was Brahmā. He received this Vedic knowledge and imparted it to Nārada and other disciples and sons, and they also distributed it to their disciples.

"In this way, the Vedic knowledge comes down by disciplic succession. It is also confirmed in the *Bhagavad-gītā* that Vedic knowledge is understood in this way. If you make experimental endeavor, you come to the same conclusion, but just to save time you should accept...The Vedas instruct that in order to understand transcendental knowledge, we have to hear from the authority. Transcendental knowledge is knowledge from beyond this universe."

(Lecture by Śrīla Bhaktivedānta Svāmī Mahārāja.
London, October 6, 1969)

the most authoritative books of divine wisdom. This is especially true of the Vedic literature *Śrīmad-Bhāgavatam*, the supreme evidence.

We sometimes speculate about what we see. For example, from a distance we might see someone coming towards us and think that person to be our father. Then, as that person comes closer, we recognize that he is not actually our father but a person resembling him. Whereas the eyes do not gather conclusive evidence on their own, if they accept the vision of the authoritative Vedic literatures such as *Śrīmad-Bhāgavatam*, the Vedas, and the Upaniṣads, they can surely be trusted.

The Soul Within

According to the sages who have realized the divine knowledge of the Vedas, we are not these material bodies; we are spirit souls. The soul is presently captured in the jail of this body, as a beautiful bird is captured in a cage. Although we do not want our body to become old and die, it is bound to age; that is, if it does not die in youth. The hair on this present body will become white, the eyesight will weaken, and the day will come when the body will not be able to walk without the help of a stick. Then, one day, the soul will give it up altogether.

Within this material body there is another transcendental person. However, although that other person is within the body, He is not encaged. He is never born, and never becomes old or subject to death. Unlike us, He does not become a material child, youth, or aged person. He is the controller of the entire creation and all souls. He is God, and His position as God never changes. He is almighty. He knows past, present and future. He is omniscient and all-powerful.

Soul and Supersoul

The individual soul and the Supreme Soul live together within the body. This is confirmed in the Upaniṣads by the analogy that two friendly birds live in one tree – one bird eating the fruit of the tree and the other simply witnessing and directing. Although the individual living being, who is compared to the bird that is eating, is sitting with his friend the Supreme Soul, the individual living being cannot see Him.

(*Śrīmad-Bhāgavatam* 6.4.24,
Purport by Śrīla Bhaktivedānta Svāmī Mahārāja)

All potencies are eternally invested in that transcendental personality, the Supreme Personality of Godhead. It is because His internal power always lives within Him that He can create millions of universes, He can sport anywhere, and He can perform any herculean task. By the arrangement of this same intrinsic power, which is known in the Vedas as *svarūpa-śakti*, He manifests as His plenary and partial incarnations, such as Rāma, Balarāma, and Nṛsiṁhadeva.

The Lord also manifests His marginal energy, called *taṭasthā-śakti*, which is situated between the spiritual and material world, and which is comprised of spirit souls. Although we souls are His parts and parcels, we have now chosen to forget Him. For this reason another of His potencies, His power of delusion called *māyā*, has thrown us in this world and covered us. We are thus bewildered regarding who is God, and we are trapped in an endless cycle of birth, death, and sorrow.

A careful scrutiny of this world reveals that even high-posted personalities such as emperors, chief ministers, and presidents are suffering; everyone is suffering and no one knows why. Even if people experience some happiness in youth, they face many problems, and one day they will have to give up this body. Even if they are unable to determine whether or not God exists, they can very easily say that death exists. Even people who do not believe in God are bound to admit, "Death is sure." Eating, sleeping, mating, and defending or quarreling, they consider that they will be happy by material endeavors.

Among all species in this world, the human being possesses the most developed consciousness. Humans can perceive the future, whereas less-developed animal forms of life lack this capacity. Animals like monkeys, donkeys, and cows can anticipate the very near future, but not more than that. Let us suppose that there are many cows or goats being taken to a slaughter house. Even as they are approaching the moment of death, if they are given some morsels of grass to eat, they will quarrel over it, saying, "I will take it!" "No, I will take it!" In general, they cannot understand that they are about to die.

But as humans, we can contemplate matters of life and death; we can anticipate a future situation. Still, we are not happy. We will become happy by realizing our identity as spirit souls and that there is a realm free from the jurisdiction of birth, old age, disease, and death.

Why does one person take birth as a daughter or son of a prime minister and another take birth in a very poor family? Why is one person born beautiful and healthy, and another born lame? Why will a particular poor man later become a prime minister or president, whereas another poor man, despite great endeavor for such a position, remains impoverished? In this human body one must contemplate topics such as: "Why am I suffering?" "Why am I moving toward death?" "Who am I?" and "Who is God?" Such contemplation is the difference between an animal birth and a human birth.

All species of life, such as humans, trees, creepers, and lower animals have some sense of gratification, and they all experience some degree of love and affection. Suppose we sweetly call a dog and show him affection; he will respond, wagging his tail in happiness. If one feels and shows that love, then even a tiger or lion will not be ferocious towards him.

Everywhere there is love and affection – even in trees. If you caress a tree's leaf, the tree will be very happy. On the other hand, if you take a knife to cut its branches, the tree will tremble in fear. Little creepers show their love for trees by embracing them.

True religion is pure, divine love and affection, and the embodiment of true religion is God, known in the Vedic literature as Kṛṣṇa. God is very merciful and unlimitedly powerful, and we are His parts and parcels. If we realize this fact, we will definitely escape the chain of sorrow and suffering. This understanding, as well as the process to attain it, is called *bhakti-yoga*.

Linking Two Souls

Yoga is a Sanskrit word which means 'linking' or 'combining.' There must be two objects to form a link, and there must be a process to link those two objects. For example, if you want to join two bricks, then cement and water are needed. Similarly, *yoga* means linking or connecting two persons, the Supreme Lord Kṛṣṇa and each soul, by the process of *bhakti*, or pure devotion. In other words *yoga* is that process by which a soul can associate with Kṛṣṇa through devotion.

The soul is the Lord's part and parcel, His eternal servant. Servants of Kṛṣṇa are not like worldly servants. Service rendered to Kṛṣṇa is loving and beautiful, like the service of a friend, or of a mother and father to a son, or of one beloved to another. *Bhakti* means loving devotion, and Kṛṣṇa's servants are all very loving in their devotional service.

Having attained this human form of life, we must try to know who we really are. There are exalted personalities in this world who have realized the soul and God, and who have a transcendental link with Him. By their own practices they can show us the path to attain Him, and by our practice we can also have realization of this. Such a teacher is called *ācārya*, *guru*, holy master, or spiritual master. Such a *guru* is not subject to the delusion of this world, and therefore it is essential to attain his association.

The renowned, self-realized spiritual master, Śrīla Rūpa Gosvāmī, has explained the path to perfection: "In the beginning one must have a preliminary desire for self-realization. This will bring one to the stage of trying to associate with persons who are spiritually elevated. In the next stage one becomes initiated by an elevated spiritual master and under his instruction the neophyte devotee begins the process of devotional service. By executing devotional service under the guidance of the spiritual master, one becomes free from all material attachment, attains steadiness in self-realization, and acquires a taste for hearing about the Supreme Personality of Godhead, Śrī Kṛṣṇa. This taste gradually bestows attachment for Kṛṣṇa consciousness, which is matured in *bhāva*, or the preliminary stage of transcendental love of God. Real love for God is called *prema*, the highest perfectional stage of life" (*Bhakti-rasāmṛta-sindhu* 1.4.15–16).

It is the inherent nature of the individual soul to serve God, the Supreme Soul, and the desire or tendency to serve Him manifests by the association of His pure devotee. If we desire to serve the Supreme Godhead but after some time we fail to associate with those who are serving Him, that desire dries up. It is likened to a tree which, after developing some leaves, dies for want of water. Good association is the water of our spiritual life.

Without good association, and without this higher realization of the goal of life, human existence becomes like that of lower animals. In fact, we see that the world's leaders quarrel with each other like animals, and are even crueler than animals. Fighting with nails and teeth, animals are forced by their nature to kill a few other animals, but these humans create atom bombs and destroy the lives of millions of people and animals. Devoid of spiritual guidance, looking for love and happiness through sense gratification, and unable to control their senses, such persons want to control the world.

The Three Realms

The great saint Śrīla Jīva Gosvāmī has explained that there are three types of creation – the transcendental realm, the innumerable souls, and the millions of material worlds.

The transcendental world is beyond the world of matter; repeated birth, death, and sorrow do not exist there.

Regarding the infinite souls, they are of two categories. One category pertains to those who are liberated and are immersed in the happiness of loving service to God in the transcendental world of Vaikuṇṭha (the spiritual planetary system). The other category pertains to those souls who are in this world, who have forgotten God, and who are called conditioned souls.

In this world the soul is covered by a body composed of the five inert elements – earth, water, fire, air, and ether. When the body dies and is then burned or buried, the five elements return to their original source – earth returns to earth, fire to fire, and so on – but the soul never dies or takes birth.

Individual spirit souls are in some ways the same as God and in some ways different. As God has a beautiful body, multifarious powers, and fathomless good qualities, the living entities are also graced with these attributes. The difference is that God is infinite whereas souls are infinitesimal. The tiny souls cannot create worlds and cannot control them, whereas God orchestrates everything and is the master of the deluding energy of this world. The Supreme Lord and His numerous incarnations are beyond transformation. His incarnations are not under the control of the deluding energy and They are never subject to misery.

Conditioned souls, those who have misused their independence and have forgotten the Supreme Lord, undergo various material changes and influences. Thrown into this world by the Lord's potency of illusion, they think, "I am this body, I am the doer, I am the controller, and I am the enjoyer of this world." This mentality is the symptom of conditioned souls. Actually, all souls have emanated from the Supreme Godhead, Kṛṣṇa, and all the universes have also emanated from His power.

This world has emanated from His deluding *māyā* potency, and therefore it is also different and non-different from Him. The ancient Vedic scriptures state: "*Śakti-śaktimator abhedaḥ* – there is no difference between the potent (God) and the potency (His power)." This Vedic philosophy is called *acintya-bhedābheda-tattva*, or inconceivable, simultaneous difference and non-difference.

We cannot understand these truths by merely reading books. It is essential for us to hear such truths from devotees who have realized this knowledge. We cannot realize the Supreme Personality of Godhead or the position of our own soul by worldly knowledge, practicing *aṣṭāṅga-yoga*, performing austerities, or giving donations in charity. Transcendental realization is possible only by the practice of pure *bhakti-yoga*, engagement in transcendental loving service.

We can understand these truths by first recognizing the nature of God. If God were to have no individual form, this world and all souls could have no individual existence. If God were to have no shape or form, how could He create human bodies? The fact of His supreme personality is not only stated in the Vedic scriptures and the Bible, but also in the Koran of the Muslims: "*Inallah kalaka mein suratihi* – Khoda (or Allah) has created human bodies similar to His own form." God is a Person, He has a form, and He is very merciful. With this conviction, we can trust Him.

We can become attached to God through *bhakti-yoga*, whereas we cannot do so by mere theoretical knowledge. For example, someone may say, "By drinking water, we can quench our thirst." However, if we do not actually drink water our thirst will not dissipate. We must drink a glass of water, and then our thirst will be quenched. Suppose you are hungry; you need food. I may tell you that by eating chapatis, rice, bread, butter, and some sweets, your hunger will go away, but merely knowing this will not give you the foodstuffs or satisfy your hunger. Similarly, intellectual knowledge is not enough to practically progress in spiritual life. *Bhakti-yoga* is practical activity, and by practicing it we will realize all knowledge.

The Only Object of Love

As explained above, we all possess love and affection to some degree. A beautiful young girl and boy see each other, then they are attracted to each other, and after that they are bound by marriage. Then, if they quarrel, they may divorce and try to fulfill their desires by taking another wife or husband. Then, if they are still not happy in their householder life, they get a dog and say, "We can trust dogs. Wives and husbands may divorce us, but dogs do not do so." Then, after some time they see that the dog dies. In this way, we cannot become truly or perpetually happy by the loving exchanges in this world. The only true object of love is God. The nature of our soul is that we are reservoirs of divine love, but at present our love is impure and selfish. A man may

Service in the Mood of Friends

love his very beautiful wife, but only if she serves and obeys him. If she is quarrelsome, or if she is in love with another man, that love will be disrupted.

Thus, in our present state of bodily consciousness, our love and affection is not pure; it is mixed with selfishness. On the other hand, if we perform *bhakti-yoga* by chanting the names of God and regularly hearing about Him, His beloved devotees will guide us to develop unalloyed love for Him. Such devotees alone are truly happy. They understand the dynamic of this world and thus they have no attachment to the body. Somehow maintaining their life, they always chant, remember, and meditate on the Supreme Lord. If we associate with them, they will guide us in spiritual advancement.

The beginning stage of *bhakti-yoga* is called *sādhana-bhakti*, the stage of spiritual practice. Then, by such practice, with the development of a semblance of love and affection and with the mind and intelligence in the mode of pure goodness, the practitioner of *bhakti* reaches the stage called *bhāva-bhakti*. In *bhāva-bhakti*, a soul can somewhat realize love for Kṛṣṇa, as well as the way in which he can serve Him. Then, after some time, divine absorption in Him and love for Him manifests, and this final stage is called *prema*.

Prema is one principle, but it is divided into five moods of service: *śānta-rasa* (neutral love), *dāsya-rasa* (servitorship), *sakhya-rasa* (friendship), *vātsalya-rasa* (parental love), and *mādhurya-rasa* (amorous love). *Śānta* means love and affection toward God without any speciality of service. In *śānta-rasa* one thinks, "God is great and we are His tiny parts and parcels. We should offer obeisances to Him. He is so merciful." One in *śānta-rasa* has no worldly attachment. The devotee does not pray, "O God, give me bread and butter, give me bliss, give me liberation." *Śānta-rasa* manifests after liberation, as was the case with the four Kumāra brothers: Sanaka, Sanandana, Sanātana and Sanat Kumāra. They had no worldly attachment, but they also relished no specific mellow of love and affection for God.

In the mood of *dāsya-rasa*, one serves God as one's master. A devotee in *dāsya-rasa* thinks about Kṛṣṇa thus: "You are my master. You are the root of the entire universe, its creation and destruction." Moreover, in *dāsya-rasa* there is active service, as in the case of Hanumān, who faithfully served Lord Rāma.

Next is the mood of *sakhya-rasa*, service to Kṛṣṇa as a friend. A devotee in *sakhya-rasa* thinks, "Kṛṣṇa is my friend." There are two kinds of friends: friends in Ayodhyā and Dvārakā (the abodes of Śrī

Service in the Mood of a Parent

Kṛṣṇa's expansions, Lord Rāma and Dvārakādīśa), and friends in Vraja (the abode of Śrī Kṛṣṇa Himself). The Lord's friends in Ayodhyā and Dvārakā experience some awe and reverence along with their mood of friendship, but Śrī Kṛṣṇa's friends in Vraja are bosom friends. Kṛṣṇa and His intimate friends always show affection for each other on an equal level. Kṛṣṇa's friends can sleep on the same bed as Him. They can eat and then share their food with Him, and He also eats and then shares His remnants with them. They do not consider that He is God.

One can also think, "Kṛṣṇa is my son." This relationship, called *vātsalya-rasa*, is more exalted than the previous relationships. If we want to serve God in a parental mood, we can serve Him as His own parents. The father will take his son on his lap, embrace Him, and give Him sweets to eat. Even if the father has become old, still he wants to serve his son. The idea of the Supreme Personality of Godhead as our father opposes our desire for loving service, because if God is the father, He would have to serve us. We tell our father, "Oh father, please supply this, please supply that. Give me water, give me bread." On the other hand, if we think of God as our son, then we wish to serve Him.

Superior to parental love is amorous or conjugal love, which is called *mādhurya-rasa*. *Mādhurya-rasa* is divided into two separate moods: married or wedded love, and unwedded love. Those who are married to Kṛṣṇa by Vedic *mantra* and by law are exemplified by Kṛṣṇa's queens, headed by Rukmiṇī and Satyabhāmā. The other mood is unwedded love, and the young women in this category have no cause for their loving relation with Kṛṣṇa other than love and affection itself. This supreme stage of ecstatic love, called paramour love (*upapati-bhāva*), is exemplified by the *gopīs* of Vraja.

Bhakti-yoga is very easy to practice. You can chant the name of God in the day or in the night, whether you are Hindu, Muslim, Christian, or any other religious denomination. Even animals can hear when you chant loudly, and they are also spiritually benefited. You can chant the names of God – "Hare Kṛṣṇa" – if you are poor, and you can chant if you are wealthy. You can chant after bathing or without having bathed at all; before, after, or during meals; sitting or standing, or in any other condition. There is no dependence on wealth or situation. The essence of all Vedic scriptures is the Hare Kṛṣṇa *mantra*: "Hare Kṛṣṇa, Hare Kṛṣṇa, Kṛṣṇa Kṛṣṇa, Hare Hare, Hare Rāma, Hare Rāma, Rāma Rāma, Hare Hare."

We have invented divisions, thinking, "This is India, this is America, this is Australia," and thus we create passports and visas. But

Service in the Mood of Beloveds

God is one without a second. We can chant to Him and pray to Him to be merciful to us. This chanting of the holy name is the supreme process for perfection of life.

[*This lecture was given on December 27, 1998, in Perth, Australia, on the disappearance day of the great saint Śrīla Jīva Gosvāmī.*]

CHAPTER ONE

THE TRUTH OF THE SOUL

The subject matter regarding the established philosophical truths of the living entity (*jīva-tattva*) is very advanced. Still it is essential to know, especially for those who actively share spiritual topics with others. Lucid knowledge of philosophical truths is the foundation of a strong spiritual life.

siddhānta baliyā citte nā kara alasa
ihā ha-ite kṛṣṇe lāge sudṛḍha mānasa
(*Śrī Caitanya-caritāmṛta, Ādi-līlā* 2.117)

A sincere student should not neglect the discussion of such conclusions, considering them controversial, for such discussions strengthen the mind. Thus, one's mind becomes attached to Śrī Kṛṣṇa.

Although this subject is elevated and profound, it gradually becomes easier to understand, and over time, to read or discuss it becomes relishable. Do not be disheartened and think, "Oh, it is such a lofty topic. My mind is not able to even touch it."

We Stood on the Shoreline

In all Vaiṣṇava or devotional literature, we find someone who asks questions and someone who answers those questions. This recurring theme points to the foundation of spiritual life: humble inquiry to know the truth. God Himself set this example, as seen in the conversations between the Supreme Lord Śrī Caitanya Mahāprabhu[1] and His associates Śrīla Rāya Rāmānanda and Śrīla Sanātana Gosvāmī.

In this mood, the great king Parīkṣit Mahārāja inquires from the sage, Śrīla Śukadeva Gosvāmī: "The living entity's transcendental constitution is spiritual and conscious, whereas the Lord's deluding material potency, *māyā*, is inert and mundane. How is it, then, that the living entity became entangled in *māyā*? This is very amazing."

Śrīla Śukadeva Gosvāmī replies:

bhayaṁ dvitīyābhiniveśataḥ syād
īśād apetasya viparyayo 'smṛtiḥ
tan-māyayāto budha ābhajet taṁ
bhaktyaikayeśaṁ guru-devatātmā

(*Śrīmad-Bhāgavatam* 11.2.37)

> Fear arises when a living entity misidentifies himself as the material body because of absorption in the external, illusory energy of the Lord. When he thus turns away from the Supreme Lord, he also forgets his own constitutional position as a servant of the Lord. This bewildering, fearful condition is the effect of the potency of illusion, called *māyā*. Therefore, an intelligent person should engage unflinchingly in the unalloyed devotional service of the Lord under the guidance of a bona fide spiritual

---

1 "Śrī Caitanya Mahāprabhu, the incarnation who delivers the fallen conditioned souls in the age of Kali, is directly the Supreme Lord Śrī Kṛṣṇa Himself. Vrajendra-nandana Śrī Kṛṣṇa, overwhelmed with an intense desire to relish a particular sentiment, assumed the heartfelt ecstatic mood and bodily complexion of Śrīmatī Rādhikā, the embodiment of His own pleasure potency (*hlādinī-śakti*), and bestowed upon the entire world the gifts of His holy name and divine love for Him" (*Śrī Śikṣāṣṭaka*, Introduction).

> master, whom he should accept as his worshipful deity and as his very life and soul.

This verse indicates that Śrī Kṛṣṇa is the root of all existence. He is the Absolute Truth, 'one without a second.' He is the ultimate person; He is the first, with no second. He is the personification of complete and total existence. He manifests various potencies, unlimited living entities (*jīvas*), and innumerable worlds; and even His father Nanda Mahārāja, His Mother Yaśodā, and all of His associates are His manifestations. He is thus the worshipful Deity of all.

By the living entity's constitution, he is an eternal servant of that Supreme worshipful Lord, Śrī Kṛṣṇa. As stated in *Śrī Caitanya-caritāmṛta* (*Madhya-līlā* 20.108):

jīvera 'svarūpa' haya – kṛṣṇera 'nitya-dāsa'
kṛṣṇera 'taṭasthā-śakti' 'bhedābheda-prakāśa'

> It is the living entity's constitutional position to be an eternal servant of Kṛṣṇa, because he is the marginal energy of Kṛṣṇa and a manifestation simultaneously one with and different from Him.

As an eternal servant of Kṛṣṇa, the *jīva* soul is blissful by nature. However, in one crucial moment he looked towards the Lord's external potency, thinking that something exists besides the Lord.

Being part and parcel of Kṛṣṇa, the *jīva's* intrinsic nature is to look towards Kṛṣṇa; so why did he look towards *māyā*? The answer is that Kṛṣṇa has given the *jīva* independence. If the *jīva* misuses that independence, he is entrusted to the jurisdiction of *māyā* and punished. Grabbed by *māyā* he becomes materially absorbed, and in this predicament no other materially absorbed person can save him.

In the above-mentioned verse by Śrīla Śukadeva Gosvāmī (*Śrīmad-Bhāgavatam* 11.2.37), the words *īśād apetasya viparyayo 'smṛtiḥ* confirm that the *jīva* was standing at the line running between the transcendental world and the inert, material world. By his choice he looked to this 'lovely' *māyā*, who showed him the ways in which he could enjoy on his own, apart from Kṛṣṇa. Spellbound by *māyā*, the *jīva* thought, "It is my right to enjoy." *Māyā* immediately supplied him a subtle body (made of material mind, intelligence, and false ego) and gross body (made of bones, blood, skin, urine, stool, and so forth), and he began to think, "I am this body and everything in relation to this body is mine."

Thus, when the *jīva* turns away from Kṛṣṇa by his free will and independence, he becomes enveloped by the misconception of this bodily concept of life and becomes enamored by the beautiful forms manufactured by *māyā*. Having entered this realm of existence, he cannot find the way out by himself. The only escape is the shelter of those who know the way out. After a long time of being bound in this world of birth and death, the fortunate *jīvas* may be approached by a pure devotee saying, "What are you doing, my brothers, my sisters? You are misguided. You have derailed from the path of love of God. Come with me; I will guide you on the path to true happiness."

Only by proper association can one develop spiritual consciousness and consider the truth: "I am an eternal servant of Śrī Kṛṣṇa, and I can serve Him with love and affection like those in the spiritual realms of Vraja and Vaikuṇṭha. This world is only a shadow of that sublime spiritual consciousness of love and service."

In the *Śrīmad-Bhāgavatam* verse above, Śrīla Śukadeva Gosvāmī explains to Parīkṣit Mahārāja the importance of associating with saintly, exalted devotees of the Lord. A saintly devotee can change the heart of the misery-stricken conditioned soul in one moment.

'sādhu-saṅga', 'sādhu-saṅga' – sarva-śāstre kaya
lava-mātra sādhu-saṅge sarva-siddhi haya

(*Śrī Caitanya-caritāmṛta, Madhya-līlā* 22.54)

The verdict of all revealed scriptures is that by even a moment's association with a pure devotee, one can attain all success.

Śrīmad-Bhāgavatam declares that anyone who is sincerely chanting and remembering Kṛṣṇa under the guidance of a *sādhu* is destined to become happy. If even a neophyte devotee (*kaniṣṭha-adhikārī*) is chanting and sincerely weeping for Kṛṣṇa, lamenting his fallen state, he is destined to become happy through the shelter of saintly association. One may be entangled in numerous unwanted mentalities and habits, but if one chants sincerely, he becomes happy.

That happy devotee will show a person the spiritual path and advise him, "I know a bona fide, self-realized *guru*, and by his help I have become so joyous. Come with me; I will introduce him to you." This person is called *vartma-pradarśaka guru*, the *guru* who shows the path.

Śrī Kṛṣṇa is very merciful; He is the *guru* in the heart (*caitya-guru*). Together with the *vartma-pradarśaka guru*, He guides a person to the

bona fide, self-realized *guru*. Accepting the bona fide *guru*, that person begins to perform devotional activities (*bhajana*) in the service of Śrī Kṛṣṇa, and gradually all his unwanted habits and mentalities disappear.

In the Eleventh Canto of the *Śrīmad-Bhāgavatam*, Śrī Kṛṣṇa tells Uddhava, His foremost associate:

ekasyaiva mamāṁśasya
jīvasyaiva mahā-mate
bandho 'syāvidyayānādir
vidyayā ca tathetaraḥ

(*Śrīmad-Bhāgavatam* 11.11.4)

> O most intelligent Uddhava, the living entity, called *jīva*, is My part and parcel, but due to ignorance he has been suffering in material bondage since time immemorial. By knowledge, however, he can be liberated.

In this verse, Śrī Kṛṣṇa praises Uddhava for his intelligence. A sincere devotee of Kṛṣṇa is intelligent because he has chosen the path of *bhakti*, pure devotion. There are many so-called intelligent persons in the world, like scientists and politicians, but according to the standard of supreme intelligence – the choice to love and serve God – such persons' intelligence is lost.

According to this verse, Kṛṣṇa is telling Uddhava, "Uddhava, you should know that on this Earth, and in all material worlds, the spirit soul is My part and parcel. Wandering throughout these worlds since time immemorial, his ignorance has no calculable beginning and therefore the duration of his conditioning cannot be measured. However, by the influence of the spiritual energy known as *yogamāyā*, who is the embodiment of timeless transcendental knowledge, the conditioned soul can be liberated." What is that transcendental knowledge which liberates the soul? It is knowledge of the Supreme Lord's greatness, and the soul's eternal relationship with Him.

If someone tears a flower, the flower is no longer whole; if he tears it further, it shreds and is destroyed. The entire material world is like this – if anything in this world is divided and further divided, the whole is lost. But this principle does not apply to the spiritual realm. Kṛṣṇa remains complete even though unlimited parts and parcels emanate from Him. This reality is stated in many places in the Vedic scriptures, and one such statement is found in *Bhagavad-gītā*:

mamaivāṁśo jīva-loke
jīva-bhūtaḥ sanātanaḥ
manaḥ-ṣaṣṭhānīndriyāṇi
prakṛti-sthāni karṣati
(*Bhagavad-gītā* 15.7)

The living entities, in this conditioned world are My eternal fragmental parts. Due to conditioned life, they are struggling very hard with the six senses, which include the mind.

It is essential to understand in which way the *jīva* is part of the Supreme Whole, Śrī Kṛṣṇa, since the Lord can never be divided into parts. There is no limit to His length or width; He has no end – no top and no bottom. The entire world is within Him, yet He Himself is not divided.

For example, we can cut a pebble from a boulder, but we cannot cut anything from Kṛṣṇa. The *jīva* is not a part of Kṛṣṇa in the same way that a small piece of stone is part of a larger stone. Because Śrī Kṛṣṇa is the Complete Whole, the complete Absolute Truth, the personification of complete existence, even though so many manifestations and expansions emanate from Him, He remains the complete balance.

The Supreme Personality of Godhead Kṛṣṇa has two types of expansions. His *viṣṇu-tattva* expansions, known as *svāṁśa*, are His plenary (direct and full) incarnations. The living entities, known as *vibhinnāṁśa*, are not full or direct expansions. They are His infinitesimal, separated parts and parcels.

The following analogy helps us understand the Supreme Lord in relation to His plenary incarnations. The Lord can be compared to a ghee-lamp[2] that lights other ghee-lamps. Some lamps almost equal the light of the original and some lamps have only tiny flames; it depends on the size of the lamp. Moreover, if the flame of one ghee-lamp is used to light another, the first flame will remain the same as it was. It will not become smaller or lose potency. Similarly, although innumerable plenary incarnations have emanated from Kṛṣṇa, the original source of all incarnations, the source has not diminished in power.

oṁ pūrṇam adaḥ pūrṇam idaṁ pūrṇāt pūrṇam udacyate
pūrṇasya pūrṇam ādāya pūrṇam evāvaśiṣyate
(*Śrī Īśopaniṣad*, Invocation)

2 A ghee-lamp is a wick dipped in clarified butter, which is used for worship of the Deity.

Śrī Kṛṣṇa's Expansions

Kṛṣṇa's personal expansions (svāṁśa)
Kṛṣṇa's separated expansions (vibhināṁśa)
Kṛṣṇa
eternally liberated (nitya-mukta) jīvas
Baladeva
Kṛṣṇa's eternal associates in Goloka Vṛndāvana
Mula-Saṅkarṣaṇa
Kṛṣṇa's eternal associates in Mathurā and Dvārakā
Maha-Saṅkarṣaṇa
The eternal associates of Kṛṣṇa (as Nārāyaṇa) in Vaikuṇṭha
Kāraṇodakaśāyī Viṣṇu (Mahā-Viṣṇu)
taṭasthā-jīvas who looked towards Yogamāyā
taṭasthā-jīvas who looked towards Mahāmāyā
Garbhodakaśāyī Viṣṇu
Kṣīrodakaśāyī Viṣṇu
jīvas conditioned since time immemorial (nitya-baddha)

> The Personality of Godhead is perfect and complete, and because He is completely perfect, all emanations from Him, such as this phenomenal world, are perfectly equipped as complete wholes. Whatever is produced of the Complete Whole is also complete in itself. Because He is the Complete Whole, even though so many complete units emanate from Him, He remains the complete balance.

From the point of view of philosophical truth (*tattva*), Śrī Kṛṣṇa's plenary incarnations like Rāma and Nṛsiṁhadeva are one with Him. At the same time, from the point of view of the mellow of transcendental relationships (*rasa*), these incarnations are different. Kṛṣṇa is the origin of all incarnations, such as the *līlā-avatāras* (pastime incarnations) and the three *puruṣa-avatāras*, namely Kāraṇodakaśāyī Viṣṇu, Garbhodakaśāyī Viṣṇu, and Kṣīrodakaśāyī Viṣṇu, who control the three various aspects of material existence: creation, maintenance, and destruction. [Please see chart at the end of this chapter.]

The analogy of the ghee-lamp contributes to our understanding of Kṛṣṇa and His plenary expansions (*svāṁśa* incarnations). Now, to clarify our understanding of the Lord's expansion as the infinitesimal living entities, we may take the analogy of the *cintāmaṇi* stone[3].

The word *cintā* means 'thought' or 'desire,' and *maṇi* means 'jewel.' The *cintāmaṇi* stone manifests as much gold as a person desires, but that gold is not directly *cintāmaṇi*. Similarly, every one of us emanates from Śrī Kṛṣṇa, but we are not Kṛṣṇa Himself.

Cintāmaṇi can manifest unlimited opulence to fulfill anyone's desires; yet no matter how much gold emanates from it, that jewel remains as it was, without any transformation or diminution. Similarly, Kṛṣṇa always remains full and complete even though unlimited infinitesimal parts and parcels (*vibhinnāṁśa jīvas*) have emanated from Him.

When gold is within the *cintāmaṇi* stone it is in its original state or position, but when it manifests outside that *cintāmaṇi* it is transformed. Similarly, when the living being is within the '*cintāmaṇi*' of full Kṛṣṇa

---

3 There are many references to the *cintāmaṇi* stone in the Vedic scriptures. For example, in *Brahma-saṁhitā* (5.29, 56) Śrī Kṛṣṇa and His abode are described thus: "I worship that supreme abode of Śvetadvīpa, where the beloved heroines are a host of transcendental goddesses of fortune, and the Supreme Personality Śrī Kṛṣṇa is the only lover; where all the trees are spiritual desire-trees, and the earth is made of transcendental wish-fulfilling *cintāmaṇi* jewels."

consciousness, he has spiritual qualities like those of Kṛṣṇa; but when he is outside pure Kṛṣṇa consciousness, in other words when he is entangled in *māyā*, those qualities appear to be lost or perverted. At that time, when he is absorbed in *māyā*, only material qualities abound.

We Are Infinitesimal, He Is Infinite

ekaḥ śuddhaḥ svayaṁ-jyotir
nirguṇo 'sau guṇāśrayaḥ
sarva-go 'nāvṛtaḥ sākṣī
nirātmātmātmanaḥ paraḥ

(*Śrīmad-Bhāgavatam* 4.20.7)

> The Supreme Soul is one. He is pure, non-material, and self-effulgent. He is the reservoir of all good qualities and He is all-pervading. He is without material covering and He is the witness of all activities. He is completely distinguished from other living entities and He is transcendental to all embodied souls.

This verse describes the qualities of the Supreme Personality of Godhead, thus highlighting several distinctions between Him and the individual soul. Some say that all living entities are God, and the proponents of this belief misinterpret such Vedic aphorisms as *tat tvam asi* [meaning 'the living entity is a spiritual particle of the supreme spirit'] to mean 'you are that impersonal God;' *sarvaṁ khalv idaṁ brahma* [meaning 'there is no existence beyond *brahma*, the Absolute Truth'] to mean 'everything is God;' *prajñānaṁ brahma* [meaning 'pure knowledge is transcendental and is of the same spiritual substance as *brahma*'] to mean '*brahma* is impersonal consciousness;' and *ahaṁ brahmāsmi* [meaning 'I am not this body; I am spirit soul'] to mean 'I am that spirit whole. I am *brahma*.'

The leader of such proponents, Śaṅkarācārya, is an incarnation of Śankara, Lord Śiva. He was very clever; although he appeared to be the leader of the impersonal path, his actual purpose was to fulfill the desire of Lord Kṛṣṇa. Kṛṣṇa had instructed Śankara, "Go to the material world and hide Me from all those who are opposed to My pure devotion, those who serve and worship Me with the desire to become very powerful like the demons Hiraṇyakaśipu and Rāvaṇa. Such false devotees will create great disturbances, so keep them far away from Me. Go and delude them by misinterpreting the Vedas. Tell them this: 'Why are you worshiping Kṛṣṇa? You yourself are God in every respect. We are all one with that impersonal God.'"

Thus, impersonalism is not an idea of the Vedas themselves. In truth, we are not God, nor is God impersonal. He is a person, and we are His parts and parcels, His eternal servitors. The Supreme Personality of Godhead is one without a second, whereas the *jīvas* are unlimited in number.

What does it mean that the *jīvas* are unlimited in number? Suppose that all persons in this universe become liberated, and the material universe then becomes vacant of humans. Still, there are so many *jīvas* in the blood of even one human being that if each of those *jīvas* were to take a human body, hundreds of thousands of universes would overflow with human population. This localized example gives a hint of the unlimited number of living entities within the universe, and there are also unlimited *jīvas* in the spiritual worlds of Vaikuṇṭha and Goloka Vṛndāvana. This multiplicity is one of the prime distinctions between the *jīva* and God.

Consider this distinction as well: the individual soul is not present in an object such as a microphone, but the Paramātmā, Śrī Kṛṣṇa's form as the Supersoul, is present there. Nothing in this world exists without the presence of Paramātmā.

There are two souls present within each body – the infinitesimal *jīva* and the Lord's manifestation as Paramātmā. The *jīva* is entangled in fruitive activities (*karma*), trying to relish the fruits of his labor. The Supreme Lord is not a conditioned soul, and He is not enamored by the material energy. He is simply the witness within the *jīva's* heart.

The Supreme Lord is eternally pure, and *māyā*, or delusion, is far away from Him and His abode. *Māyā* cannot attract the Lord, but the *jīva*, being minute, can be attracted by *māyā* at any time. Śrī Kṛṣṇa is always pure and self-illuminating, whereas the *jīva* is prone to be influenced by the darkness of illusion and can thus be covered by the mistaken identity of bodily identification.

Kṛṣṇa appears personally in His beautiful form of Vrajendra-nandana, the son of Nanda Mahārāja, to those who perform *bhajana*, devotional meditation and service to Him. To those who serve the Lord in His opulent, four-handed form as Vaikuṇṭha Nārāyaṇa, He appears as Lord Nārāyaṇa. Here in this world, He resides as the witness in the heart of every individual living being, and He is also situated in each and every atom as Paramātmā. The Lord manifests in an astounding array of forms and energies, while the *jīva* is very limited; he is localized and minute.

Śrī Kṛṣṇa is the eternal Absolute Truth. *Kaṭha Upaniṣad* (2.2.13) says, "*nityo nityānāṁ cetanaś cetanānām* – of living beings He is the Supreme Living Being, and among all eternals He is the Prime Eternal." Although the *jīva* is known to be His separated part and parcel, he is not actually separate. The *jīva* has no separate existence from Kṛṣṇa and he will always be subordinate to Him, in this world and in the spiritual world.

Kṛṣṇa is free from material qualities and at the same time possesses all transcendental qualities. The *jīvas* can reach the stage of having qualities like the Lord's when, by the grace of God and *guru*, they realize their eternal nature of subordination to Him.

Our Choice to Dream

Once, the great saint Vidura went to Badrikāśrama in the Himalaya Mountains to see Maitreya Ṛṣi, a learned sage and a recipient of Śrī Kṛṣṇa's mercy. Vidura approached Maitreya Ṛṣi and inquired, "It is very amazing: although the *jīva* is a conscious being and is always connected with the Supreme Lord Kṛṣṇa's form as the Supersoul, he becomes entangled in *māyā*. How is this possible?"

Maitreya Ṛṣi replied, "I will tell you, in brief, the only reason. Kṛṣṇa possesses an inconceivable power known as *aghaṭana-ghaṭana-paṭīyasī-śakti*, the power which makes the impossible possible. It is this power that hides the Lord's mercy from the *jīva* who chooses to turn away from Him, thus compelling that *jīva* to become a conditioned soul."

Consider that *māyā* is also one of Kṛṣṇa's potencies and thus cannot do anything against His will. Ultimately, therefore, Kṛṣṇa is the cause of *māyā's* workings. Why, then, has Kṛṣṇa created such an environment that causes so many *jīvas* to suffer? The answer is that creating the material world is one of His unlimited pastimes. There is no lack in the variety of His innumerable pastimes, and this is one of them. The Lord is fully independent to do as He chooses. We cannot challenge Him, and as stated in the Vedic scriptures, we cannot understand Him by argument or logic.

acintyāḥ khalu ye bhāvā na tāṁs tarkeṇa yojayet

(*Mahābhārata, Bhīṣma-parva* 5.22)

Vidura and the Sage Maitreya

> We should not try to understand things beyond our material conception by argument and counter-argument.

It is not possible to understand transcendental matters with the limited, mundane mind, and therefore we rely on the descriptions of that realm from the Vedas. We rely on the essence of the Vedas, which is the *Śrīmad-Bhāgavatam*, and on the great saints known as the Six Gosvāmīs, who have given us the essence of *Śrīmad-Bhāgavatam* in their own writings.

As mentioned above, only by the influence of Śrī Kṛṣṇa's inconceivable energy that makes the impossible possible does the *jīva* become bewildered by *māyā*, under the sway of the conceptions 'I,' 'me,' and 'mine,' which are based on the illusion of bodily identification. In his natural state, in his constitutional form, the *jīva* is pure. Although he is minute, he is an atomic portion of *cit-śakti*, Lord Kṛṣṇa's own transcendental potency.[4] He is now conditioned by a material body, but there is nothing material – no *māyā* – in his natural, spiritual constitution.

Material conditioning is called 'bondage,' but this bondage is not real. It is not reality because it does not touch the transcendental soul. When a man sleeps at night, he may dream that his head is being cut off, but when he wakes up he sees that nothing has happened. Similarly, by the mercy of *guru* and Kṛṣṇa, when we awaken to Kṛṣṇa consciousness we think, "What was I seeing all that time? It was just like a dream." If suffering comes to you, you need not be upset or nervous. Just remember that this apparent suffering is due to being under illusion, like living in a dream.

Maitreya Ṛṣi continued to explain to Vidura that where there is no sun there is darkness; but in truth, darkness does not exist, for it is simply the absence of light. Similarly, where there is no service to Kṛṣṇa, who is like the sun, there is *māyā*, or darkness.

Maitreya gave the following analogy: On a moonlit night, the moon in the sky and a tree standing on the bank of a pond are both reflected in the water. When the wind blows and there are ripples upon the surface of the water, it seems as though the moon and the tree are swaying back and forth. In truth, however, both are solid and still; they are not trembling at all. Similarly, in this world we accept reflection as reality. We appear to be suffering in various material conditions, but actually we are transcendental to matter.

---

[4] Please see the chart on Lord Kṛṣṇa's potencies (*śaktis*) in Chapter Two.

Although it is not possible to understand with material senses or mind, the *jīva* is an eternal servant of Kṛṣṇa even if in his conditioned state it appears that he is not. Here is yet another analogy: If one places a cloth over a watch, one cannot see any movement of the hands of the watch – but there is movement. Similarly, we perceive only our bodily and mental activities. We cannot understand that there is an eternal soul inside the body, without whom the body would not be able to function. We are conscious, infinitesimal parts and parcels of the Lord, somehow serving the Lord even in this stage of bondage although we do not realize it.

For example, the demon Kaṁsa was serving Kṛṣṇa in an indirect way. Kaṁsa's atrocities were an integral cause for Kṛṣṇa's appearance in this world; if there were no Kaṁsa, there would be no sweet pastimes of Śrī Kṛṣṇa in Vṛndāvana. Similarly, Rāvaṇa's atrocities were an integral cause for the appearance of Lord Rāma; if there were no Rāvaṇa, the enemy of Lord Rāma, there would be no sweet pastimes of Lord Rāma in this world.

Similarly, the conditioned *jīva* is serving the Lord, but indirectly. At present he is serving the Lord's deluding *māyā* potency. He is now in a dream, dreaming that he is his various material bodies.

Our Awakening

Hidden in the heart of the material body, every *jīva* possesses a beautiful, marvellous form. It is with this transcendental form (called *siddha-deha*) that the *jīva* can serve Kṛṣṇa directly. Although this spiritual form is now covered, by the mercy of *guru* and Kṛṣṇa all unwanted habits and mentalities gradually disappear and it is gradually revealed. When one reaches the stage of *bhāva*, spiritual emotion (also known as *svarūpa-siddhi*[5]), devotion that is transcendental to the modes of material nature manifests in the heart and one can awaken to the realization of his or her own divine form. Then, receiving the mercy of Śrī Kṛṣṇa, one becomes totally freed from this gross material body, mind, intelligence, false ego, and contaminated consciousness.

Regarding Śrī Kṛṣṇa Himself, He never has a material body. He did not leave a material body behind when He left this planet and disappeared from the world's vision. Not only is Kṛṣṇa's form transcendental to any

[5] *Svarūpa-siddhi* is the stage in which a devotee's *svarūpa*, or internal spiritual form and identity, becomes manifest in his heart. This comes at the stage of *bhāva-bhakti*.

kind of material body, it is the very cause of all spiritual and material worlds.

In order to understand these deep subject matters and realize our original, internal self, let us aspire to attain the mercy of the bona fide spiritual master, and through him, aspire to perform *bhajana*.

evaṁ-vrataḥ sva-priya-nāma-kīrtyā
jātānurāgo druta-citta uccaiḥ
hasaty atho roditi rauti gāyaty
unmāda-van nṛtyati loka-bāhyaḥ

(*Śrīmad-Bhāgavatam* 11.2.4)

> By chanting the holy name of the Supreme Lord, one comes to the stage of love of Godhead. Then the devotee is fixed in his vow as an eternal servant of the Lord, and he gradually becomes very much attached to a particular name and form of the Lord. As his heart melts with ecstatic love, he laughs very loudly or cries or shouts. Sometimes he sings and dances like a madman, for he is indifferent to public opinion.

Such a pure devotee has no shyness in regard to expressing his devotion. He chants loudly, unaware of his environment and unaware of whether or not he is dressed. Constantly remembering the pastimes of Kṛṣṇa, sometimes he weeps, "Kṛṣṇa, where are You?" and sometimes he rolls on the ground, laughing. Ordinary people consider him mad, but he is simply experiencing love of God. This spiritual realization is our true position and it is the aim and object of our life. Let us endeavor to engage our mind in hearing (*śravaṇaṁ*), worshiping (*arcanaṁ*), and especially in chanting the holy names of the Lord (*nāma-saṅkīrtanaṁ*).

Question: Is the *jīva* conscious of what he is doing when he chooses to turn away from Kṛṣṇa and become enamored by *māyā*?

Śrīla Nārāyaṇa Gosvāmī Mahārāja: No, he is unaware of the implications of his choice. He thinks, "I am doing the best thing for myself. I will enjoy." He is like a baby trying to capture fire with his bare little hands. He believes that the fire is something he can eat, whereas that fire will devour him. Similarly, the *jīva* looks towards this world for enjoyment, but is devoured by the cycle of repeated births and deaths, sorrows, and suffering.

If you are always engaged in the practices of *bhakti*, then *māyā* – forgetfulness of your relationship with the Lord – will not be able to attract you.

[This discourse, given on June 15, 2005 in Badger, California, is based on Śrīla Bhaktivinoda Ṭhākura's book, Śrī Śrīmad Bhāgavata Arka Marīcimāla, which means "A Garland of Śrīmad-Bhāgavatam Verses."]

The Three Viṣṇu Incarnations [Puruṣa-Avatāras]

The three *puruṣa-avatāras* are the Lords of the universal creation. They are responsible for generating, maintaining, and destroying the entire material cosmos. They are the Supersoul of everything that exists. (The word *viṣṇu* indicates "He who is all-pervading, omnipresent.")

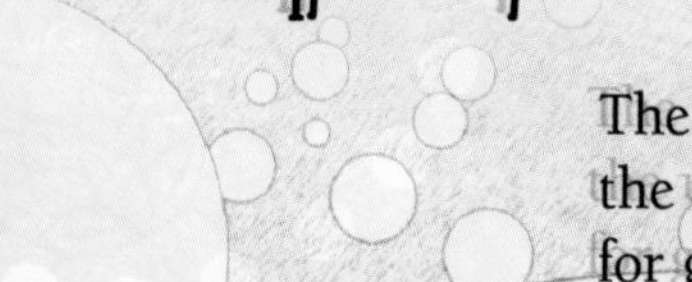

(Sources: *Śrīmad-Bhāgavatam* 1.3.2, purport; *Śrīmad-Bhāgavatam* 2.5.33, purport; *Śrī Caitanya-caritāmṛta*, *Ādi-līlā* 2.52, purport; *Śrī Caitanya-caritāmṛta*, *Madhya-līlā* 2.244, purport; *Śrī Caitanya-caritāmṛta*, *Madhya-līlā* 20.251; *Room Conversation*, Geneve, June 4, 1974.)

Śrī Mahā-Viṣṇu

The first *puruṣa-avatāra* is called Mahā-Viṣṇu or Kāraṇodakaśāyī Viṣṇu. He lies down within the Kāraṇa (Causal) Ocean, and is the creator of the total material energy. As He breathes, innumerable universes emanate from the pores of His body. He glances over the material nature (represented here as Durgā), impregnating it with those living entities who have emanated from His glance and have chosen to go to there. He is the original Supersoul of the entire material creation, which is the aggregate of material universes.

Śrī Garbhodakaśāyī-Viṣṇu

The second *puruṣa-avatāra* is Garbhodakaśāyī Viṣṇu. He enters each and every universe, where He lies down on the Garbha Ocean, which emanated from the perspiration of His own body. Thus, He is the Supersoul within each individual universe. From His navel springs the stem of a lotus, and on the flower petals of that lotus Lord Brahmā, the first living entity within the universe, is born. He places Lord Brahmā in charge of manifesting the Vedas as well as creating all the material objects and all the forms of living beings within that universe.

Śrī Kṣīrodakaśāyī-Viṣṇu

The third *puruṣa-avatāra* is Kṣīrodakaśāyī Viṣṇu. Within each universe He enters into each and every atom of the material creation, and also into the hearts of all the living entities within the creation. Thus, He is known as the Supersoul of all the individual living beings and the Supersoul in all material objects. He is the witness of all activities, from Him come knowledge, remembrance, and forgetfulness, and He awards the results of material activities.

CHAPTER TWO

A MAP OF THE WORLDS

How and why did this world come into existence? We must know the answer to this question. The answer is given in the first verse of *Śrīmad-Bhāgavatam*, and it is the central theme of this discussion:

> *janmādy asya yato 'nvayād itarataś*
> *cārtheṣv abhijñaḥ svarāṭ*
> *tene brahma hṛdā ya ādi-kavaye*
> *muhyanti yat sūrayaḥ*
> *tejo-vāri-mṛdāṁ yathā vinimayo*
> *yatra tri-sargo 'mṛṣā*
> *dhāmnā svena sadā nirasta-kuhakaṁ*
> *satyaṁ paraṁ dhīmahi*

O my Lord, Śrī Kṛṣṇa, son of Vasudeva, O all-pervading Personality of Godhead, I offer my respectful obeisances unto You. I meditate upon Śrī Kṛṣṇa because He is the Absolute Truth and the primeval cause of all causes of the

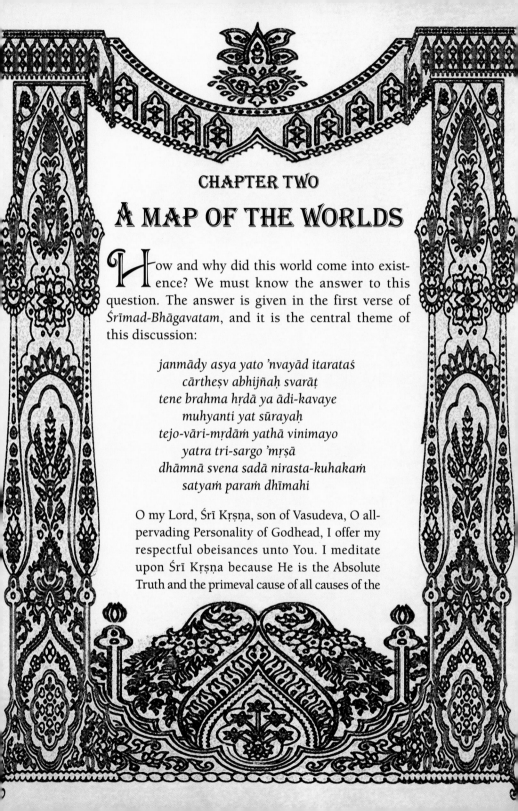

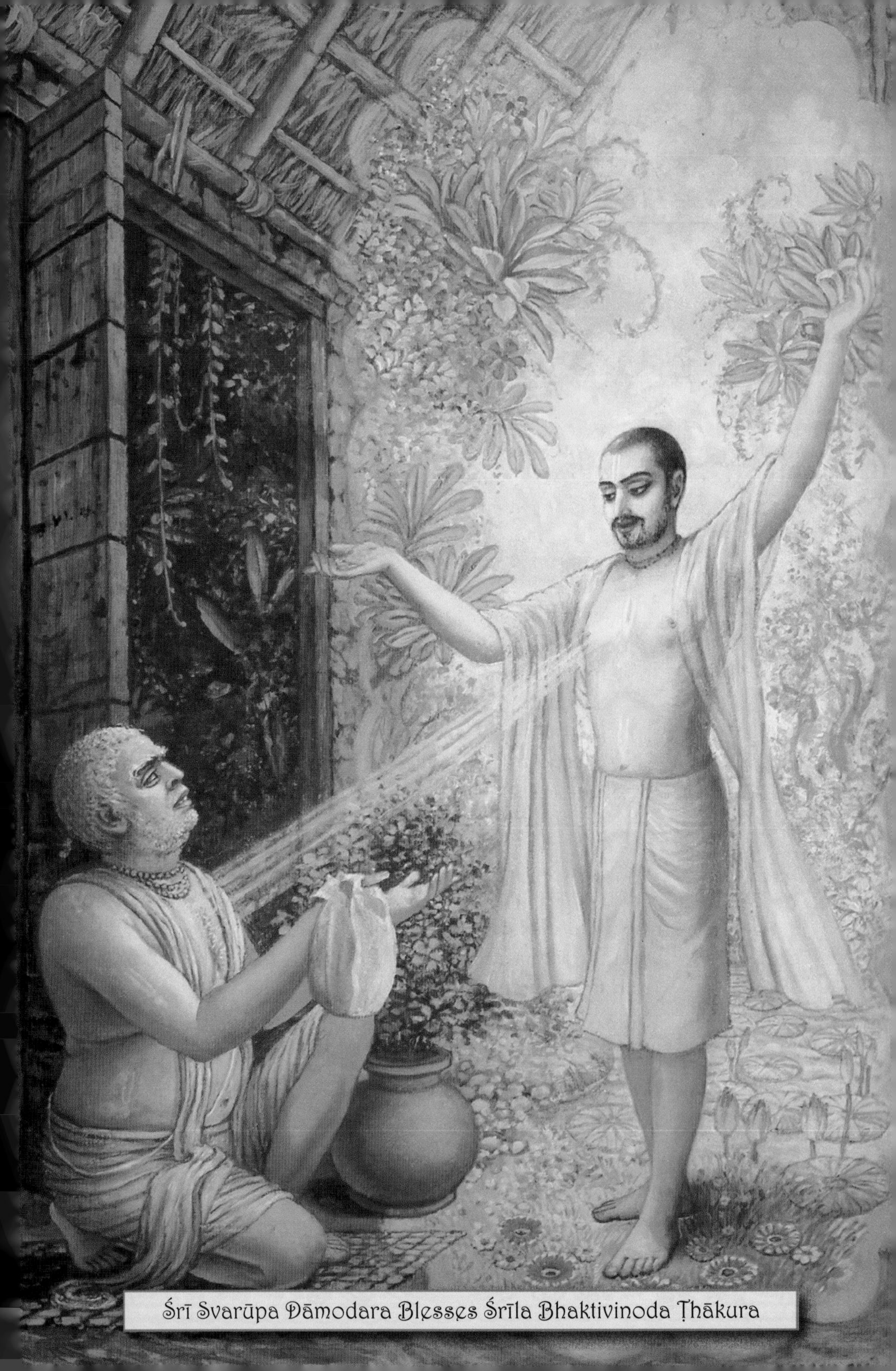

Śrī Svarūpa Dāmodara Blesses Śrīla Bhaktivinoda Ṭhākura

> creation, sustenance, and destruction of the manifested universes. He is directly and indirectly conscious of all manifestations, and He is independent because there is no other cause beyond Him. It is He only who first imparted the Vedic knowledge unto the heart of Brahmāji, the original living being. By Him, even the great sages and demigods are placed into illusion, as one is bewildered by the illusory representations of water seen in fire or land seen on water. Only because of Him do the material universes, temporarily manifested by the reactions of the three modes of nature, appear factual although they are unreal. I therefore meditate upon Him, Śrī Kṛṣṇa, who is eternally existent in the transcendental abode, which is forever free from the illusory representations of the material world. I meditate upon Him, for He is the Absolute Truth.

Śrī Svarūpa Dāmodara expounded upon this important verse to Śrīla Bhaktivinoda Ṭhākura, who in turn expanded that explanation in his book, *Śrī Bhāgavata Arka Marīcimāla*. I am further delineating the teachings of this significant verse according to the teachings of these two previous *ācāryas*. Although this is a very deep subject, we should acquaint ourselves with its important philosophy.

One Without a Second

In this world there are unlimited living entities in the 8,400,000 species of life, and it is impossible to fathom the extent of the varieties of their natures and qualities. All these conditioned living entities are expansions of Śrī Kṛṣṇa's energy.

At the same time, Kṛṣṇa has innumerable associates in the transcendental world – His parents Nanda Bābā and Mother Yaśodā, His many cowherd friends such as Dāmā, Śrīdama, Subala, and Madhumaṅgala, and His millions of *gopī* beloveds – with their innumerable natures and qualities.

Kṛṣṇa has numberless expansions in both the spiritual and material worlds. Yet, the *Śrīmad-Bhāgavatam* states that the Absolute Truth, Śrī Kṛṣṇa, is one-without-a-second (*advaya-jñāna*). This means He is devoid of duality, He is the sum-total of all existence and there is no one besides Him. In light of the previous statements, which mention the extent and variety of conditioned living entities and transcendental associates, why has the *Śrīmad-Bhāgavatam* stated that Kṛṣṇa is one without a second?

[**Editorial note:** *As mentioned in 'A Note from the Editors' at the beginning of this book, Śrīla Nārāyaṇa Gosvāmī Mahārāja uses several Sanskrit terms from the Vedic literatures. There are no exact English equivalents for these spiritually scientific terms. Therefore, for precision of the original depth of meaning, in addition to the English translation we have kept the original Sanskrit terms. As these terms are used throughout this book in different contexts, you will soon be able to understand and relish them. If you are new to this subject and feel it is too cumbersome to read all the Sanskrit terms, feel free to skip over them until you feel more comfortable with them. We are especially mentioning this here, because many Sanskrit terms come up in the next few paragraphs.*]

Kṛṣṇa is one without a second because nothing, and no one, has any independent existence from Him; everything and everyone depends upon Him for existence. In the transcendental world, He expands as His own personal power (*cit-śakti*, or *svarūpa-śakti*), which is also known as His internal power (*antaraṅga-śakti*).[1] The living entities are manifestations of His marginal energy (*jīva-śakti*, or *taṭasthā-śakti*), which is situated between the transcendental and material worlds. Finally, in this material world, His illusory power called *māyā-śakti* manifests the innumerable varieties of inert matter visible to us. None of these powers, or potencies, has any independent existence from Him.

In this verse, not only is Śrī Kṛṣṇa described as one-without-a-second, but His power (*śakti*) is one-without-a-second as well. At the same time, His power is known by various names, such as the internal potency (*antaraṅga-śakti*), the pleasure potency (*hlādinī-śakti*) and the transcendental or spiritual potency (*cit-śakti*, or *svarūpa-śakti*). There are different names for the one *śakti*.[2]

The living entities (*jīva-śakti*, or *taṭasthā-śakti*) and this inert world (*māyā-śakti*) are not different from the non-dual spiritual potency (*cit-śakti* or *svarūpa-śakti*), in the sense that they have no independent

1 "The *cit-śakti*, which is also called *svarūpa-śakti* or *antaraṅga-śakti*, displays many varied manifestations. It sustains the kingdom of God and its paraphernalia" (*Śrī Caitanya-caritāmṛta, Ādi-līlā* 2.101).

2 See the chart on Lord Kṛṣṇa's potencies (*śaktis*) on pages 48 and 49.

existence from it. When that internal, transcendental potency manifests the millions of infinitesimal *jīvas*, then, according to its activity, it is called *taṭasthā-śakti*. When the shadow of that same internal potency manifests this material world and its varieties of inert matter, then, according to its activity, it is called *bahiraṅgā-śakti* (the external energy), or *māyā-śakti* (the deluding material energy), or simply *māyā*. But ultimately, that internal, spiritual potency is one.

When the marginal energy (the living entities) comes in contact with *māyā-śakti* (the external energy), it manifests as the world of the living entities. *Māyā-śakti* has manifested this inert, temporary world, with its varieties of bodies, minds, natures, and so on.

In this world we are under the illusion of *māyā*, and there is a prominence of *māyā*, so we consider that this phantasmagoric world is full of *māyā*. Ultimately, though, as mentioned above, *māyā* is a shadow manifestation of Kṛṣṇa's intrinsic internal potency, His *svarūpa-śakti* or *antaraṅga-śakti*, whose embodiment is Śrīmatī Rādhikā.[3] This is because *māyā* is a power, or *śakti*, and all *śaktis* are transformations of *svarūpa-śakti*.

However, if we say that *māyā-śakti* refers directly to Śrīmatī Rādhikā Herself, this would be a misunderstanding. If we say that the form of *māyā* is Rādhikā Herself, this is incorrect, but if we say that *māyā* (personified as Durgā-devī) is a shadow expansion of Rādhikā and therefore has no independent existence from Her, this is correct.[4]

In this way, it is not that there are many *śaktis*; there is only one *śakti*, but it has different names according to various functions. Moreover, there is no duality in *śakti* (the power) and *śaktimān* (the possessor of the power). "*Śakti-śaktimatayor abheda* – Śrī Kṛṣṇa and His power are non-different or non-dual." They are one. [Pease see chart of Kṛṣṇa's energies on pages 48 and 49.]

---

3 "The *śaktis* (potencies) of God exist in two ways. When the potencies of the Lord are situated within His form and are one with it, they are manifest as potency alone without shape. When they are manifest in the form of the presiding deity of the *śakti*, they appear as the associates of the Lord and render all of their varieties of service; then they are called personified" (*Bhakti Prajñāna Keśava Gosvāmī – His Life and Precepts*, Part Five).

4 The following statement by Śrī Durgā can be found in the *Sammohana-tantra*: "The name Durgā, by which I am known, is Her name. The qualities for which I am famous are Her qualities. The majesty with which I am resplendent is Her majesty. That Mahā-Lakṣmī, Śrī Rādhā, is non-different from Śrī Kṛṣṇa. She is His dearmost sweetheart and the crest-jewel of His beloveds."

Pūrṇa-śakti and Pūrṇa-śaktimān, Śrī Śrī Rādhā-Kṛṣṇa

The Sacred Supreme Power

Śrī Kṛṣṇa is *pūrṇa-śaktimān*, the supreme energetic in His highest original form, and Śrīmatī Rādhikā is *pūrṇa-śakti*, His supreme energy in Her highest, original form. Also, Śrīmatī Rādhikā may be known as *pūrṇa-svarūpa-śakti*, the absolute embodiment of the original divine energy of the Lord and identical with Him. For example, musk is recognizable by and inseparable from its inherent fragrance. Similarly, fire is known by and is inseparable from its heat. Similarly, Śrīmatī Rādhikā and Śrī Kṛṣṇa, relishing Their transcendental pastimes, are eternally distinct personalities, but simultaneously non-different and inseparable. The three active potencies – *cit-śakti*, *jīva-śakti*, and *māyā-śakti* – emanate from the *svarūpa-śakti*. Another name of the *cit-śakti* is *antaraṅgā-śakti*, the internal spiritual potency, and another term for the jīva-śakti is the *taṭasthā-śakti*, the marginal energy. The synonym for the *māyā-śakti* is *bahiraṅgā-śakti*, the external energy. Although the *svarūpa-śakti* is one, She executes activities through these three extensions. All the eternal, inherent qualities of the *svarūpa-śakti* are fully manifest in the *cit-śakti*; they are minutely present in the *jīva-śakti*; and are perversely reflected in the *māyā-śakti*.

(*Jaiva-dharma*, Chapter 14)

A Fact of Wonder

The word *anvayād* in the above-mentioned first verse of *Śrīmad-Bhāgavatam* means 'direct.' This indicates that all potencies manifest directly from Śrī Kṛṣṇa. The word *itarataś*, meaning 'indirect,' indicates the existence of something very strange – a fact of wonder. Although the *jīva* is part and parcel of Kṛṣṇa and is therefore spiritual and conscious, he is now bound by *māyā* and is influenced by inert material energy. Although the soul is not his body, he thinks, "I am this body." How is this possible, since consciousness is superior to dull matter? Although it is not possible for the *jīva* to be bound by the inferior material energy, nevertheless it takes place. This is a fact of wonder.

When Śrī Kṛṣṇa created the *jīvas*, He gave them a very valuable gift called independence. We chose to misuse our independence, and now we are being rectified in the prison of this material world by its prison-warden, Māyā-devī.

Overview of Śrī Krsna's Potencies (Śaktis)

Kṛṣṇa is called sarva-śaktimān. Sarva-śaktimān means the possesor (mān) of all (sarva) potencies (śakti).

His one spiritual potency has many different names. The main names are:

- PARĀ-ŚAKTI, *meaning 'supreme potency'*
- SVARŪPA-ŚAKTI, *meaning 'personal, complete, intrinsic potency'*
- CIT-ŚAKTI, *meaning 'transcendental, spiritual, knowledge potency'*

Kṛṣṇa's original svarūpa-śakti is one, but it manifests in different ways, according to:

- Its function
- Its Activity

Three Activities of Svarūpa-śakti

IN OTHER WORDS, ALTHOUGH SVARŪPA-ŚAKTI IS ONE, SHE ACTS IN THE THREE FOLLOWING WAYS:

as CIT-ŚAKTI *svarūpa-śakti*	*as* JĪVA-ŚAKTI	*as* MĀYĀ-ŚAKTI *acit-śakti (a-cit = not-cit)*
OTHER NAMES: *antaraṅga-śakti* *internal energy*	OTHER NAMES: *taṭastha-śakti* *marginal energy*	OTHER NAMES: *bahiraṅga-sakti* *external energy*
ACTIVITY: *manifests the Holy Dhāmas, like Vaikuṇṭha, Goloka, Vraja, etc.*	ACTIVITY: *manifests the aggregate of unlimited jīvas*	ACTIVITY: *manifests the mundane world of inert material creations, like the unlimited material universes*
CORRESPONDING REALM OF EXISTENCE: *cit-sarga* *the transcendental realm*	CORRESPONDING REALM OF EXISTENCE: *jīva-sarga* *realm of living entities*	CORRESPONDING REALM OF EXISTENCE: *jaḍa-sarga* *realm of inert matter*

All the eternal characteristics of svarūpa-śakti are completely present in cit-śakti, present to a minute degree in jīva-śakti, and present in a distorted way (as a perverted reflection) in māyā-śakti.

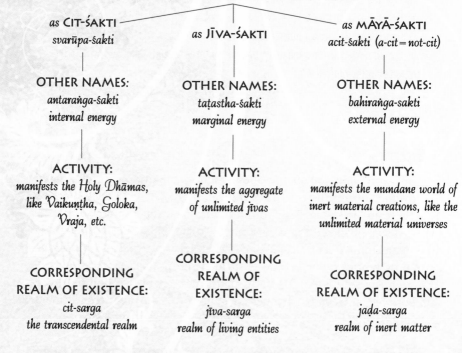

Three Functions of Svarūpa-śakti

KṚṢṆA'S ORIGINAL, CONSTITUTIONAL FORM, OR SVARŪPA, IS COMPOSED OF SAT (ETERNITY), CIT (KNOWLEDGE), AND ĀNANDA (BLISS) THEREFORE, HIS POTENCY, OR SVARŪPA-ŚAKTI, ALSO MANIFESTS IN THREE FORMS:

KṚṢṆA is SAT *(full of eternity)*	KṚṢṆA is CIT *(full of knowledge)*	KṚṢṆA is ĀNANDA *(full of bliss)*
KṚṢṆA *has* SANDHINĪ-ŚAKTI *(existence potency)*	KṚṢṆA *has* SAṀVIT-ŚAKTI *(knowledge potency)*	KṚṢṆA *has* HLĀDINĪ-ŚAKTI *(pleasure potency)*

The three aspects or functions of svarūpa-śakti (hlādinī, saṁvit, and sandhinī) completely influence all the activities of the cit-śakti, jīva-śakti, and māyā-śakti. Both jīva-śakti and māyā-śakti originate from Kṛṣṇa's original svarūpa-śakti, in the sense that jīva-śakti is an atomic part of svarūpa-śakti, and māyā-śakti is a perverted reflection of it.

THE ACTIVITIES OF / INFLUENCES	CIT-ŚAKTI or SVARŪPA-ŚAKTI	JĪVA-ŚAKTI	MĀYĀ-ŚAKTI
HLĀDINI	makes Kṛṣṇa joyful. By this *śakti*, both Kṛṣṇa (the embodiment of bliss) and His devotees taste pleasure (*cidānanda*). The essence of *hlādinī* is *prema*, and the concentrated essence of *prema* is called *mahābhāva*. The embodiment of this *mahābhāva* is Śrīmatī Rādhikā. She gives happiness to Kṛṣṇa in all ways: (1) in Her own transcendental form (2) by manifesting eight ecstatic symptoms (*bhāvas*), personified as the eight principal *sakhīs* (3) by manifesting four moods, personified as the four different groups of *sakhīs*	manifests as *brahmānanda*, the spiritual bliss of the *jīva*	manifests as mundane pleasure (*jaḍānanda*)
SAṀVIT	manifests all the various moods in the relationships of the devotees with Kṛṣṇa. Through this *saṁvit*-potency, Kṛṣṇa performs activities such as attracting the gopīs by playing on His flute, taking the cows for grazing, etc.	manifests as transcendental knowledge	manifests as material knowledge
SANDHINI	manifests everything in Kṛṣṇa's spiritual abode that consists of water, earth, etc., such as villages, forests, gardens, etc. All the places of Kṛṣṇa's pastimes, all the transcendental objects used in Kṛṣṇa's pastimes, as well as the transcendental bodies of Kṛṣṇa, Śrīmatī Rādhikā, all the Vrajavāsīs, all the animals, etc.	manifests the *jīva's* minute transcendental form	manifests the entire material universe, consisting of fourteen planetary systems, and the material bodies of the *jīvas*

(Source: *Jaiva-dharma*, Chapter 14)

There are twenty-eight principles[5] (*tattvas*) in the manifestation of this world, and none of them have any separate existence from the Supreme Lord. Although the *jīva* does not know how this world was created or how he was covered by *māyā*, Kṛṣṇa knows everything. By the influence of Kṛṣṇa's *māyā*, even great demigods like Brahmā and Śaṅkara (Śiva) may become bewildered, for even they are unable to measure the depth of power in His energy.

Because Kṛṣṇa is served by His *svarūpa-śakti*, His complete power personified as Śrīmatī Rādhikā, He is complete. It is stated in *Śrī Īśopaniṣad*:

> *oṁ pūrṇam adaḥ pūrṇam idaṁ pūrṇāt pūrṇam udacyate*
> *pūrṇasya pūrṇam ādāya pūrṇam evāvaśiṣyate*

> The Personality of Godhead is perfect and complete, and because He is completely perfect, all emanations from Him, such as this phenomenal world, are perfectly equipped as complete wholes. Whatever is produced from the Complete Whole is also complete in itself; and because He is the Complete Whole, even though so many complete units emanate from Him, He remains the complete balance.

The Supreme Lord is always complete, infinite, and independent; no one can control Him. He mercifully inspired Lord Brahmā, the original Vedic scholar (*ādi-kavi*), in the four 'nutshell' verses of the *Śrīmad-Bhāgavatam* called *catuḥ-ślokī*. Thus, Brahmā realized the Lord's glories by the Lord's mercy, and then manifested the Vedas with their unlimited knowledge. Even the world's greatly learned scholars become bewildered regarding the expanse of this Vedic knowledge. They cannot understand how Kṛṣṇa is controlling all of His energies and how these energies are working under His direction.

[5] The twenty-eight principles are: (1) the unmanifest material nature (*prakṛti*), (2) Mahā-Viṣṇu (or Kāraṇodakaśāyī Viṣṇu), (3) the unmanifest material world in the form of the aggregate of material ingredients (*mahat-tattva*), (4) the Supersoul (Paramātmā, or Kṣīrodakaśāyī Viṣṇu), (5) the living entity (*jīva*), (6) false ego, (7) intelligence, (8) mind, (9-13) the five gross elements (ether, air, fire, water, earth), (14-18) the five sense objects (sound, touch, form, taste, smell), (19-23) the five organs of sense perception (ear, skin, eyes, tongue, nose), and (24-28) the five working sense organs (hands, feet, mouth, anus, genitals).

Three Worlds

The word *tri-sargaḥ* in the above-mentioned *Śrīmad-Bhāgavatam* verse (1.1.1) refers to the three kinds of creation: the transcendental realm (*cit-sarga*), the realm of the living entities (*jīva-sarga*), and the material realm, or the realm of inert matter (*jaḍa-sarga*). *Cit-sarga*, the transcendental world, begins from the Vaikuṇṭha planets and goes up to the highest of the Lord's abodes, Goloka Vṛndāvana. In Vṛndāvana, Nanda Bābā, Mother Yaśodā, the cowherd boys, the *gopīs*, the trees, creepers, rivers, and mountains are all transcendental. Everything and everyone there is full of eternal life, unending bliss, and unfathomable knowledge (*sat-cit-ānanda*).

Love in Friendship

Because they would massage Kṛṣṇa's legs with great love, the *sakhās*, Kṛṣṇa's cowherd friends, are referred to as *mahātmās*, great souls. There are millions of *sakhās* and all are exalted. Some would fan Him, but not with a *cāmara*; with a fan made of leaves and peacock feathers they would fan Him with great love. They serve Kṛṣṇa by providing their own laps as pillows for His head – can such good fortune be seen anywhere else? Their affection for Kṛṣṇa is supremely natural, in the mood of *nara-līlā*, which means they consider Him to be an ordinary child. Seeing how Kṛṣṇa has exerted Himself in wrestling with them and in taking the cows out to graze, the *sakhās* serve Him with tender feelings in order to remove His exhaustion...To remove even one drop of perspiration from Kṛṣṇa's brow they are prepared to give up their very lives.

(*Bhakti-rasāyana*, Chapter 10)

Śrīla Raghunātha dāsa Gosvāmī prays:

yat kiñcit tṛṇa-gulma-kīkaṭa-mukhaṁ goṣṭhe samastaṁ hi tat
sarvānandamayaṁ mukunda-dayitaṁ līlānukūlaṁ param
śāstrair eva muhur muhuḥ sphuṭam idam niṣṭaṅkitaṁ yācñyā
brahmāder api saspṛheṇa tad idaṁ sarvaṁ mayā vandyate

(*Stavāvalī, Vraja- vilāsa-stava* 102)

With great longing I worship all the living entities of Vraja, including the grass, bushes, flies, and birds, which are filled with transcendental bliss. Their fortune is so great that it is aspired for by personalities like Śrī Brahmā and Uddhava. *Śrīmad-Bhāgavatam* and other *śāstras* have repeatedly and clearly propounded their glories. They are very dear to Śrī Mukunda and assist in His pastimes.

Forever in Love

In this way the cows and calves, due to excessive joy, forget themselves and get lost in gazing at the one who adorns His moon-like face with the *veṇu*. As soon as they see Vrajendra-nandana, His sweet and incomparable beautiful form manifests in their hearts, and their eyes fill with tears of joy. Thus, they cannot even see Him although He is standing right in front of them. They can only hear and relish the *veṇu's* wonderful *rasa*-filled sound through their ears. They remain absolutely still, being intoxicated from tasting the nectar of their internal vision of that most attractive form. It seems that these cows, who are the embodiment of the nectar of *vātsalya-prema* (motherly love), make their lives successful by taking Vrajendra-nandana in the laps of their hearts, being unable to do so outwardly. As a result, they drown in ecstatic bliss.

(*Veṇu-gīta*, Chapter 13)

In this world there is no example of *cit-sarga* (the spiritual realm) and there is no perfect analogy to explain it. Still, commenting upon this verse from the *Bhāgavatam*, Śrīla Bhaktivinoda Ṭhākura cites the analogy of fire in order to help us gradually understand.

What is fire? Fire is a *śakti*, or potency. Although we cannot see fire despite the fact that it is everywhere (in its invisible feature as a potency), by the striking of matches or the rubbing together of two stones or pieces of wood, flames become visible. In other words, fire manifests when there is an appropriate cause for it to do so.

In a similar way, the Lord's spiritual potency is transcendental and cannot be seen or experienced by material senses. His spiritual abode, Goloka Vṛndāvana, is ever present in the transcendental realm, far beyond the purview of our sense perception. As fire sometimes manifests, so Kṛṣṇa and His incarnations like Lord Rāmacandra and Lord Nṛsiṁhadeva appear in this world from time to time. Kṛṣṇa comes especially to show favor to His devotees, and at that time He performs an unlimited variety of activities to please them.

The analogy of the fire has been given in relation to the spiritual realm. Regarding the realm of the living entities, this crucial *Śrīmad-Bhāgavatam* verse gives the analogy of water. In a very cold environment water becomes ice, and if that ice is thrown at someone, it may injure that person or even fracture his bones. On the other hand, in water's natural state, if a man is very thirsty he can drink it and find it sweet.

Similarly, as water's natural state is liquidity, the *jīva's* natural state is to be an eternal servant of Kṛṣṇa. By constitution, the *jīva* serves Kṛṣṇa and is joyous in that service. When he misuses the independence given by Kṛṣṇa, *māyā* throws him very far away from Kṛṣṇa and gives him gross and subtle bodies whereby he becomes like ice. He is frozen, out of his own nature, at which time he thinks, "I am this body, and the happiness and suffering of this body is mine."

When the conditioned *jīva* becomes advanced in spiritual life, he sees that there is in fact no bondage and no liberation from that bondage. In reality he is always liberated, but at present he is in the illusion that he is bound. It is only by the mercy of *guru*, and then the mercy of Kṛṣṇa, that he is able to emerge from this bodily conception of bondage.

The analogy of fire elucidates the nature of the transcendental realm (*cit-sarga*), and the second analogy, of water, illustrates the nature of the living entities (*jīva-sarga*). Now, consider the analogy of earth in order to understand the creation of this world of inert matter (*jaḍa-sarga*).

In this material world, more than fire or water, earth is the prominent element; almost everything is made of earth. For example, an earthen pot is made of earth. It can carry water if it has been first baked in a kiln, but still it is earth. In fact, gold, copper, coal, and diamonds are also manifestations of the element earth.[6] One can manufacture a variety of products with various functions, all seemingly different, but these products are all basically earth.

This analogy is given to express the principle of *māyā-śakti*, the *māyā* creation. Just as the pot, gold, copper, etc. appear to be separate elements whereas they are nothing but earth, similarly, everything in the material world is composed of *māyā*. Although this world is made of *māyā-śakti* and is thus perishable and illusory, by the influence of Śrī Kṛṣṇa's *acintya-śakti* (His inconceivable power) it appears to be a permanent truth.

6 *Bhagavad-gītā* states that there are five gross material elements: earth, water, fire, air, and ether. Diamonds, copper, and gold are not mentioned as being separate elements.

Faith in the Spiritual Realm

The above-mentioned *Śrīmad-Bhāgavatam* verse states: *dhāmnā svena sadā nirasta-kuhakaṁ*. This phrase means that the abode of Lord Kṛṣṇa is completely free from *māyā*. That realm is animated only by Yogamāyā, who is the manifestation of the Lord's superior spiritual energy (*parā-śakti*) and who enlivens all the residents with pure love.

Land of Transcendental Potency

This *yogamāyā* and *mahāmāyā* are called the superior and inferior potencies, respectively. They are perceived as two forms. Actually they are one, but the original is superior and its shadow is inferior. ... In Goloka, Kṛṣṇa's *rāsa-līlā*, Kṛṣṇa's taking birth, devotees serving Kṛṣṇa, Kṛṣṇa's form, the *gopīs'* forms, the trees and plants there – everything is manifest by the influence of *yogamāyā* and is true and eternal."

(*Going Beyond Vaikuṇṭha*, Chapter 8)

Only the spiritual pleasure potency (*hlādinī-śakti*), the eternal existence potency (*sandhinī-śakti*), and the transcendental knowledge potency (*saṁvit-śakti*), which are the three aspects of *svarūpa-śakti*, are present there. The illusion (*māyā*) which creates this material world is not present in the spiritual realm.

Thus, those who reside there never fall to this material world. It is not that the *jīvas* of this world have forgotten that spiritual abode and come here. Rather, they have forgotten that they are originally manifest from the borderline region called *taṭasthā*, which lies between the material and spiritual worlds.

The phrase *satyaṁ paraṁ* means that Śrī Kṛṣṇa, Vrajendra-nandana Syamasundara, the youthful son of the king of Vraja, who possesses a dazzling cloudlike complexion, is *paraṁ-satya*, the Supreme Truth. The word *dhīmahi*, meaning 'I meditate,' indicates, "I meditate on that Supreme Truth. May He be merciful and kindly manifest in my heart." Or, "I meditate upon the Supreme Absolute Truth Śrī Kṛṣṇa, along with the embodiment of His *svarūpa-śakti*, Śrīmatī Rādhikā, and Her bodily expansions, the *gopīs*." "*Dhāmnā svena sadā* – That Absolute Truth is eternally present in Goloka Vṛndāvana, and sometimes He manifests in the material world with His associates."

GOLOKA VṚNDAVANA
MATHURĀ/DVĀRAKĀ
AYODHYĀ
VAIKUṆṬHA PLANETS
BRAHMAJYOTI
CAUSAL OCEAN
ONE MATERIAL UNIVERSE
JADA-JAGAT
GARBHODAKA OCEAN

In the *Bhagavad-gītā* (15.6) Śrī Kṛṣṇa states: "*Yad gatvā na nivartante tad dhāma paramaṁ mama* – those who reach that supreme abode of Mine never return to this material world." As mentioned above, the Lord's associates come here now and then, but only to fulfill His mission. By practicing great austerities for millions of births, one may go to Goloka Vṛndāvana. Since there is no *māyā* in Vṛndāvana, how can one be interested in anything but Kṛṣṇa? How can anyone fall from there? Rather, Yogamāyā assists all the residents of that abode to lovingly serve Him forever.

By Śrī Kṛṣṇa's unlimited power He manifests the transcendental world, the world of *jīvas* and the myriad material universes, and simultaneously He maintains His own separate and independent existence. Śrīla Vyāsadeva, the author of this foundational *Śrīmad-Bhāgavatam* verse, is offering obeisances to that Absolute Truth, Śrī Kṛṣṇa.

In conclusion, consider the analogy that when a person takes a bath, most of the water disappears from his body and goes down the drain. Yet, some water remains on the body, and that is enough to cleanse it. Similarly, although this subject is profound and difficult to grasp at first, please endeavor to understand. Allow to remain with you whatever knowledge you can grasp.

[*This discourse was given on June 14, 2005, in Badger, California, on the subject of Śrīla Bhaktivinoda Ṭhākura's book, Bhāgavata Arka Marīcimāla. The sub-section, Faith In That Realm, is an excerpt from Śrīla Nārāyaṇa Gosvāmī Mahārāja's book, Secret Truths of the Bhāgavatam.*]

CHAPTER THREE

THE ORIGIN OF THE LIVING ENTITY

In this discourse, Śrīla Bhaktivedānta Nārāyaṇa Gosvāmī Mahārāja discusses a conversation that took place between Śrī Caitanya Mahāprabhu and Śrīla Sanātana Gosvāmī as described in the Śrī Caitanya-caritāmṛta. Herein, Śrīla Sanātana Gosvāmī is playing the role of a conditioned soul who is seeking divine self-awareness and freedom from material miseries. He has inquired from Śrī Caitanya Mahāprabhu about his own true identity, which is beyond the body.

The Crest-jewel of Inquiry

Śrīla Sanātana Gosvāmī inquired from Śrī Caitanya Mahāprabhu, "I have come to this world, but I do not know who I am. Who am I?"

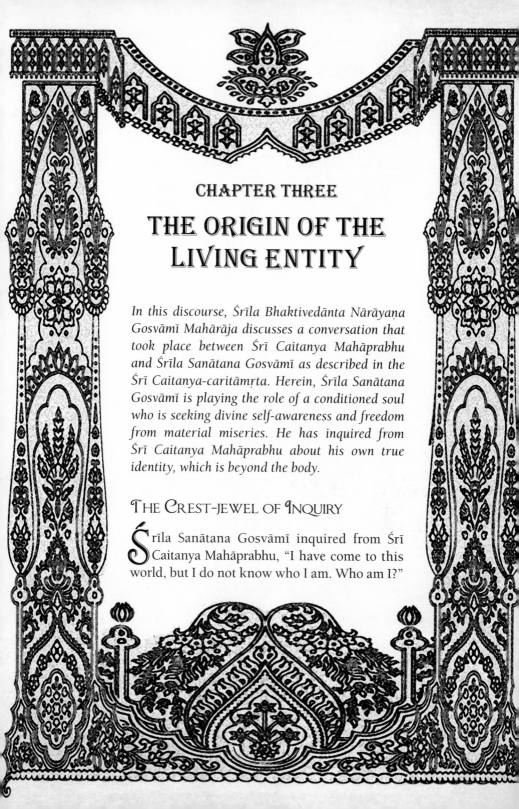

Śrīla Sanātana Gosvāmī questions Śrī Caitanya Mahāprabhu

In order to understand this subject, we will turn to the translations of Śrīla Bhaktivedānta Svāmī Mahārāja. In *Śrī Caitanya-caritāmṛta, Madhya-līlā* 20.102-103 his translation states:

> Who am I? Why do the threefold miseries always give me trouble? If I do not know this, how can I be benefited? Actually, I do not know how to inquire about the goal of life and the process for obtaining it. Being merciful upon me, please explain all these truths.

None of us know who we are by spiritual constitution. Someone may consider, "I am Īśa Prabhu," another may think, "I am Keśava Prabhu," and others may conjecture that they are this or that person. Therefore, in order to indicate our true identity, Śrīla Sanātana Gosvāmī humbly questioned Śrī Caitanya Mahāprabhu.

Mahāprabhu replied, "You know everything, but you are inquiring about your true identity so as to uplift others. Although a saintly person knows everything, he remains very humble and tries to confirm his statements by asking the higher authorities."

> *kṛṣṇa-sakti dhara tumi, jana tattva-bhava*
> *jani' dardhya lagi' puche,-sadhura svabhava*
>
> (*Śrī Caitanya-caritāmṛta, Madhya-līlā* 20.105)

> Since you possess Lord Kṛṣṇa's potency, you certainly know these things. However, it is the nature of a *sādhu* to inquire. Although he knows these things, the *sādhu* inquires for the sake of strictness.

Mahāprabhu continued, "You are not really Sanātana, in the sense that you are not this physical body."

> *jīvera 'svarūpa' haya——kṛṣṇera 'nitya-dāsa'*
> *kṛṣṇera 'taṭasthā-śakti' 'bhedābheda-prakāśa'*
>
> *sūryāṁśa-kiraṇa, yaiche agni-jvālā-caya*
> *svābhāvika kṛṣṇera tina-prakāra 'śakti' haya*
>
> (*Śrī Caitanya-caritāmṛta, Madhya-līlā* 20.108–109)

> It is the living entity's constitutional position to be an eternal servant of Kṛṣṇa, because he is the marginal energy of Kṛṣṇa – a manifestation simultaneously one with and different from

the Lord, like a molecular particle of sunshine or spark of fire. Kṛṣṇa has three varieties of energy.[1]

Śrī Caitanya Mahāprabhu explained that by spiritual constitution, all those who have life – such as human beings, birds, animals, trees and creepers, and even worms and insects – are all eternal servants of Lord Kṛṣṇa. All souls are transformations of the Lord's marginal potency (*taṭasthā-śakti parināma*). They are not direct transformations of *svarūpa-śakti*.

Śrī Caitanya Mahāprabhu continued:

kṛṣṇa bhuli' sei jīva anādi-bahirmukha
ataeva māyā tāre deya saṁsāra-duḥkha

(*Śrī Caitanya-caritāmṛta, Madhya-līlā* 20.117)

Forgetting Kṛṣṇa, the living entity has been attracted by the external feature from time immemorial. Therefore, the illusory energy *māyā* gives him all kinds of misery in this material existence.

Śrīla Kṛṣṇadāsa Kavirāja is quoting the version of Śrī Caitanya Mahāprabhu. The *jīva,* the eternal servant of Kṛṣṇa, is Kṛṣṇa's mar-ginal potency (*taṭasthā-śakti*). Essential to understand and remember is that he is not pure *svarūpa-śakti,* or internal potency. *Taṭasthā-śakti* is one of the energies of *svarūpa-śakti*, but it is not full.

Svarūpa-śakti has three functions (*vṛttis*), namely transcendental happiness (*hlādinī*), divine knowledge (*saṁvit*), and spiritual existence

1 "Śrīla Bhaktivinoda Ṭhākura explains these verses as follows: Śrī Sanātana Gosvāmī asked Śrī Caitanya Mahāprabhu, 'Who am I?' In answer, the Lord replied, 'You are a pure living entity. You are neither the gross material body nor the subtle body composed of mind and intelligence. Actually you are a spirit soul, eternally part and parcel of the Supreme Soul, Kṛṣṇa. Therefore you are His eternal servant. You belong to Kṛṣṇa's marginal potency.

"There are two worlds – the spiritual world and the material world – and you are situated between the material and spiritual potencies. You have a relationship with both the material and the spiritual world; therefore you are called the marginal potency. You are related with Kṛṣṇa as simultaneously one and different from Him. Because you are spirit soul, you are one in quality with the Supreme Personality of Godhead, but because you are a very minute particle of spirit soul, you are different from the Supreme Soul'" (*Śrī Caitanya-caritāmṛta, Madhya-līlā* 20.108–109, purport).

(*sandhinī*). It is from *svarūpa-śakti* that Lord Nṛsiṁha, Lord Rāma, and other direct incarnations of Kṛṣṇa manifest, and these incarnations are called *svāṁśa*, Kṛṣṇa's personal expansions. [*Sva* means 'own' or 'plenary' or 'direct,' and *aṁśa* means 'part' or 'expansion.'] This is not true for the *vibhinnāṁśa-tattva jīvas* [*vibhinna* means 'separated' and *aṁśa* means 'portion.']

svāṁśa-vibhinnāṁśa-rūpe hañā vistāra
ananta vaikuṇṭha-brahmāṇḍe karena vihāra

(*Śrī Caitanya-caritāmṛta, Madhya-līlā* 22.9)

Kṛṣṇa expands Himself in many forms. Some of them are personal expansions and some are separate expansions. Thus He performs pastimes in both the spiritual and material worlds. The spiritual worlds are the Vaikuṇṭha planets, and the material universes are *brahmāṇḍas*, gigantic globes governed by Lord Brahmā.

A question arises: if all souls are eternal servants of Śrī Kṛṣṇa, how could they have become averse to Him? Why did they turn away from Him? The answer is that the *jīvas* who became averse had not yet realized their constitutional position of eternal service.

Two Kinds of Souls

There are two categories of *jīvas*, as stated in *Śrī Caitanya-caritāmṛta, Madhya-līlā* 22.10–13:

sei vibhinnāṁśa jīva – dui ta' prakāra
eka – 'nitya-mukta', eka – 'nitya-saṁsāra'

(*Śrī Caitanya-caritāmṛta, Madhya-līlā* 22.10)

The living entities, the *jīvas*, are divided into two categories. Some are *nitya-mukta*, eternally liberated, never having been conditioned, and others are perpetually conditioned (*nitya-saṁsāra,* or *nitya-baddha*).

The meaning of *nitya-saṁsāra* in this verse is not 'forever conditioned.' It means that the time we have been conditioned is so vast that it cannot be calculated.

Only Two Kinds of Souls

"There are two categories of *vibhinnāṃśa jīvas*, not three. The *jīvas* who manifest in the spiritual world are eternally liberated (*nitya-mukta*) *vibhinnāṃśa jīvas*; and the *jīvas* who manifest in the *taṭasthā* region and who look from there towards the spiritual world are also eternally liberated (*nitya-mukta*) *vibhinnāṃśa jīvas*. The *jīvas* who look towards the material world from the *taṭasthā* region are called conditioned souls, or *nitya-baddha* (or *nitya-saṃsāra*) *vibhinnāṃśa jīvas*."

(Continued in Part Four, Overview)

'nitya-mukta' – nitya kṛṣṇa-carane unmukha
'kṛṣṇa-parisada' nama, bhunje seva-sukha

(*Śrī Caitanya-caritāmṛta, Madhya-līlā* 22.11)

Those who are eternally liberated are always awake to Kṛṣṇa consciousness, and they render transcendental loving service at the feet of Lord Kṛṣṇa. They are to be considered eternal associates of Kṛṣṇa, and they are eternally enjoying the transcendental bliss of serving Him."

This is a prominent point to understand. The liberated *jīvas* are eternal associates of Śrī Kṛṣṇa in His abode, always engaged in serving Him and relishing the sweetness of their service to Him. In the Lord's abode, the potency that bewilders the conditioned soul and encourages him to identify with his body is not present.

Never to the River

"There are many living entities who are eternally liberated. They never come to this world. It is just like the ocean and the rivers. In the river you will find fishes and in the ocean you will find fishes. Sometimes it may be that the fishes of the river may go to the ocean, but the fishes of the ocean never come to the river – they never come to the river. There is no place for them there."

(Lecture by Śrīla Bhaktivedānta Svāmī Mahārāja.
New York, January 8, 1967)

Only Yogamāyā, the spiritual potency that nourishes the service mood of liberated souls, is present there. There is nothing in the spiritual world to make one forget Kṛṣṇa, and therefore the Lord's associates are never liable to forget Him or become averse to Him. The love and affection of these associates is always fresh and ever-new; it is ever-unfolding. Even if the 'newness' of the love and affection reaches its limit and there is no room for further newness, still, it becomes ever-increasingly new and fresh.

In regard to the second category of *jīva*:

> *nitya-baddha' – kṛṣṇa haite nitya-bahirmukha*
> *'nitya-saṁsāra', bhuñje narakādi duḥkha*
>
> (*Śrī Caitanya-caritāmṛta, Madhya-līlā* 22.12)

> Apart from the ever-liberated devotees, there are the conditioned souls, who always turn away from the service of the Lord. They are perpetually conditioned in this material world and are thus subjected to the material tribulations brought about by different bodily forms in hellish conditions.

> *sei doṣe māyā-piśācī daṇḍa kare tāre*
> *ādhyātmikādi tāpa-traya tāre jāri' māre*
>
> (*Śrī Caitanya-caritāmṛta, Madhya-līlā* 22.13)

> Due to his being opposed to Kṛṣṇa consciousness, the conditioned soul is punished by the witch of the external energy, *māyā*. He is thus ready to suffer the threefold miseries brought about by the body and mind, the inimical behavior of other living entities, and natural disturbances caused by the demigods.

The souls in the second category – the conditioned souls – have never directly associated with Kṛṣṇa. They have never relished His service, and that is why they are called *nitya-bahirmukha*, or conditioned from beginningless time.

The above-mentioned verse states that the souls in the second category are being punished by *māyā*. Why are they being punished? What have they done wrong? Their defect is that they have chosen to turn away from Kṛṣṇa. They preferred to look towards the material world for pleasure; in this way it is considered that they are opposed to Kṛṣṇa consciousness.

Still, although they have never relished the sweetness of serving Kṛṣṇa nor do they possess knowledge about such service, they are Kṛṣṇa's *taṭasthā-śakti*, His marginal energy. They are His eternal servants by their constitutional position.

A certain type of *jīva* manifests in the spiritual world – from Kṛṣṇa's first expansion, Śrī Baladeva. The *jīvas* who manifest from Baladeva are called *nitya-unmukha*, meaning that they are always serving Kṛṣṇa. Although all *taṭasthā-śakti jīvas* are servants by constitution, the second kind of *jīva* has not come from Goloka Vṛndāvana. The conditioned souls of this world have never been in Goloka Vṛndāvana. They are coming from Kāraṇodakaśāyī Viṣṇu[2], in the realm between the spiritual and material world.

Śrīla Jīva Gosvāmī clarifies our understanding of the two kinds of *jīvas*. He states in his *Paramātma-sandharbha*:

> *tad evam anantā eva jīvākhyās taṭasthāḥ śaktayaḥ / tatra tāsāṁ varga-dvayam / eko vargo' nādita eva bhagavad-unmukhaḥ / anyas tv anādita eva bhagavat-parāṅmukhaḥ / svabhāvatas tadīya-jñāna-bhāvāt tadīya-jñānābhāvāt ca*
>
> (*Paramātma-sandarbha*, *Anuccheda* 47, Text 1)

> Thus the Lord's marginal potency is comprised of individual spirit souls. Although these individual spirit souls are limitless in number, they may be divided into two groups: (1) the souls who from time immemorial are favorable to the Supreme Lord; and (2) the rebellious souls who from time immemorial are averse to the Supreme Lord. One group is aware of the Lord's glories and the other group is not aware of them.

Here, Śrīla Jīva Gosvāmī explains that there are unlimited *jīvas* emanating from *taṭasthā-śakti*, and from there some have turned away from Kṛṣṇa. They turned away from Kṛṣṇa and chose to enter the material world, which is a 'dream-place' (*svapna-sthāna*). In the material world it appears that one person is aware of the world around him, another is dreaming, and another is fast asleep without dreaming at all. Actually, everyone here is dreaming, because this entire place is a dream-place. The *jīvas'* sleep in this dream-place is not so deep that they are fully unconscious, because they are part of the spiritual conscious

---

[2] Please see the chart of the three *puruṣa-avatāras* in Chapter One.

substance (*cit-vastu*) even when they are not liberated. Rather, they are experiencing a dream of material designations.

Regarding the souls coming from the divine light-filled glance of Kāraṇodakaśāyī Viṣṇu: Within that light, Kṛṣṇa in His form as Viṣṇu gives them the intelligence and freedom to consider, "What should I do?" There is a very fine, imaginary line between the transcendental and material worlds. Kṛṣṇa gives the *jīvas* some freedom, saying in effect, "From here you can look towards this world of *māyā* and you can also look towards the spiritual world. What you choose depends upon you. I will give you a moment to decide."

Certain *jīvas* looked from the *taṭasthā* region towards the spiritual world and were attracted there. Yogamāyā at once gave them the power of *bhakti* to go there, to serve Kṛṣṇa for eternity. Others looked toward the material world, they were attracted, they decided to relish it, and thus they were granted their desire.

The *jīvas* in this region were within the body of Kāraṇodakaśāyī Viṣṇu, in seed form, and when they came out through His glance, some fell in *māyā*. This truth has been substantiated in *Śrī Brahma-saṁhitā*:

> The Lord of the mundane world, Mahā-Viṣṇu (Kāraṇodakaśāyī Viṣṇu), possesses thousands upon thousands of heads, eyes, and hands. He is the source of thousands upon thousands of incarnations in His thousands upon thousands of subjective portions. He generates thousands upon thousands of individual souls.
>
> (*Śrī Brahma-Samhita*, Text 11)

> An unlimited number of atomic conscious particles emerge from the spiritual rays of Paramātmā as the aggregate of the living entities. These innumerable *jīvas* have no relation with the mundane world when they come to know themselves to be the eternal servants of the Supreme Lord. At that time, they are incorporated into the realm of Vaikuṇṭha.
>
> (*Śrī Brahma Samhita*, Text 16, purport)

> The *svarūpa-śakti*, or internal potency of Kṛṣṇa, which is spiritual, functioning as His own personal power, has manifested His pastimes of Goloka. By Her grace, individual souls who are constituents of the marginal potency can have admission into even those pastimes.
>
> (*Śrī Brahma-Samhita*, Text 6, purport)

Everything Is Present in the Divine Seed

Spiritual identity is already present within the soul, in seed-form. Consider the analogy of a mango seed. If you plant a mango seed in fertile ground and give it water, gradually a sprout will emerge. After a few days, some leaves will unfurl and later some branches will begin to grow. After a few years, the plant will become quite large, with an abundance of leaves, branches, and flowers. One day, mangos will begin to swell on its branches, and then they will ripen and become sweet and juicy.

Everything needed to produce a mango tree is present within the mango seed. The potency of the leaves, branches, and fruits is dormant within the seed, as well as the number of leaves and the sweetness of the fruit.

Similarly, the personal form of the soul is now present in a latent state. Everything about the soul's spiritual form, dress, nature, dwelling place, and service is present within the soul, even though the pure transcendental form has not developed and was never previously developed.

Potency of Divine Seed

In further reference to your question about the form of the spirit soul of the conditioned living entity, there is a spiritual form always, but it develops fully only when the living entity goes back to Vaikuṇṭha. This form develops according to the desire of the living entity. Until this perfectional stage is reached, the form is lying dormant, as the form of the tree is lying dormant in the seed.

(Letter from Śrīla Bhaktivedānta Svāmī Mahārāja,
Los Angeles, August 8, 1969.)

Śrī Kṛṣṇa states in the *Bhagavad-gītā* (15.6): *Yad gatvā na nivartante tad dhāma paramaṁ mama*. This indicates that by practicing *bhakti-yoga* for thousands upon thousands of lifetimes, one's spiritual form is developed.Thus, one is liberated and granted the benediction of entrance into the spiritual world, from which he will never return to this world. Those from this world who are liberated by practicing *bhakti-yoga* are serving Kṛṣṇa in Vaikuṇṭha in His forms as Rāma, Nṛsiṁha, Kalki, or

In God's Abode

The conclusion is that no one falls from the spiritual world, or Vaikuṇṭha-planet, for it is the eternal abode.

(*Śrīmad-Bhagavatam* 3.16.26, Purport by Śrīla Bhaktivedānta Svāmī Mahārāja)

Vāmana, or in Goloka as Mathureśa or Kṛṣṇa. They are all liberated. They will never return to the world of repeated birth and death. Śrīla Bhaktivedānta Svāmī Mahārāja writes in his translation of the above mentioned verse:

> That supreme abode of Mine is not illumined by the sun or moon, nor by fire or electricity. Those who reach it never return to this material world.
>
> (*Bhagavad-gītā* 15.6, purport)

Question: Someone may say, "Yes, we accept what Kṛṣṇa spoke in the *Bhagavad-gītā* – that once going to Vaikuṇṭha from this world, we don't return to this world. But we *did* fall from there before we first came to this world."

Śrīla Nārāyaṇa Gosvāmī Mahārāja: If this were true, the principle stated in the *Bhagavad-gītā* and other scriptures would still be a fallacy. Our scriptures propound only reality. For those souls who are already serving in that realm, there is no *māyā* at all. There is no chance of becoming averse to Kṛṣṇa. For one who is eternally in that realm and for one who has attained that realm from this material world – both kinds of souls never fall, for there is no *māyā* in God's abode.

In this connection we should try to follow the teachings of Śrīla Jīva Gosvāmī, our *tattva-ācārya,* as well as the teachings of our disciplic line of spiritual masters such as Śrīla Baladeva Vidyābhūṣaṇa, Śrīla Viśvanātha Cakravartī Ṭhākura, and especially Śrīla Bhaktivinoda Ṭhākura[3]. If there is any confusion when reading the words of a particular bona fide *guru*, we can reconcile and clarify our understanding by taking help of the words of the other bona fide *gurus* in our disciplic line.

---

3 Please see Part Five, *About the Authors*, for a brief sketch of the life and glory of Śrīla Bhaktivinoda Ṭhākura.

Jīva Gosvāmī is a very bona fide *guru*. He has explained this subject and all other spiritual subjects in his Sandarbhas, leaving no scope for doubt. We will have to read his words in order to reconcile, and in this way we will be able to see the compatibility, consistency, and harmony in the teaching of all our *ācāryas*.

It is also essential to read the books of the Seventh Gosvāmī, Śrīla Bhaktivinoda Ṭhākura, who is also a bona fide *guru* like Jīva Gosvāmī and Rūpa Gosvāmī. He clearly elucidates these truths of the soul in his book, *Jaiva-dharma*. There, he writes that innumerable eternal souls have emanated from Baladeva Prabhu in Goloka Vṛndāvana, like the *sakhas*, Nanda Bābā, and other associates. Regarding the *gopīs* there, unlimited *gopīs* are bodily manifestations (*nitya-siddha kāyavyūha-rūpa*) of Śrīmatī Rādhikā. Those *gopīs* who are not Her bodily manifestations are coming from Baladeva; they are also eternally liberated and eternally serving Kṛṣṇa.

Śrīla Bhaktivinoda Ṭhākura explains that this principle is also applicable in Dvārakā and Vaikuṇṭha. In Dvārakā, the *jīvas* are coming from Baladeva Prabhu's expansion, Mūla-Saṅkarṣaṇa, and in Vaikuṇṭha they are coming from His expansion known as Mahā-Saṅkarṣaṇa.

All these eternal souls are serving in one of two ways: in Kṛṣṇa's sweet, human-like pastimes (*mādhurya-līlā*); or in His opulent pastimes (*aiśvarya-līlā*) as Dvārakādīśa, the prince of Dvārakā, and Nārāyaṇa, the Lord of Vaikuṇṭha. Regarding those *jīvas* manifested from Kāraṇodakaśāyī Viṣṇu in the *taṭasthā* region or marginal line, they are two kinds: some liberated (those who turned towards the spiritual world) and some conditioned (those who turned towards the material world).

Śrīla Bhaktivedānta Svāmī Mahārāja has accepted this line of *guru-paramparā*, more than us. He is a realized soul. He never says anything different from the words of our previous *ācāryas*. Śrīla Bhaktivinoda Ṭhākura has accepted all the previous *ācāryas* in the line of Śrīla Rūpa Gosvāmī, Śrīla Bhaktisiddhānta Sarasvatī Gosvāmī Thākura has accepted Śrīla Bhaktivinoda Ṭhākura, and Śrīla Bhaktivedānta Svāmī Mahārāja has accepted his Gurudeva, Śrīla Bhaktisiddhānta Sarasvatī Gosvāmī Thākura. With this understanding, we can reconcile.

[*This discourse was given on June 2, 2000 in Badger, California.*]

CHAPTER FOUR

NO ONE FALLS FROM THE ETERNAL ABODE

Let us turn to an excerpt from Śrīla Bhaktivinoda Ṭhākura's book, *Śrī Jaiva-dharma*. The scene in the following excerpt takes place on the island of Godruma in Śrī Navadvīpa-dhāma, where Sannyāsī Ṭhākura asked a question to his *guru*, Paramahaṁsa Bābāji Mahārāja.

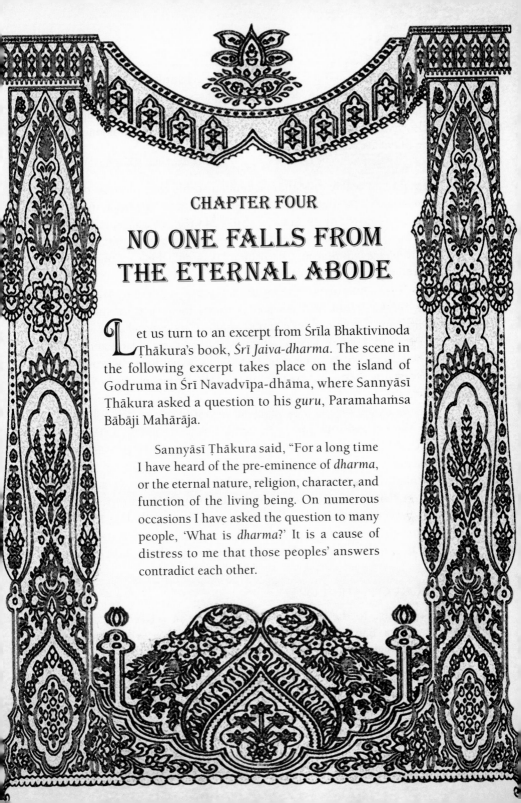

> Sannyāsī Ṭhākura said, "For a long time I have heard of the pre-eminence of *dharma*, or the eternal nature, religion, character, and function of the living being. On numerous occasions I have asked the question to many people, 'What is *dharma*?' It is a cause of distress to me that those peoples' answers contradict each other.

> "So please tell me, what is the true constitutional *dharma* of the *jīvas*, and why do different teachers explain the nature of *dharma* in such diverse ways? If *dharma* is one, why don't all learned teachers cultivate that universal *dharma* which is one without a second?"
>
> (*Jaiva-dharma*, Chapter 1)

Paramahaṁsa Bābāji Mahārāja replied to his disciple that *dharma* is one. The only real *dharma* is love and affection for the Supreme Lord, which is also known in the ancient Vedas as *vaiṣṇava-dharma* (devotion to the Supreme Lord), *sanātana-dharma* (the eternal function of the soul), and *bhagavad-dharma* (the principles of *dharma* as enunciated by the Supreme Lord Śrī Kṛṣṇa Himself).

This love sometimes transforms, as water sometimes transforms into ice, fog, or steam. When water is in the form of ice it may cause injury if thrown at someone, whereas water in its natural state will not do so. Similarly love for Kṛṣṇa, which is the intrinsic nature and mood of the *jīva*, has now become transformed. Now we love each other, or we love our dogs, cats, our own bodies, or the bodies of our boyfriends or girlfriends.

This so-called love is false *dharma*, meaning that it has nothing to do with the natural function of the soul. Love originates in the Lord's abode, Goloka Vṛndāvana; its root is there. That pure love is in the heart of every living being, but it has been transformed, as water is transformed into ice under certain conditions. Although we are under the notion that we love each other, the love experienced in this world is but a perverted reflection of real love and is actually lust for sense gratification. Love in its pure state is love and affection for Kṛṣṇa, and it originates in the hearts of the *gopīs* and other residents of Vṛndāvana.

We 'Forgot' the Lord

In response to the question of his disciple in relation to *dharma*, Paramahaṁsa Bābāji Mahārāja quoted verses from Śrīla Kṛṣṇadāsa Kavirāja Gosvāmī's book, *Śrī Caitanya-caritāmṛta*:

> *jīvera 'svarūpa' haya——kṛṣṇera 'nitya-dāsa'*
> *kṛṣṇera 'taṭasthā-śakti' 'bhedābheda-prakāśa'*
> *sūryāṁśa-kiraṇa, yaiche agni-jvālā-caya*
> *svābhāvika kṛṣṇera tina-prakāra 'śakti' haya*
>
> (*Śrī Caitanya-caritāmṛta, Madhya-līlā* 20.108–109)

It is the living entity's constitutional position to be an eternal servant of Kṛṣṇa, because he is the marginal energy of Kṛṣṇa and a manifestation simultaneously one with and different from the Lord, like a molecular particle of sunshine or fire. Kṛṣṇa has three varieties of energy.

> *kṛṣṇa bhuli' sei jīva anādi-bahirmukha*
> *ataeva māyā tāre deya saṁsāra-duḥkha*
> (*Śrī Caitanya-caritāmṛta, Madhya-līlā* 20.117)

Forgetting Kṛṣṇa, the living entity has been attracted by the external feature from time immemorial. Therefore, the illusory energy *māyā* gives him all kinds of misery in his material existence.

The words *kṛṣṇa bhuli* in the above-mentioned verse apparently mean 'forgetting Kṛṣṇa,' but what is the deeper understanding? Does it mean that the *jīva* was once engaged in Kṛṣṇa's service in His spiritual abode, and has now forgotten that service?

The intended meaning is very different. All mundane languages have defects, and therefore they cannot purely express the nature of our constitutional form (*svarūpa*). To clarify the meaning, Śrīla Kṛṣṇadāsa Kavirāja Gosvāmī writes *kṛṣṇera 'taṭasthā-śakti' 'bhedābheda-prakāśa*, meaning that the *jīva* is a manifestation of Kṛṣṇa's marginal energy.

Different Sources, Different Destinations

Please note this down carefully in your notebooks and in your hearts. *Jaiva-dharma*, Chapter Sixteen, states:

> Innumerable *jīvas* appear from Śrī Baladeva Prabhu to serve Vṛndāvana-vihārī Śrī Kṛṣṇa as His eternal associates in Goloka Vṛndāvana; and others appear from Śrī Saṅkarṣaṇa to serve the Lord of Vaikuṇṭha, Śrī Nārāyaṇa, in the spiritual sky. Eternally relishing *rasa*, engaged in the service of their worshipful Lord, these *jīvas* always remain fixed in their constitutional position. They always strive to please the Supreme Personality of Godhead and are always favorable to Him. By virtue of the spiritual potency, they have the strength to stay fixed in their devotion and they have no connection with the material energy.

> In fact, they are unaware that there is a deluding energy called *māyā*. Inasmuch as they reside in the spiritual world, *māyā* stays far from them and does not affect them at all.
>
> Always absorbed in the bliss of serving their worshipful Lord, they are eternally liberated and completely unaware of material happiness and distress. Their life is love alone, and they are not even conscious of misery, death, or fear.

The residents of the spiritual world are liberated, which means that they have no awareness of *māyā* and this material world. Who *is* aware? We *jīvas* in this material world are aware.

We have come from the *taṭasthā*-region, from a manifestation of Baladeva Prabhu called Kāraṇodakaśāyī Viṣṇu, the incarnation of the Lord who is situated on the marginal line between the spiritual and material worlds, in the Causal Ocean.

Lord Kṛṣṇa has created the *jīva* as an independent being, whose independence is a special jewel. If the *jīva* uses his independence well, he quickly progresses towards Vaikuṇṭha, and if he misuses it, he suffers.

Consider this analogy. If tiny, round mustard seeds are dropped upon the sharp edge of the blade of a sword, some seeds will fall to one side and some will fall to the other. Like those mustard seeds that fall to one side or the other, from the *taṭasthā-śakti* region the *jīvas* are either elevated to the spiritual world or degraded to this material world. After emanating from the glance of Kāraṇodakaśāyī Viṣṇu,

if they look towards Goloka Vṛndāvana, *yogamāyā* at once helps them to go there. On the other hand, those who look towards the material world are attracted by *mahāmāyā*, whereupon *mahāmāyā* drags them to this inert netherworld. Kṛṣṇa is not at fault for this; it is their free will to look here or there.

Of course, no analogy can give a perfect understanding of spiritual truth, but there are some similarities to help us understand. The sharp edge of the knife represents the *taṭasthā* region and the mustard seeds represent the innumerable *jīvas*. Like the edge of the knife, the *taṭasthā* region is not a place of rest. The *jīva* cannot stay there; he has to quickly decide his destination. What is not similar in this analogy is that, unlike the *jīvas,* the mustard seeds are not conscious and therefore they have no ability to choose.

Kṛṣṇa did not create this world with a desire that the *jīvas* should suffer. Rather, the material creation is one of the very valuable, pleasant, and sweet pastimes of Kṛṣṇa, which the *jīva* can understand and appreciate only when he transcends his materially conditioned consciousness and attains an advanced stage of Kṛṣṇa consciousness.[1]

Kṛṣṇa personally states in the *Bhagavad-gītā*:

na tad bhāsayate sūryo
na śaśāṅko na pāvakaḥ
yad gatvā na nivartante
tad dhāma paramaṁ mama

(*Bhagavad-gītā* 15.6)

That supreme abode of Mine is not illumined by the sun or moon, nor by fire or electricity. Those who reach it never return to this material world.

A person who seriously chants, remembers, and follows the process of devotional service passes through the stages of initial faith (*śraddhā*), steadiness (*niṣṭhā*), taste (*ruci*), attachment to the process of devotion and to Śrī Kṛṣṇa Himself (*āsakti*), spiritual emotions (*bhāva*), and pure love (*prema*). When he attains *prema*, he is then qualified to enter Goloka Vṛndāvana and to serve Lord Kṛṣṇa there. Once he attains this position, he is free from the possibility of falling back down to this world.

1 Please see Part Two, *Jaiva-dharma*, Chapter Sixteen, for a more elaborate explanation of this.

Truly Liberated Souls Remain Liberated

It is quite absurd to think that liberated souls in Goloka Vṛndāvana could ever be covered by *māyā*. In this regard, Canto Six of the *Śrīmad-Bhāgavatam* describes the history of the Lord's associate, Citraketu Mahārāja. A casual reading of this history may give the impression that Citraketu Mahārāja fell down from the spiritual world (Vaikuṇṭha), and one may take that impression as proof that the *jīva* falls from there. However, Citraketu Mahārāja never fell from his position as the Lord's associate.

Citraketu Mahārāja went to see his friend and god-brother Lord Śiva, who was sitting with his wife, the very beautiful Pārvatī. Lord Śiva, who is also an eternally liberated soul, was naked, Pārvatī was sitting on his lap, and the two of them were surrounded by an assembly of Siddhas, Cāraṇas, and great sages.

Citraketu began to joke with his friend: "What are you doing? You are completely naked and this beautiful young lady is sitting on your lap. What will everyone think?" He was laughing and Śiva was smiling, but Pārvatī could not tolerate his teasing. She immediately cursed him, declaring, "You will become a demon."

Hearing this undeserved curse from Pārvatī, Śiva told her, "He is a liberated soul. Whether he is in this world or in the spiritual world, he will always be a pure devotee; he cannot be transformed into anything else. He has the power to resist your curse, and had he so wished, he could have also cursed you. Just see how humble he is. Because he is a Vaiṣṇava he is beyond hankering and lamentation, and therefore he has tolerated your words and accepted your curse."

Citraketu Mahārāja intentionally and willingly agreed to accept the body of a demon in order to establish this truth: Whether a devotee is in this world or in hell, he will glorify his Lord and give instructions to everyone to serve Him. It was for this reason that he took his next birth as the 'demon' Vṛtrāsura and spent a short time in that body.

While in the body of that demon, he was engaged in a fight with his enemy, the demigod Indra. During the battle he told Indra, "Kill me. I cannot serve my Lord in this body." After having attempted to kill Vṛtrāsura and failing, Indra thought in great wonder, "How will I be able to kill him? He is telling me to do so, but I cannot." Even Indra's thunderbolt was powerless.

Vṛtrāsura prayed to the Lord (*Śrīmad-Bhāgavatam* 6.11.26):

> O lotus-eyed Lord, as baby birds that have not yet developed their wings always look for their mother to return and feed them; as small calves tied with ropes await anxiously the time of milking, when they will be allowed to drink the milk of their mothers; or as a morose wife whose husband is away from home always longs for him to return so that she can satisfy him in all respects – I always yearn for the opportunity to render direct service unto You.

In this highly elevated verse, Vṛtrāsura reveals that his mood in service to Kṛṣṇa was like that of the *gopīs*. In fact, by this prayer of Vṛtrāsura, Śrīla Vyāsadeva and Śukadeva Gosvāmī have glorified the love and affection of the *gopīs*. Citraketu Mahārāja did not fall from Vaikuṇṭha. He purposefully came to this material world to establish certain truths.

Śrīmad-Bhāgavatam also relates the history of the saint Bharata Mahārāja.[2] It is sometimes assumed that Bharata Mahārāja had fallen from his exalted devotional platform of *bhāva-bhakti*, the preliminary stage of love of God, and therefore he took his next birth as a deer. Actually, Bharata Mahārāja performed this pastime only to give particular lessons to conditioned souls like us. He wanted to demonstrate that no matter how elevated one might consider himself to be, one must be very cautious in the matter of cultivating pure *bhakti*; otherwise one falls down.

Another example of a vastly misunderstood 'fall' is Jaya and Vijaya, the doorkeepers of Vaikuṇṭha.[3] They desired to satisfy Lord Nārāyaṇa's wish to taste the mood of combat. The Lord then attracted the four Kumāras to visit Him in Vaikuṇṭha specifically to curse Jaya and Vijaya to descend to this world so that He would have the opportunity to fight with them.

Neither anger, nor lust, nor any debased qualities are present in Vaikuṇṭha. In the instance of the so-called cursing of Jaya and Vijaya, Lord Nārāyaṇa had personally inspired His transcendental potency *yogamāyā* to make the four Kumāras angry, which caused them to curse Jaya and Vijaya. After having cursed them, the four Kumāras immediately lamented, but Lord Nārāyaṇa assured them, "Do not worry. I personally wanted this to happen. Jaya and Vijaya will manifest

---

2 See glossary for a brief history of Bharata Mahārāja.

3 See glossary for a brief history of Jaya and Vijaya.

as demons in the material world for three lifetimes, and I will perform pastimes with them in the spirit of chivalry. In the meantime, they will simultaneously remain in their original forms in the spiritual world." Thus, Jaya and Vijaya continued to reside in Vaikuṇṭha in their original forms, and their manifestations came to this phenomenal world to act as demons.

Being pure devotees, Jaya and Vijaya are able to manifest manifold forms, just as Kṛṣṇa's mother, Yaśodā, has unlimited forms. Nārada Ṛṣi also has millions of forms, in Vaikuṇṭha, in Dvārakā, and throughout the infinite universes. Lord Brahmā has said that a person may be able to count the stars in the sky and the sands on the Earth, but he will not be able to fully glorify the sweet pastimes of Kṛṣṇa and His associates. We cannot imagine such things.[4]

While no souls fall from Goloka Vṛndāvana or Vaikuṇṭha at any time or in any circumstance, they may come to this world with Kṛṣṇa to assist in His pastimes, as did His cowherd friends Śrīdāmā and Subala. Or, Kṛṣṇa may send a liberated soul, His associate, to this world, telling him, "Go there and help the conditioned souls." A liberated soul in this world has a greater understanding of the overwhelming anxiety and suffering of the conditioned living entities than those liberated souls who are in Goloka, because he realizes the reality of the spiritual world and simultaneously sees this world.

No one is happy in this world. Even those in the prime of youth are unsatisfied, and they will never become satisfied. They will have to grow old and die, and when they die they will not be able to take with them anything they have collected during their lifetime. So try to remember Kṛṣṇa and follow this tenet: God is one, religion is one, and that one religion is love and affection for the Supreme Godhead, Śrī Kṛṣṇa.

Question: You mentioned that Kṛṣṇa's associates go with Him to the innumerable universes and they also have expansions. Is this also

---

[4] "There are Vaikuṇṭha planets in the spiritual world, and the devotees there are all liberated. These devotees are *akṣara*, which means they do not fall down into the material world. They remain in the spiritual world of the Vaikuṇṭhas. They are also persons like us, but they are eternal persons, complete with full knowledge and bliss. That is the difference between them and us. That is *tattva-jñāna*. In other words, these associates of the Lord, Jaya and Vijaya, descended to the material world to serve the Lord by fulfilling His desire to fight. Otherwise, as Mahārāja Yudhiṣṭhira says, *aśraddheya ivābhāti*: the statement that a servant of the Lord could fall from Vaikuṇṭha seems unbelievable" (*Śrīmad-Bhāgavatam* 7.1.35, purport).

possible for the living entity who was once conditioned but becomes perfect by the practice of devotional service? If we become perfect, do we also accompany Kṛṣṇa to all those universes?

Śrīla Nārāyaṇa Gosvāmī Mahārāja: Yes. If you become perfect like Kṛṣṇa's associates, you can do so.[5] Perfect devotees, those who constantly meditate upon the daily twenty-four-hour transcendental loving pastimes of Śrī Rādhā and Kṛṣṇa (*aṣṭa-kālīya-līlā*), will attain Goloka Vṛndāvana.

Those who worship Gaura-Nityānanda Prabhu and constantly meditate upon Their pastimes will go to Śvetadvīpa, which is Caitanya Mahāprabhu's abode of Navadvīpa as it is manifest in Goloka. [This Śvetadvīpa is different from the island which lies in the Ocean of Milk.]

Those who remember both Gauranga and Rādhā-Kṛṣṇa, and want to serve both, have two constitutional forms and go to both abodes.[6] Beyond the infinite material universes, Śvetadvīpa and Goloka Vṛndāvana are gloriously manifest, and such perfect, liberated souls reside in both these abodes.

[*This discourse was given on February 16, 2002, in Murwillumbah, Australia, as part of a series of classes on Śrīla Bhaktivinoda Ṭhākura's Jaiva-dharma.*]

5 The associates of Śrī Śrī Rādhā-Kṛṣṇa and Mahāprabhu in the spiritual world also assist Them in Their divine pastimes that are performed throughout the myriad material universes.

6 For more information on this topic, please read Part Two, *Jaiva-dharma*, Chapter Seventeen).

CHAPTER FIVE

MOON ON THE BRANCH

In the Sanskrit language, the logic used to explain that which is beyond our understanding is called, *śākhā-candra-nyāya*, or 'moon-on-the-branch logic.'

One may ask, "Where is the moon?" And someone may reply, "Look over there, the moon is sitting on the branch of that tree." In truth, the moon is millions of miles away from the Earth, and its position in the sky is indicated by pointing to it as it apparently sits on the branch.

Similarly, regarding eternal, spiritual existence, mundane language can only give a scant indication of the truth. No example or analogy can fully explain it. By way of illustration, one may say, "Śrī Kṛṣṇa is beautiful; His complexion is black like that of a fresh rain-cloud or *tamāla* tree." However, is He actually black like a cloud or a *tamāla* tree? Can any comparison be completely accurate? His beauty is unparalleled.

Beyond Material Words

Whatever we say or describe in the material world is under the jurisdiction of material time and space. When we say, "The *jīvas* were created," "The spiritual world was manifested," or "There is no influence of *māyā* in creating the form of the *jīvas*," material time is bound to influence our language and statements. This influence of material time is inevitable in our conditioned state, so we cannot remove it from our descriptions of the atomic *jīva* and spiritual objects. The conception of past, present, and future always enters our descriptions in some way or another.

Still, those who can discriminate properly can understand the application of the eternal present when they comprehend the purport of the descriptions of the spiritual world. Be very careful in this matter. Give up the inevitable baseness, the aspect of the description that is fit to be rejected, and have spiritual realization.

(*Jaiva-dharma*, Chapter 15)

In the same way, mundane language cannot fully explain *jīva-tattva*, the truth of the eternal living entity. By the regular performance of *bhajana*, by daily chanting the Hare Kṛṣṇa *mahā-mantra*, and by hearing *hari-kathā* (narrations about Kṛṣṇa and His associates) with a strong belief in the goal of life, we will advance in devotion. Then, according to our level of advancement, we will be able to realize all established philosophical truths.

Arguments based on mundane logic will not satisfy us, for one logical argument may defeat other arguments, and yet another logical argument will defeat all of the previous ones. Mundane logic and argument have no entrance into the spiritual atmosphere. As stated by Śrīla Bhaktivinoda Ṭhākura:

tathā pratyakṣādi-pramiti-sahitaṁ sādhayati naḥ
na yuktis tarkākhyā praviśati tathā śakti-rahitā

(*Daśa-mūla* 1)

Reasoning that is based only on logic is always crippled when evaluating inconceivable subject matters, since logic and argument have no access in the realm of the inconceivable.

In *Jaiva-dharma*, Sannyāsī Ṭhākura humbly asks his spiritual master, Paramahaṁsa Bābājī Mahārāja, "Prabhu, I want to know about the eternal soul. I want to realize the truth; I am not satisfied by only having intellectual knowledge. I want to be truly satisfied." Paramahaṁsa Bābājī Mahārāja replied, "Śrīla Kṛṣṇadāsa Kavirāja Gosvāmī, who was an object of Śrī Nityānanda Prabhu's mercy, showed me a manuscript he had written in his own handwriting. In that divine compilation, *Śrī Caitanya-caritāmṛta*, Śrī Caitanya Mahāprabhu instructed us on this subject:

jīvera svarūpa haya kṛṣṇera nitya-dāsa,
kṛṣṇera taṭasthā-śakti bhedābheda prakāśa

(*Śrī Caitanya-caritāmṛta, Madhya-līlā* 20.108)

The constitutional nature of the *jīva* is to be an eternal servant of Śrī Kṛṣṇa. He is the marginal potency of Kṛṣṇa, and is a manifestation simultaneously one with Him and different from Him.

kṛṣṇa bhuli' sei jīva anādi-bahirmukha
ataeva māyā tāre deya saṁsāra-duḥkha

(*Śrī Caitanya-caritāmṛta, Madhya-līlā* 20.117)

> The *jīva* who has forgotten Kṛṣṇa has been preoccupied with the external potency since a time without beginning. Consequently, Kṛṣṇa's illusory potency, *māyā*, gives him misery in the form of material existence.

What is the harm in believing that this verse confirms the *jīva's* previous residence in Goloka and his falldown from there to the material world? The harm is this: If it is possible to fall from the spiritual world, if one were vulnerable there, then what use would it be to engage in spiritual practices (*sādhana*) and devotional absorption (*bhajana*) for attainment of that abode? If, by the performance of *bhajana* one attains the spiritual world and later falls back to the material world, what would be the use of endeavoring with great determination to reach there? There would be no use; it would be better to stay here in the material world. Moreover, the idea of the *jīvas*' fall-down from Goloka Vṛndāvana suggests that the deluding material potency also exists there.

Causal Ocean

The Virajā, or Causal Ocean, is the border between the spiritual world and material world. The material energy is situated on one shore of that ocean and cannot enter onto the other shore, which is the spiritual sky.

(*Śrī Caitanya-caritāmṛta, Madhya-līlā* 20.269)

The idea that *māyā* is present in Goloka implies that even Kṛṣṇa's cowherd friends like Sudāmā, Śrīdāmā, and Madhumaṅgala, His parents Mother Yaśodā and Nanda Bābā, and all the *gopīs* including Śrīmatī Rādhikā may also forget Kṛṣṇa and fall down from there. But it is not possible for them to forget Kṛṣṇa.

Here, by the influence of the material energy, we have a certain vocabulary and we use certain words – like *kṛṣṇa bhuli*, meaning 'forgetting Kṛṣṇa.' We can purify our understanding of those words by performing *sādhana-bhajana*. We cannot understand spiritual topics through words alone because, as mentioned above, mundane language does not extend beyond matter. Nevertheless language is our tool for expression, and therefore we require the help of pure devotees to assist us in comprehending it.

Nārada Muni Did Not Fall

The verses of *Śrī Caitanya-caritāmṛta*, *Śrīmad-Bhāgavatam*, and other Vedic scriptures are full of profound purports and require careful explanation. For example, it is sometimes thought that the great sage Nārada Muni, although a liberated soul, occasionally falls into *māyā*. In reality, his apparent fall-downs are his pastimes of role-playing, performed for the purpose of serving the Lord in His various incarnations. All of his pastimes are performed to please the Lord, and also to teach lessons to all of us.

In the following pastime, Nārada Muni conquered Kāmadeva (Cupid) and then proudly thought, "Oh, even my own *guru*, Śaṅkara (Lord Śiva), ran after *māyā*. When Kṛṣṇa assumed His female form as the goddess Mohinī-mūrti, Śiva became enraptured and ran after Her, oblivious to Her real identity."[1] Śrī Nārada Muni gloated, "On the other hand, when Kāmadeva came to me, he could not attract me at all."

Nārada approached Lord Śiva and boasted, "I have conquered Kāmadeva." Lord Śiva laughed and said, "Don't tell Lord Brahmā and Lord Nārāyaṇa." Not listening, he then went to Lord Brahmā, bragging in the same way. Lord Brahmā thought, "A thorn of false ego has entered him. It must be removed." Brahmā replied, "Very good, but don't tell Lord Nārāyaṇa." Not listening, Nārada finally approached Lord Nārāyaṇa.

Listening to Nārada's self-praise, Lord Nārāyaṇa considered, "False ego, like a disease, has now infected his heart. His disease is like piles, and he will not be cured without an operation. I must remove this condition; I must operate." Hiding His real feelings, He replied to Nārada, "You are My best devotee. I am very proud of you."

While Nārada was returning to this universe after his visit with the Lord, he saw a magnificent kingdom in which there lived a king and his beautiful daughter. Delighted, Śrī Nārada thought, "I have never before seen such stunning beauty!" Approaching the king, he said, "I know astrology. I want to see the hand of your daughter so that I can tell you her future." He then read on the princess's palm that the

1 "In *Bhagavad-gītā* (7.14) it is said: '*daivī hy eṣā guṇa-mayī mama māyā duratyayā* – The external potency of the Supreme Personality of Godhead is extremely strong.' Indeed, everyone is fully captivated by her activities. Lord Śambhu (Śiva) was not to be captivated by the external potency, but because Lord Viṣṇu wanted to captivate Him also, He exhibited His internal potency to act the way that His external potency acts to captivate ordinary living entities. Lord Viṣṇu can captivate anyone, even such a strong personality as Lord Śambhu" (*Śrīmad-Bhāgavatam* 8.12.21, purport).

man she marries would possess all the qualities of greatness, in full. Wondering, "How can I marry this girl?" he left and began to meditate on his worshipful Lord Nārāyaṇa.

Nārāyaṇa at once appeared in his meditation and inquired, "What benediction do you wish?" Nārada prayed, "Please help me. I want to marry the king's daughter. Please give me a face as beautiful as Yours." Lord Nārāyaṇa replied, "All auspiciousness to you. All blessings unto you. I will do what is best for you."

Now, convinced and satisfied that Lord Nārāyaṇa had fulfilled his desire, Nārada returned to the king's palace. It so happened that the king was then in the midst of performing his daughter's *svayaṁvara*, the ceremony in which a princess chooses her husband. The king's daughter was holding a garland, preparing to place it on the neck of the man who would most attract her, whom she would choose to marry.

Nārada followed the princess as she perused the various contestants, showing his face in hope that she would offer him the garland. However, whenever he came into her view, she looked at him in disgust and walked on. Still, trying to attract her attention, he continued to pursue her.

The associates of Lord Śiva were present on that occasion and, seeing Nārada's repeated attempts, told him, "Oh, you are so beautiful!" Nārada believed that he was being praised, but he was actually being ridiculed.

In the meantime, Lord Nārāyaṇa arrived at the palace on His bird carrier, Garuḍa, and as soon as the princess saw Him she adorned His neck with her garland. Then, without a moment's delay, Lord Nārāyaṇa placed her on His lap and they quickly flew away on Garuḍa.

Nārada deliberated, "What a wicked person! I have served Him selflessly throughout my life. Only one time did I request from Him a favor – I wished to marry this girl and I asked Him for a countenance as attractive as His own. I will now see what type of face He has given me!" Then, looking in a mirror, he saw that he had the face of a baboon.

Angry and upset, Nārada immediately flew to Vaikuṇṭha, where he saw that very princess on Lakṣmī-devī's seat. "You have cheated me!" He rebuked, "I curse You that You will weep just as I am weeping over this lady. Your wife will be taken away from You, and to retrieve her You will have to take the help of monkeys!"

At the next moment Lord Nārāyaṇa removed the illusion created by His *yogamāyā* potency, and Nārada saw that the girl who had enchanted him was actually Lakṣmī-devī herself.

"I performed this operation only to remove your false ego and pride," Lord Nārāyaṇa explained kindly. Nārada at once fell to the Lord's lotus feet and apologized profusely.

This transcendental pastime became the cause of Lord Śrī Rāmacandra's appearance. It manifested to teach conditioned souls what to do and what not to do. We should not think that Nārada was previously in Goloka Vṛndāvana or Vaikuṇṭha and was later covered by *māyā*. By the wish of Śrī Kṛṣṇa, devotees can do anything to fulfill His desires.

Liberation in an Instant

Question: Why does the living entity have minute independence?

Śrīla Nārāyaṇa Gosvāmī Mahārāja: This is because he is a conscious being; he is not unconscious. Independence is the symptom of the conscious entity, who always has independence whether he is here in bondage or liberated in the spiritual world.

Question: Using his independence, the living entity has a choice to go from the *taṭasthā* region to Goloka, or from the *taṭasthā* region to the material world.

Generally, one learns to differentiate between *māyā* and Kṛṣṇa by associating with pure devotees. Since the *jīva* does not have the association of pure devotees in the *taṭasthā* region, how could he know what is *māyā* and what is Kṛṣṇa? How could he know how to make the proper choice?

Śrīla Nārāyaṇa Gosvāmī Mahārāja: Kṛṣṇa wants everyone to come to Him and serve Him in the spiritual world. He never wants anyone to be separated from Him and thus be unhappy. He arranges whatever is favorable for the *jīvas* to easily attain Him. Knowing everything and being all-powerful, if He sees that a soul has some small but sincere desire to serve Him, He arranges everything in such a way that that soul can go to the spiritual world and associate with Him there. Śrīla Sanātana Gosvāmī's book, *Bṛhad-bhāgavatāmṛta*, describes how the Lord makes elaborate arrangements for the living entity to come to the spiritual world.

'Revival' of Our Relationship with Kṛṣṇa

Question: If we spirit souls have not fallen from Kṛṣṇa's pastimes in Goloka Vṛndāvana, why do the scriptures say that we 'revive' our relationship with Kṛṣṇa, or that we have 'forgotten' that relationship? If we have never experienced it, where is the question of 'reviving' or 'forgetting' it?

Śrīla Nārāyaṇa Gosvāmī Mahārāja: We can understand this by the following verse:

kṛṣṇa bhuli' sei jīva anādi-bahirmukha
ataeva māyā tāre deya saṁsāra-duḥkha

(*Śrī Caitanya-caritāmṛta, Madhya-līlā* 20.117)

> Forgetting Kṛṣṇa, the living entity has been attracted by the external feature from time immemorial. Therefore, the illusory energy, *māyā*, gives him all kinds of misery in his material existence.

The answer to your question has been given by the word *anādi*. *Anādi* means 'no *ādi*,' or 'no beginning.' This means that the conditioned *jīva* has never met Kṛṣṇa.

Question: Why is the word 'forgotten' used so often?

Śrīla Nārāyaṇa Gosvāmī Mahārāja: This word and other words like it have been used for beginners, for those who have no true understanding of spiritual consciousness. Moreover, there is no other word.

That You Can Remember

Devotee: ...if we've never been with Kṛṣṇa, if we've never been in Kṛṣṇa-loka, then how is it that we start 'remembering' His pastimes and His form?

Prabhupāda: You remember Kṛṣṇa's pastimes by hearing *Śrīmad-Bhāgavatam*. You can hear Kṛṣṇa's pastimes. That you can remember.

Devotee: But how can we remember if we've never known them before?

Prabhupāda: How you can remember?

Devotee: If we haven't known it.

Prabhupāda: You can know it by hearing from *Śrīmad-Bhāgavatam*. Why we are citing so many scriptures, like *Śrīmad-Bhāgavatam* and *Bhagavad-gītā*? Just to remember.

(Room Conversation with Śrīla Bhaktivedānta Svāmī Mahārāja. Boston, April 27, 1969)

Someone may say, "The sun is sitting on the branches of that tree." This is said just to give an indication regarding the direction in which the sun can be perceived. If the sun were actually sitting on the branches, the tree would turn to ashes in less than a moment.

Similarly, verses that contain words like 'forget' and 'revive' give us a mere indication of spiritual truth. It is certain that if one is able to see Kṛṣṇa, he will never be prone to fall in the trap of *māyā*. This would not be possible. If a true *sādhaka* (advanced spiritual practitioner) does not fall in the trap of *māyā*, then what to speak of a *siddha*, a perfect, liberated soul, who is always immersed in tasting the nectar of Śrī Kṛṣṇa's personal service?

If a *jīva* is present in Goloka Vṛndāvana, how is it possible for him to forget Kṛṣṇa? The following *Bhagavad-gītā* verse describes the devotee situated in *prema-bhakti*, who, in his *siddha*-form, is an associate of Kṛṣṇa in the spiritual realm:

viṣayā vinivartante nirāhārasya dehinaḥ
rasa-varjaṁ raso 'py asya paraṁ dṛṣṭvā nivartate

(*Bhagavad-gītā* 2.59)

The embodied soul may be artificially restricted from sense enjoyment by withdrawing the senses from their objects, but his

> taste for sense objects remains. However, one who experiences a higher taste is fixed in consciousness. A devotee of the Lord automatically refrains because of a superior taste.

If one sees a beautiful object but then beholds something he considers to be more beautiful, he will be attracted to the latter. If a person has a taste to enjoy certain objects, but then gets a higher taste for a superior object, his lower taste will automatically disappear.

It is because of their higher taste that pure Gauḍīya Vaiṣṇavas, who follow in the footsteps of Śrī Caitanya Mahāprabhu, do not require to labor even slightly to control their mind. Rather, they easily control it by always engaging it in hearing *hari-kathā*, chanting, and remembering Śrī Kṛṣṇa.

Rasa-varjaṁ raso 'py asya paraṁ dṛṣṭvā nivartate. Spiritual *rasa* (the mellow flavor experienced in one's relationship with Kṛṣṇa) is more tasteful than this worldly *rasa* (the taste in a mundane relationship). The mind is made of matter and therefore always engages in worldly *rasa*. However, if it experiences a more beautiful taste, loving service to Śrī Kṛṣṇa, it has no incentive to think about this world.

A Higher Taste

Possessing the highest divine love, *mahābhāva*, the *gopīs'* minds and hearts became so absorbed in Kṛṣṇa that they could no longer be considered their own. As a piece of cotton placed on a few drops of water immediately absorbs the water into it, the 'water of the *gopīs'* hearts' was immediately absorbed into the 'Kṛṣṇa-cotton' in such a way that it was as if their individual existences were lost...

Singing about His virtues more and more, the *gopīs* at once became *tadātmika*, or one in heart, with Kṛṣṇa. They completely forgot their own bodies, bodily relations, homes, and everything else. They were unremittingly searching for Kṛṣṇa, asking the vines, trees, *tulasī*, and deer if they had seen Him...Taking on Śrī Kṛṣṇa's identity, they began imitating His activities and saying to one another, 'How beautiful is my gait! How beautifully do I play the flute!" Fully absorbed in Kṛṣṇa their natures had changed, just as iron put into a fire develops the qualities of the fire.'

(*Bhakti-rasāyana*, Chapter 15)

In this way, even without the pure devotee's conscious desire to control his mind, it is automatically controlled by his giving it more compelling topics of thought. The material world is somewhat beautiful, but Śrī Kṛṣṇa and the *gopīs* and Goloka Vṛndāvana are far more beautiful.

In this world there are so many *rasas*, but they are actually like poison. While first tasting them they seem sweet, but in time the taste becomes insipid. For example, when a man and woman try to enjoy an intimate relationship, their relationship seems sweet at the beginning but invariably turns sour. A mango is very delicious, but if one eats more mangos than he can digest, that mango will act like poison. One may like ghee (clarified butter), but if he takes more ghee than he can digest, it acts like poison. We encounter this phenomenon whenever we try to enjoy in this world. If one can engage his mind always, in all ways, in Śrī Kṛṣṇa, his mind will automatically be controlled and he will never be deluded by *māyā*.

[*"Moon on the Branch" was spoken on December 15, 2001, in Paderborn, Germany. The subsection "'Revival' of our Relationship with Kṛṣṇa" is a transcription of a darśana given in June, 1992, in Vṛndāvana, India.*]

CHAPTER SIX

BOTH, CHOICE AND CHANCE

The following chapter is an excerpt from two morning walk conversations. In all the other chapters, the indented quotes are part of the discourses and discussions. However, the nature of morning walks is that the topics are diverse and quickly travel from one theme to another. We have therefore added relevant indented quotes in order to assist with the flow and clarity of the presentation.

A Chance to Choose

Question: When the *jīvas* first come into this world from Kāraṇodakaśāyī Viṣṇu's glance, they receive either a human body or a non-human body. In the human species, the *jīva* performs materialistic activities and consequently suffers or enjoys the fruits of his work.

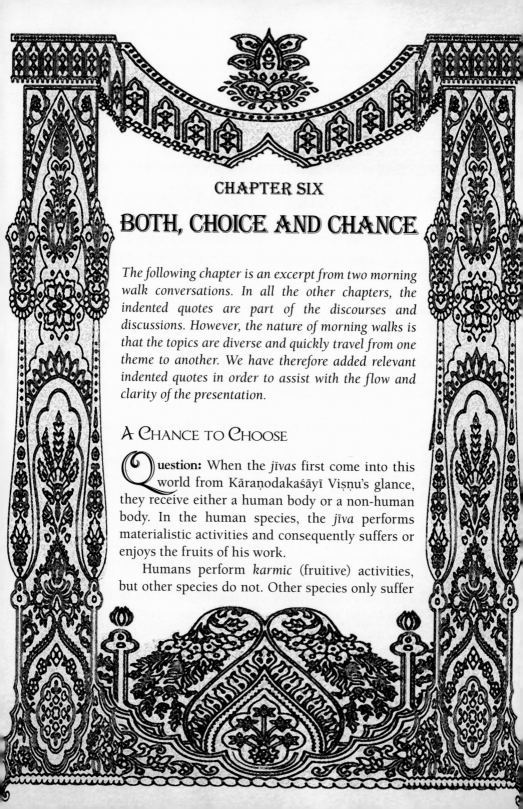

Humans perform *karmic* (fruitive) activities, but other species do not. Other species only suffer the results of the *karmic* actions which they performed when they were previously humans.

Does this mean that all *jīvas* first come into this world from the *taṭasthā* region as human beings, and then, due to their *karma*, they enter into other species?

Śrīla Nārāyaṇa Gosvāmī Mahārāja: No, this is not the process. The species in which the *jīva* takes birth depends on Kṛṣṇa. The *jīva* gets a body according to the degree of his desire to enjoy this world. If he has a strong desire to enjoy independently from Kṛṣṇa, he takes birth in the animal species. If his desire to be independent is moderate, he takes a human birth. So, the *jīva's* appearance in different species depends on the will of Kṛṣṇa, and also according to the degree of his desire to enjoy separately from Kṛṣṇa.

Question: The *jīva* has no *karma* when he first decides to come to this world?

Śrīla Nārāyaṇa Gosvāmī Mahārāja: He has no *karma* at that time, but he has independence in the sense of free will.

> Kṛṣṇa's qualities are also present in the *jīvas*, but only in a minute quantity. Kṛṣṇa is supremely independent, so the desire to be independent is eternally present in the *jīvas* as well. When the *jīva* uses his independence correctly, he remains disposed towards Kṛṣṇa, but when he misuses it, he becomes indifferent to Him. It is just this indifference that gives rise to the desire in the *jīva's* heart to enjoy *māyā*.
>
> (*Jaiva-dharma*, Chapter 15)

It is not that all independence is the same; there is gradation. Some *jīvas* desire a little independence, or a small sense of autonomy, while others desire total independence.

Question: In your class yesterday, you described how the living entities in the *taṭasthā-śakti* region fall to this material world. You gave the analogy of mustard seeds landing on the sharp blade of a knife and then falling on one side of the knife or the other. You said that, like those mustard seeds, the *jīva* can go either to the material world or the spiritual world. I am trying to understand if this happens because of our minute independence, or by chance, that we come here.

Śrīla Nārāyaṇa Gosvāmī Mahārāja: Independence was first, and chance is second. Without independence, how can the *jīva* look toward either *yogamāyā* or *mahāmāyā*?

Question: So it is a choice, Gurudeva? The *jīva* is responsible?
Śrīla Nārāyaṇa Gosvāmī Mahārāja: Yes; the *jīva* has independence, and Kṛṣṇa never interferes with that. Here is an analogy to help explain this principle. In the government, there is a magistrate for each district. If a person does something for the benefit of the public he will be rewarded by that magistrate, and if he commits a crime he will be punished.

There are some people who know that if they commit a crime they will be punished or even put to death; yet they commit the crime. There are numerous culprits who go to jail, and when they are released they commit the crime again because they like to be in jail. Some *jīvas* are like that; even though they suffer repeatedly in this material world, they are ignorantly attached to remaining here.
Question: In *Jaiva-dharma* it is said that when Kṛṣṇa situates Himself in the *taṭasthā-śakti*, He manifests the *jīva*. What does this mean?
Śrīla Nārāyaṇa Gosvāmī Mahārāja: At this time, Kṛṣṇa is only with His *taṭasthā-śakti*. He has somehow hidden His *cit-śakti* (transcendental potency), *hlādinī-śakti* (spiritual pleasure potency), and all other potencies. When all other potencies are hidden, then the *jīva* manifests.

> Śrī Kṛṣṇa establishes Himself in each of His *śaktis*, and manifests His *svarūpa* according to the nature of that *śakti*. When He is situated in the *cit-svarūpa*, He manifests His essential *svarūpa*, both as Śrī Kṛṣṇa Himself, and also as Nārāyaṇa, the Lord of Vaikuṇṭha. When He is situated in the *jīva-śakti*, He manifests His *svarūpa* as His *vilāsa-mūrti* (pastime expansion) of Vraja, Baladeva. When He situates Himself in the *māyā-śakti*, He manifests the three Viṣṇu forms: Kāraṇodakaśāyī, Garbhodakaśāyī and Kṣīrodakaśāyī.
>
> In His Kṛṣṇa form, He manifests all the spiritual affairs to the superlative degree. In His Baladeva svarūpa as *śeṣa-tattva*, He manifests *nitya-mukta-pārṣada-jīvas* (eternally liberated associates) who render eight types of service to Kṛṣṇa Himself, the origin of *śeṣa-tattva*. Again, as *śeṣa-rūpa* Saṅkarṣaṇa in Vaikuṇṭha, He manifests eight types of servants to render eight kinds of services as eternally liberated associates of Nārāyaṇa. Mahā-Viṣṇu, who is an expansion of Saṅkarṣaṇa, situates Himself in the heart of the *jīva-śakti*, and as Paramātmā, manifests the *jīvas* in the material world.
>
> These *jīvas* are susceptible to the influence of *māyā*, and unless they attain the shelter of the *hlādinī-śakti* by Bhagavān's

> mercy, it is possible that they will be defeated by *māyā*. The countless conditioned *jīvas* who have been illusioned by *māyā* are under the control of the three modes of material nature. Bearing all this in mind, the *siddhānta* is that it is only the *jīva-śakti*, and not the *cit-śakti*, that manifests the *jīvas*.
>
> (*Jaiva-dharma*, Chapter 15)

The head of *taṭasthā-śakti* is Baladeva Prabhu. Kāraṇodakaśāyī Viṣṇu, who manifests the innumerable *jīvas* in the region between the material and spiritual worlds, is an expansion of Mahā-Saṅkarṣaṇa in Vaikuṇṭha, and Mahā-Saṅkarṣaṇa is an expansion of Baladeva.

So, your question was, "What is the meaning of the statement, 'When Kṛṣṇa situates Himself in the *taṭasthā-śakti*, He manifests the *jīva*?' The answer is that Kṛṣṇa manifests His form as Baladeva, and Baladeva manifests the *jīva*.

Question: Are the *jīvas* who manifest from Kāraṇodakaśāyī Viṣṇu significantly different from those who directly manifest from Mahā-Saṅkarṣaṇa in Vaikuṇṭha or Baladeva in Vraja?

Śrīla Nārāyaṇa Gosvāmī Mahārāja: Their qualities are the same, except that those who emanate from Baladeva and Mahā-Saṅkarṣaṇa in the spiritual world have the eternal shelter of *cit-śakti*.

> There are also innumerable atomic conscious *jīvas* who emanate as rays in Kāraṇodakaśāyī Māhā-Viṣṇu's glance upon His *māyā-śakti*. Since these *jīvas* are situated next to *māyā*, they perceive her wonderful workings. Although they have all the qualities of the *jīvas* I have already described, because of their minute and marginal nature, they sometimes look to the spiritual world and sometimes to the material world.
>
> (*Jaiva-dharma*, Chapter 16)

A Chance at the Imaginary Line

Question: If the *jīva* is conscious and transcendental (*cit*), how is it that he manifests via the *taṭasthā-śakti* and not the *cit-śakti*, since the *taṭasthā-śakti* is inferior to the *cit-śakti*?

Śrīla Nārāyaṇa Gosvāmī Mahārāja: The *jīva* is actually *cit-śakti*. The philosophy of *taṭasthā-śakti* has been given only as an indication. In actuality there is no specific geographic area between the spiritual and material worlds called *taṭasthā*. *Taṭasthā* as a line between the two worlds is imaginary. There is certainly *jīva-śakti* and *taṭasthā-śakti*, but the concept of *taṭasthā* as a geographical place is provisional. *Taṭasthā-śakti* is ultimately also *cit-śakti*, in the sense that the *jīva* is conscious (*cit*), not inert (*acit*).

> The *taṭa-rekha*, the marginal line lying between the water of a river and its bank, is both water and land, being situated where the two meet. Since the divine *taṭasthā-śakti* is situated at the margin of matter and spirit, it displays the characteristics of both matter and spirit. It is one principle, yet it displays two natures.
>
> The *jīva* is a spiritual spark, a product of the higher spiritual nature, yet being the divine *taṭasthā-śakti*, he has a nature that enables him to relate to the mundane material energy and be always prone to coming under her influence. Thus, on one hand, the *jīva* cannot be wholly likened to the pure spiritual nature, which is transcendental to and entirely beyond the influence of the material nature. Nevertheless, he cannot be categorized as material since, by his intrinsic constitution, he is spiritual.
>
> (*Jaiva-dharma*, Chapter 1)

The Right Choice Was Enough

Question: In regard to those *jīvas* who look towards Kṛṣṇa and the spiritual world from the *taṭasthā-śakti*, from where does their eligibility come to make such a choice? One's choices in one's present life are generally made according to one's *sukṛti* (past and present spiritual pious activities) and *saṁskāras* (impressions on the heart, coming from past pious or impious acts.)

Śrīla Nārāyaṇa Gosvāmī Mahārāja: At that time there are neither *sukṛtis* nor *saṁskāras* (impressions on the heart, or reformatory procedures).

Question: Nothing?

Śrīla Nārāyaṇa Gosvāmī Mahārāja: Nothing, nothing. The very act of their looking toward the Vaikuṇṭha planets is their *sādhana* (spiritual practices), *sukṛti*, and *saṁskāra*. There is no other *sukṛti* or *saṁskāra* required. Those *jīvas* used their independence properly, and that is sufficient.

> Whatever we say or describe in the material world is under the jurisdiction of material time and space. When we say, "The

jīvas were created," or "The spiritual world was manifested," or "There is no influence of *māyā* in creating the form of the *jīvas*," material time is bound to influence our language and statements. This is inevitable in our conditioned state, so we cannot remove the influence of material time from our descriptions of the atomic *jīva* and spiritual objects. The conception of past, present, and future always enters them in some way or another.

Still, those who can discriminate properly can understand the application of the eternal present when they comprehend the purport of the descriptions of the spiritual world. Be very careful in this matter. Give up the inevitable baseness, the aspect of the description that is fit to be rejected, and attain spiritual realization.

I advise you not to inquire about this philosophical subject from anyone, but to realize it yourself. I have just given you an indication or semblance.

(*Jaiva-dharma*, Chapter 15)

The Potency of the Lord's Potency

Question: Śrīla Gurudeva, in your class yesterday you said that our *sampradāya* (line of disciplic succession), the disciplic line of Śrī Caitanya Mahāprabhu, has a speciality that is not present in the other Vaiṣṇava *sampradāyas*.

The teaching in the other Vaiṣṇava *sampradāyas* is that the *jīva* is actually part and parcel of Kṛṣṇa's body. But in our *sampradāya*, the teaching is that the *jīva* is coming from Kṛṣṇa's spiritual potency (*śakti*), not directly from Kṛṣṇa's body. I thought that all four Vaiṣṇava *sampradāyas* accepted the fact that the Supreme Lord has potencies, and that the *jīva* is one of His potencies.

Śrīla Nārāyaṇa Gosvāmī Mahārāja: Proponents of the other *sampradāyas* know that the *jīva* is one of the Lord's potencies, and they have written this; but their understanding is that the marginal potency, the living entity, is directly coming from Kṛṣṇa's body. They do not accept that the *jīva* is a manifestation of Kṛṣṇa's potency called *jīva-śakti*, which in turn is a partial manifestation of the spiritual potency called *cit-śakti*.

They have not accepted the philosophy of *śakti-pariṇāma-vāda*, which is the understanding that all manifestations are transformations of the Supreme Lord's potencies. Only Śrī Caitanya Mahāprabhu and His *sampradāya* have accepted this philosophy.

Śrīla Madhvācārya accepted the theory of *vastu-pariṇāma-vāda*. He wrote that the *jīva* and this material world are compared to two separate adjectives qualifying a noun, the noun in this analogy being *brahma* (meaning, the Absolute Truth). He wrote that the material world is the external body of *brahma* and the *jīva* is *brahma's* subtle body, as the mind, intelligence, and false ego comprise our subtle body. Madhvācārya gave this analogy to create the understanding that Reality is one, but with specialities. It is clear that although he accepts the philosophy that Kṛṣṇa and Viṣṇu have *śakti*, he has not accepted *śakti-pariṇāma-vāda*. In other words, he accepted the false idea that Kṛṣṇa Himself is transformed, whereas it is actually His divine potency that is transformed.

The philosophies of Śrī Viṣṇusvāmī, Śrī Nimbāditya (Nimbārka), and Rāmānujācārya are similar to that of Śrī Madhvācārya, in the sense that they have also accepted the philosophy of *vastu-pariṇāma-vāda*. According to their philosophy, Kṛṣṇa's own form is transformed. Śrī Caitanya Mahāprabhu did not approve of this philosophy. He preached *śakti-pariṇāma-vāda*.

A Chance for the Lord's Sweet Pastimes

Question: In *Jaiva-dharma*, Śrīla Bhaktivinoda Ṭhākura says that the *jīva's* going through material existence is Kṛṣṇa's pastime. I don't understand this. Even though suffering takes place in the mind, nevertheless, the *jīva* is suffering. It seems that this is very cruel of Kṛṣṇa.

Śrīla Nārāyaṇa Gosvāmī Mahārāja: If you read *Jaiva-dharma* thoroughly, you will see that this is one of Kṛṣṇa's sweet pastimes.

Question: But the *jīva* does not think, "This is a sweet pastime." He thinks, "This is suffering." Moreover, this suffering is not by his choice. You said yesterday that the *jīva's* misuse of independence is compared to mustard seeds falling on the blade of a knife and then falling on one side of the blade or the other. It seems like chance, not choice, that the *jīva* is suffering here in this material world. How can we reconcile this? How is 'chance' Kṛṣṇa's pastime?

Śrīla Nārāyaṇa Gosvāmī Mahārāja: Kṛṣṇa has given independence to all *jīvas*, and He does not want to take that away. The *jīva* looks here and there; because he has eyes, he must look somewhere. If it happens that he looks towards the transcendental world he is attracted to *yogamāyā*, and if he looks toward *mahāmāyā* he is attracted to this world.

Question: This cannot be the *jīva's* conscious choice, because he does not have experience of Kṛṣṇa and the spiritual world.

Śrīla Nārāyaṇa Gosvāmī Mahārāja: He has no experience, but Kṛṣṇa has given him independence, and by that independence he looks where he wants to go.

> **Vrajanātha**: Lord Kṛṣṇa is overflowing with mercy, so why did He make the *jīva* so weak that he became entangled in *māyā*?"
> **Śrī Raghunātha dāsa Bābāji**: It is true that He is overflowing with mercy, but He is also overflowing with desire to perform pastimes. Desiring various pastimes to be enacted in different situations, Śrī Kṛṣṇa made the *jīvas* eligible for all conditions, from the marginal state to the highest state of the *gopīs'* love for Kṛṣṇa called *mahābhāva*. To facilitate the *jīvas'* progress practically and steadfastly towards becoming qualified for His service, He has also created the lower levels of material existence – beginning from the lowest inert matter up to false ego – which is the cause of unlimited obstruction in attaining supreme bliss.
>
> Having fallen from their constitutional position, the *jīvas* who are entangled in *māyā* are indifferent to Kṛṣṇa and engrossed in personal sense gratification. However, Śrī Kṛṣṇa is the reservoir of mercy. The more the *jīva* becomes fallen, the more Kṛṣṇa provides him with opportunities to attain the highest spiritual perfection. He brings this about by appearing before him along with His spiritual abode and eternal associates. Those *jīvas* who take advantage of this merciful opportunity and sincerely endeavor to attain the higher position gradually reach the spiritual world and attain a state similar to that of Śrī Hari's eternal associates."
>
> **Vrajanātha**: Why must the *jīvas* suffer for the sake of the Lord's pastimes?
>
> **Śrī Raghunātha dāsa Bābāji**: The *jīvas* possess some independence. This is actually a sign of God's special mercy upon them. Inert objects are very insignificant and worthless because they have no such independent desire. The *jīva* has attained sovereignty of the inert world only because of this independent desire.
>
> Misery and happiness are conditions of the mind. Thus, what we may consider misery is happiness for one engrossed in it. Since all varieties of material sense gratification finally result in nothing but misery, a materialistic person only achieves

suffering. When that suffering becomes excessive, it gives rise to a search for happiness. From that desire discrimination arises, and from discrimination, the tendency for inquiry is born. As a result of this, one attains the association of saintly devotees, whereupon *śraddhā* (faith in serving Kṛṣṇa) develops. When *śraddhā* is born, the *jīva* ascends to a higher stage, namely the path of devotional service to the Lord.

Gold is purified by heating and hammering. Being indifferent to Kṛṣṇa, the *jīva* has become impure through engaging in mundane sense gratification. Therefore, he must be purified by being beaten with the hammers of misery on the anvil of this material world. By this process, the misery of the *jīvas* averse to Kṛṣṇa finally culminates in happiness. Suffering is therefore just a sign of God's mercy. That is why far-sighted people see the suffering of *jīvas* in Lord Kṛṣṇa's pastimes as auspicious, though the near-sighted can only see it as an inauspicious source of misery.

(*Jaiva Dharma*, Chapter 16)

Try to read Śrīla Bhaktivinoda Ṭhākura's *Jaiva-dharma* thoroughly, and strive to follow its teachings. You must know that you cannot reconcile these philosophical principles by material intelligence. Perform *bhajana* and aspire to increase your advancement in devotional service. Then, when you become advanced, all your doubts and questions will automatically be answered.

No Control over Freedom

Question: When we go on our morning walk, we see billions of blades of grass. What kind of *karma* makes one fall from a human birth all the way down to the birth of a blade of grass?

Śrīla Nārāyaṇa Gosvāmī Mahārāja: It happens by free will. I have already given the analogy of a very small mustard seed. If that seed is thrown on the edge of a sword's blade, it will immediately fall on one side or the other. It will not remain on the blade's edge. Even without suffering or enjoying the fruit of *karma*, it will go to one side or the other.

Similarly, even if the soul is not subjected to the pain or pleasure resulting from one's past activities, because his nature is to be *taṭasthā* (marginal), he must always choose one path or the other. He cannot remain in the *taṭasthā* realm.

Question: But where is the free will? It seems like there is no free will. The *jīvas* are falling here or there without choice.

Śrīla Nārāyaṇa Gosvāmī Mahārāja: Kṛṣṇa has given them independence, free will, both in the realm of *taṭasthā-śakti* and as conditioned souls. That independence must always be with them. Even when they become liberated, that *taṭasthā-bhāva*, the mood of free will to choose, will be present within them.

Question: But when he hits that demarcation – that sharp edge of the blade – going this way or that way…

Śrīla Nārāyaṇa Gosvāmī Mahārāja: As I mentioned earlier, material analogies are not perfect in all respects. The mustard seed is not conscious, whereas in all situations the *jīva* has his natural, intrinsic marginal nature. Kṛṣṇa never interferes with his freedom. Wherever he wants to go, he can go.

Question: The human form is a platform on which one performs *karma*. How does one fall from human life all the way down to being a blade of grass?

Śrīla Nārāyaṇa Gosvāmī Mahārāja: Freedom has so many possibilities. Someone may think, "I want to be a blade of grass." You cannot control a person's freedom. One may think, "I will be a mountain," or "I will be river," or "I will be a human," or "I will be a tiger." There is no control over the freedom of another living being.

Question: Who would want to be a blade of grass?

Śrīla Nārāyaṇa Gosvāmī Mahārāja: Uddhava wanted to be a blade of grass in Vṛndāvana. Why would he not want to be a blade of grass? In that way Kṛṣṇa and the *gopīs* would walk by him and he would be bathed by the dust of their lotus feet.

Question: At the time of the *jīva's* choosing which way to turn, he may look left and right. What does he see exactly?

Śrīla Nārāyaṇa Gosvāmī Mahārāja: He sees that in this world all are enjoying sense gratification. Moreover, since the *jīva* is independent in all stages of his existence, he may enthusiastically take to the process of Kṛṣṇa consciousness and then later on change his mind. Later on he may think, "Oh, sense gratification is very, very good. It is more rewarding than Kṛṣṇa's service. There is nothing of value in Kṛṣṇa's service."

Question: Sometimes it is said that the *jīva* falls to this world by chance, and sometimes it is said that his fall is his own fault. Which is correct?

Śrīla Nārāyaṇa Gosvāmī Mahārāja: Try to understand that both are the same.

[Except for the section called "No Control Over Freedom," this chapter is a collection of excerpts from a conversation with Śrīla Nārāyaṇa Gosvāmī Mahārāja during his morning walk in Badger, California, on June 14, 2008. "No Control Over Freedom" was spoken on a morning walk in Venice, Italy, on June 9, 2009.]

CHAPTER SEVEN

INCONCEIVABLE JĪVA-TATTVA

Question: There is a verse in *Śrī Caitanya-caritāmṛta* which says that the *jīva* in this world is eternally conditioned. The words *nitya-saṁsāra* means 'eternally conditioned.'

'nitya-baddha' – kṛṣṇa haite nitya-bahirmukha
'nitya-saṁsāra', bhuñje narakādi duḥkha

(*Śrī Caitanya-caritāmṛta, Madhya-līlā*, 22.13)

Śrīla Nārāyaṇa Gosvāmī Mahārāja: The *jīva* is not eternally conditioned. In this particular verse, *nitya* does not mean 'eternal.' *Nitya* also means 'perpetually,' 'constantly' or 'regularly.'[1] In this connection it means

---

1 "We are therefore stressing, 'Always hear, always read, always hear.' *Nityaṁ bhāgavata-sevayā* (*Śrīmad-Bhāgavatam* 1.2.18). *Nitya*. If you can constantly, twenty-four hours, hear and chant… 'Hear' means somebody chants, or you chant yourself, or hear,

anādi, or 'beginningless,' meaning that the *jīva* has been conditioned since time immemorial.[2] If it meant 'eternal' in the true sense, we would have no scope to get out of *māyā*. A careful translation of the verse reveals this truth.

Question: The *anādi-baddha-jīva*, the living entity who has been conditioned since time immemorial, never had any direct relationship with Kṛṣṇa?

Śrīla Nārāyaṇa Gosvāmī Mahārāja: Everything about the *jīva's* relationship with Kṛṣṇa is present in his *svarūpa*, but he has never experienced that relationship. It cannot be said that in a seed there is no tree, no fruit, no branches, and no leaves. Everything is latent within a seed, but we cannot see it. This is also true of the *jīva*.

The *mukta-mahāpuruṣa*, or liberated, self-realized soul, sees that every soul in this world is serving Kṛṣṇa. But we see that we are conditioned souls; our vision does not encompass spiritual reality.

No mundane words can describe the form of the soul, because it is beyond our comprehension. *Māyā* is not present in the *ātmā*, and to help us understand this I will give the analogy of the sun and the clouds. The sun is compared here with the spirit soul, and *māyā* is compared with the clouds. Although there are clouds outside the sun, there are no clouds in the sun itself. Those on the ground see the clouds, but those who are above the clouds always see the sun; they do not see clouds. Similarly, although we conditioned souls cannot see the soul serving Kṛṣṇa, self-realized souls like Śrī Nārada Ṛṣi can see that we are always serving even though we are conditioned.

What I am explaining to you now is only for you at this stage of your spiritual life. Strive to perform *harināma*, the chanting of the pure holy names of Kṛṣṇa, and beg for mercy so that you will come out of *māyā* and realize all these truths. Without the chanting of the holy names, the experience of transcendence is not possible.

A devotee who has come to the stage of *nirdhūta-kaṣāya* (the advanced stage of *bhāva-bhakti*, in which all impurities are gone from one's heart but one still has a material body) or *bhagavat-pārṣada-deha-prāpta* (the

---

or some of your colleagues may chant, you hear" (Lecture by Śrīla Bhaktivedānta Svāmī Mahārāja on *Śrīmad-Bhāgavatam* 5.5.6. Vṛndāvana, October 28, 1976).

2 "The *nitya-dharma* of the *jīva* is servitorship to Kṛṣṇa. When he forgets this, he is subjected to the tyranny of *māyā*, and from that very moment he becomes diverted from Kṛṣṇa. The fall of the *jīva* does not take place within the context of material time. Accordingly, the words *anādi-bahirmukha* are used, meaning that the *jīva* has been diverted since time without beginning" (*Jaiva-dharma*, Chapter 1).

stage in which one has the spiritual body of an eternal associate of the Lord)[3] realizes that there is actually no *māyā*. On the other hand, for a conditioned soul there is no realization of liberation. Kṛṣṇa's associates can realize the transcendental reality, whereas conditioned souls can only imagine it.

Śrīla Bhaktivinoda Ṭhākura writes in *Jaiva-dharma* that devotees who perform *harināma* and beg mercy from Śrī Kṛṣṇa and Śrī Caitanya Mahāprabhu may realize transcendence (*cit-vastu*). Kṛṣṇa is the complete *cit-vastu*, or Complete Transcendental Entity, whereas the *jīva* is the infinitesimal *cit-vastu*, or minute spirit spark.

In *śāstra*, numerous *siddhāntas*, philosophical conclusions, have been explained for certain devotees at certain stages of their spiritual

---

3 *Siddha-mahāpuruṣas* are of three types: (1) *bhagavat-pārṣada-deha-prāpta* (those who have obtained perfected spiritual bodies as eternal associates of the Lord), (2) *nirdhūta-kaṣāya* (those who have thrown off all material impurities), and (3) *mūrcchita-kaṣāya* (those in whom a trace of material contamination still lies dormant).

(1) *Bhagavat-pārṣada-deha-prāpta*:

After giving up the gross material body, those who have perfected themselves through the practice of *bhakti* obtain *sat-cit-ānanda* spiritual forms, which are just suitable for the service of the Lord as associates (*pārṣadas*). Such persons are the best of all *uttama-bhāgavatas*.

(2) *Nirdhūta-kaṣāya*:

Those who, although still residing within the gross material body made of five elements, have no trace of material desire nor any material impressions (*saṁskāras*) within their hearts are called *nirdhūta-kaṣāya* (those who have thrown off all material impurities). They belong to the intermediate class of *uttama-bhāgavatas*.

(3) *Mūrcchita-kaṣāya*:

Those *siddha-mahāpuruṣas* pursuing the path of *bhakti* in whose hearts there remains a trace of desire and impressions based on the material mode of goodness are known as *mūrcchita-kaṣāya*. Due to the influence of their *bhakti-yoga*, these desires and impressions remain in a dormant or unconscious state. As soon as there is a favorable opportunity, their worshipful object, Śrī Bhagavān, somehow causes their desire to be consumed and attracts them to His lotus feet. Such elevated souls belong to the preliminary stage (*kaniṣṭha*) of *uttama-bhāgavatas*. Devarṣi Nārada is an example of the topmost *uttama-bhāgavata*. Śukadeva Gosvāmī belongs to the intermediate stage of *uttama-bhāgavatas* (*nirdhūta-kaṣāya*). Śrī Nārada in his previous birth as the son of a maidservant is an example of the preliminary stage of *uttama-bhāgavatas* (*mūrcchita-kaṣāya*).

The association and mercy of these three kinds of *maha-bhāgavatas* is the cause of the manifestation of *śraddhā*.

(*Śrī Bhakti-rasāmṛta-sindhu-bindu*, Verse 3, *Śrī Bindu-vikāśinī-vṛtti*, comment) life. It is not that all *siddhānta* is for all persons at all stages of their development in devotion. There is *siddhānta* for *kaniṣṭha* Vaiṣṇavas (neophytes in *bhakti*), *madhyama* Vaiṣṇavas (those devotees in the intermediate stage), and *uttama* Vaiṣṇavas (those devotees who have crossed over *māyā*). In the *Śrīmad-Bhāgavatam*, many categories of *siddhānta* are given for various classes of persons.

Chant, "Hare Kṛṣṇa, Hare Kṛṣṇa, Kṛṣṇa Kṛṣṇa, Hare Hare, Hare Rāma, Hare Rāma, Rāma Rāma, Hare Hare." Try to do *bhajana* and realize all these transcendental truths. Mundane logic and reasoning will never truly answer the questions about the individual soul and his relationship with the Supreme Soul.

Question: Śrīla Jīva Gosvāmī says that one acquires *bhakti* by association or by mercy. Can you explain this further?

Śrīla Nārāyaṇa Gosvāmī Mahārāja: The attainment of *bhakti* is dependent on whom we associate with. It depends on whether we associate with a *kaniṣṭha* Vaiṣṇava, a *madhyama* Vaiṣṇava, or an *uttama* Vaiṣṇava .

A *madhyama* Vaiṣṇava can only give *siddhānta*. He cannot speak from an experience of spiritual realization. If we want realization, it is necessary to hear and associate with realized souls, namely the three kinds of *uttama* Vaiṣṇavas. The association of a *madhyama* Vaiṣṇava can take us to the entrance of regulated devotional practice (*sādhana-bhakti*), and by his mercy he can lead us to a realized soul, an *uttama* Vaiṣṇava.

["Inconceivable Jīva-tattva" is an excerpt of a conversation between Śrīla Nārāyaṇa Gosvāmī Mahārāja and a group of ISKCON GBC sannyāsīs and other senior ISKCON members. This conversation took place on March 29, 1993.]

Part Two

JAIVA-DHARMA

INTRODUCTION TO
JAIVA-DHARMA

I am very happy and satisfied that Śrīla Bhaktivinoda Ṭhākura's *Jaiva-dharma* has been published and printed in English. It is a very authentic book for understanding fundamental philosophical truths, the process to attain the perfection of *kṛṣṇa-prema*, and finally the attainment of *kṛṣṇa-prema* itself.

When I first published it in Hindi, I thought that it must also be translated into English for the benefit of the entire world, for it would bring about a spiritual revolution. Now that it is published and will be distributed throughout the world, that revolution of new thought will surely manifest and the erroneous impressions about *jīva-tattva*, *bhakti-tattva*, and all other important philosophical truths will be clarified. Those who read this book under the guidance of a qualified Vaiṣṇava will capture its glories.

Śrīla Bhaktivinoda Ṭhākura adopted the same process in his *Jaiva-dharma* that had been adopted by Śrīla Vyāsadeva in *Śrīmad-Bhāgavatam*; that is, he presented *tattva* in such an interesting and enlivening way that the book appears like a novel.

But it is not a novel; it is factual history. Śrīla Bhaktivinoda Ṭhākura saw the series of historic divine events in his *samādhi* (mystic trance), and then he systematically wrote it down. He was able to do this because, besides realizing these events, he also realized all of the written documents of Śrīla Rūpa Gosvāmī, Śrīla Sanātana Gosvāmī, Śrīla Raghunātha dāsa Gosvāmī, Śrīla Jīva Gosvāmī, Śrīla Visvanātha Cakravartī Ṭhākura, the teachings of Caitanya Mahāprabhu, and the teachings of all the *ācāryas* in His line.

If one wants to enter the spiritual realm, he must read *Jaiva-dharma* thoroughly, under the guidance of an exalted realized Vaiṣṇava, not only one time but one hundred times.

[*A glorification of Jaiva-dharma by Śrīla Bhaktivedānta Nārāyaṇa Gosvāmī Mahārāja, spoken in September, 2001, in Mathurā, India.*]

CHAPTER FIFTEEN
JĪVA-TATTVA

The following three chapters from Śrīla Bhaktivinoda Ṭhākura's Jaiva-dharma contain all the beautiful conclusive truths about the soul – the transcendental particle of spirit, who is simultaneously within the body and beyond it. Herein you will be fortunate to meet the ideal guru, Śrī Raghunātha dāsa Bābājī, and his ideal disciple, Vrajanātha, in the ideal and divine setting of Śrī Dhāma Māyāpura.

The next day, Vrajanātha reached the courtyard of Śrīvāsa Paṇḍita's house earlier than on previous days. The Vaiṣṇavas from Godruma had also come before evening to see the Deities' *sandhyā-āratī* ceremony. Śrī Premadāsa Paramahaṁsa Bābājī, Vaiṣṇava dāsa, Advaita dāsa, and other Vaiṣṇavas were already seated on the small platform in front of the Deities, where the devotees observe the ceremony.

When Vrajanātha saw the transcendental moods of the Vaiṣṇavas from Godruma, he was struck with wonder and thought, "I will perfect my life by having their association as soon as possible." At the same time, when those Vaiṣṇavas saw Vrajanātha's humble and devotional disposition, all of them bestowed their blessings on him.

When the *āratī* ceremony was over, Vrajanātha and the elderly Bābājī began to walk southwards together, in the direction of Godruma. Raghunātha dāsa Bābājī saw that tears were continuously falling from Vrajanātha's eyes and, feeling very affectionate towards him, asked lovingly, "Why are you weeping?"

Vrajanātha said, "Master, when I remember your sweet instructions, my heart becomes restless and the whole world seems to be empty. My heart is eager to take shelter at Śrī Gaurāṅga-deva's [Śrī Caitanya Mahāprabhu's] lotus feet. Being merciful, please tell me of my true identity and why I have come to this world."

Śrī Raghunātha dāsa Bābājī: My dear son, you have blessed me by asking such a question. On the auspicious day that the *jīva* asks this question, certainly good fortune arises in his life. Kindly hear the fifth verse of *Daśa-mūla*, and all your doubts will vanish.

sphuliṅgāḥ ṛddhāgner iva cid-aṇavo jīvā-nicayāḥ
hareḥ sūryasyaivāpṛthag api tu tad-bheda-viṣayāḥ
vaśe māyā yasya prakṛti-patir eveśvara iha
sa jīvo mukto 'pi prakṛti-vaśā-yogyaḥ sva-guṇataḥ

> Just as sparks burst out from a blazing fire, so the innumerable *jīvas* are like spiritual particles in the rays of the spiritual sun, Śrī Hari. Though non-different from Him, they are simultaneously eternally different. The eternal difference between the *jīva* and God is that God is the lord and master of His illusory potency, whereas the *jīva* has the potential to fall under her control, even in his liberated stage, due to his constitutional nature.

Vrajanātha: This philosophical conclusion which you have presented is certainly unique and unparalleled, yet I would like to hear some Vedic evidence in relation to it. Lord Caitanya's statements are certainly Veda (Vedic knowledge); still, people will be bound to accept His teachings if the Upaniṣads can substantiate them.

Śrī Raghunātha dāsa Bābājī: This truth is described in many places in the Vedas. I will cite a few references:

yathāgneḥ kṣudrā visphuliṅgā vyuccaranti
evam evāsmad ātmanaḥ sarvāṇi bhūtāni vyuccaranti

Bṛhad-āraṇyaka Upaniṣad (2.1.20)

Innumerable *jīvas* emanate from the Supreme Personality of Godhead, just like tiny sparks from a fire.

tasya vā etasya puruṣasya dve eva sthāne / bhavata
idañ ca paraloka-sthānañ ca / sandhyaṁ tṛtīyaṁ
svapna-sthānaṁ / tasmin sandhye sthāne tiṣṭhann
ete ubhe / sthāne paśyatīdañ ca paraloka-sthānañ ca

Bṛhad-āraṇyaka Upaniṣad (4.3.9)

The *jīva* has the possibility of two residences – the material realm and the spiritual realm – both of which he may seek. He is situated in a third position, which is a dreamlike condition (*svapna-sthāna*) and is the juncture (*taṭasthā*) between the other two. From that middle position he is able to see both the material and the spiritual worlds.

This verse describes the marginal nature of *jīva-śakti*. Again, it is said in *Bṛhad-āraṇyaka Upaniṣad* (4.3.18):

tad yathā mahā-matsya ubhe kule 'nusañcarati /
pūrvañ cāparañ caivam evāyaṁ puruṣa etāv ubhāv
antāv / anu sañcarati svapnāntañ ca buddhāntañ ca

The symptoms of the marginal existence are like those of a huge aquatic who is capable of living on both the eastern and western sides of the river at his own will. The *jīva* soul, situated within the waters of the Causal Ocean, which lies between the material and spiritual worlds, is able to reside in both the dream world of matter and the spiritual world of divine wakefulness.

Vrajanātha: What is the Vedic understanding of the word *taṭasthā*?

Śrī Raghunātha dāsa Bābājī: The borderline between the ocean and the land is called the shore (*taṭa*); but the place that touches the ocean is actually nothing but land, so where is the shore? The *taṭa* is the line of demarcation separating the ocean and the land, and it is so fine that it cannot be seen with the gross eyes. If we compare the transcendental realm to the ocean and the material world to the land, then *taṭa* is the subtle line that divides the two. The *jīva-śakti* is situated at that place.

The countless atomic particles that float in the rays of the sun give an inkling of the real position of the *jīva*. Situated in the middle place, they see the spiritual world on one side and the material universe created by *māyā* (the Lord's deluding material potency) on the other. The Lord's spiritual potency on one side is unlimited, and the material potency on the other side is enormous. In between them are situated the innumerable extremely minute *jīvas*. The *jīvas* arise from Śrī Kṛṣṇa's marginal potency; hence their nature is also marginal.

Vrajanātha: What is the marginal nature?

Śrī Raghunātha dāsa Bābājī: It is the nature that enables the *jīva* to be situated between both worlds, and to see both. It is the *jīva's* tendency to become subordinate to the control of either of the potencies. Sometimes the shore is submerged in the river because of erosion, and then again it becomes one with the land because the river changes its course. In a similar way, if the *jīva* looks towards Kṛṣṇa – that is, towards the spiritual world – he is influenced by Kṛṣṇa's internal energy. He then enters the spiritual world and serves Śrī Kṛṣṇa in his pure, fully conscious spiritual form. However, if he looks towards *māyā*, he becomes opposed to Kṛṣṇa and is bound by the net of *māyā*. This dual-faceted nature is called the marginal nature.

Vrajanātha: Is there any illusory material component (*māyā-śakti*) in the *jīva's* original constitution?

Śrī Raghunātha dāsa Bābājī: No, the *jīva* is created solely from the *cit-śakti* (transcendental, or spiritual, potency). He can be defeated, or covered, by *māyā*, because he is minute by nature and lacks spiritual power. However, there is not even a scent of *māyā* in his existence.

Vrajanātha: I have heard from my teacher that when a fraction of *brahma*, the all-pervasive spiritual Absolute Truth, is covered by *māyā*, it becomes the *jīva*. He explained the sky to be always indivisible, but when a part of it is enclosed in a pot, it becomes like a pot of sky. Similarly, the *jīva* is constitutionally nothing but *brahma*, but when that *brahma* is covered by *māyā*, the false ego of being a *jīva* develops. Is this conception correct?

Śrī Raghunātha dāsa Bābājī: This doctrine is simply Māyāvāda. How can *māyā* touch transcendental *brahma*? The Māyāvādīs propose that *brahma* has no potency. If potency is supposed to be non-existent, how can *māyā* – which is potency – possibly approach *brahma*?

Conversely, if we accept the transcendental potency (*cit-śakti*) of *brahma*, how can the material potency, *māyā-śakti*, who is insignificant, defeat that transcendental potency and create the *jīva* from *brahma*? Moreover, how can *māyā* be assertive when she has no independent potency and will? *Brahma* can never be deluded by *māyā's* shroud of illusion. Furthermore, *brahma* is indivisible, so how can such a *brahma* be fragmented? The idea that *māyā* can act upon *brahma* is not acceptable.

Māyā plays no role in the creation of the *jīvas*. Admittedly the *jīva* is atomic, but even so, the *jīva* is still a reality superior to *māyā*.

Vrajanātha: Once, another teacher said that the *jīva* is nothing but a reflection of *brahma*. The sun is reflected in water, and similarly, *brahma* is seen as *jīva* when it is reflected in *māyā*. What do you think of this conception?

Śrī Raghunātha dāsa Bābājī: Again, this is simply an example of Māyāvāda philosophy. *Brahma* has no limit, and a limitless entity can never be reflected. The idea of limiting *brahma* is opposed to the conclusions of the Vedas, so this illogical theory of reflection should be utterly rejected.

Vrajanātha: A scholar of debate once told me that in reality there is no substance known as *jīva*. One only thinks himself a *jīva* because of illusion, and when the illusion is removed, there is only one indivisible *brahma*. Is there any truth to this concept?

Śrī Raghunātha dāsa Bābājī: This is also a Māyāvāda doctrine, which has no foundation at all. According to scripture, "*ekam evādvitīyam* – there is nothing apart from *brahma*." If this is so, whence has illusion come, and who is supposed to be in illusion? If you say that *brahma* is under illusion, in effect you are saying *brahma* is not actually *brahma*, which means great, but rather is insignificant. Furthermore, if you propose that illusion is a separate and independent entity, you negate the non-dual nature of *brahma*.

Vrajanātha: Once an influential scholar arrived in Navadvīpa, and in a conference of scholars he tried to establish that only the *jīva* exists. His theory was that the *jīva* creates everything in his dreams, and it is because of this that he enjoys happiness and suffers distress. Then, when the dream breaks, he sees that he is nothing but *brahma*. To what extent is this idea correct?

Śrī Raghunātha dāsa Bābājī: This is, again, Māyāvāda. If, as they say, *brahma* is undifferentiated, how can it possibly produce the *jīva* and his dreaming state? Māyāvādīs use examples such as the illusion of seeing mother-of-pearl (the shining inner surface of a pearl oyster shell) as gold, and the illusion of taking a rope to be a snake. Through such arguments, their philosophy cannot provide a consistent basis for non-dual oneness. All these arguments are traps of illusion.

Vrajanātha: So *māyā* has nothing whatsoever to do with creating the constitutional form of the *jīvas* – this has to be accepted. At the same time, I have also clearly understood that the *jīva* is by nature subject to the influence of *māyā*. Now I would like to know, did the *cit-śakti* directly create the *jīvas* with their marginal nature?

Śrī Raghunātha dāsa Bābājī: No, the *cit-śakti* is the complete potency of Kṛṣṇa, and its manifestations are all eternally perfect beings (*nitya-siddha*). The *jīva* coming from the the *taṭasthā* region is not *nitya-siddha*, although when he performs regulated devotional services (*sādhana*), he can become perfect by the performance of such services (*sādhana-siddha*) and enjoy transcendental happiness like the *nitya-siddhas*. Śrīmatī Rādhikā has four types of *sakhīs* who are *nitya-siddha*, and they are direct expansions (*kāya-vyūha*) of the personified *cit-śakti*, Śrīmatī Rādhikā Herself.

All *jīvas* have manifested from Śrī Kṛṣṇa's *jīva-śakti*. The *cit-śakti* is His complete potency, whereas the *jīva-śakti* is His incomplete potency. The complete entities are all transformations of the complete potency, and the innumerable atomic, conscious *jīvas* are transformations of the incomplete potency.

Kṛṣṇa establishes Himself in each of His *śaktis*, and manifests His svarūpa according to the nature of that *śakti*. When He is situated in the *cit-svarūpa*, He manifests His essential *svarūpa*, both as Śrī Kṛṣṇa Himself, and also as Nārāyaṇa, the Lord of Vaikuṇṭha; when He is situated in the *jīva-śakti*, He manifests His *svarūpa* as His *vilāsa-mūrti* (pastime expansion) of Vraja, Baladeva; and when He situates Himself in the *māyā-śakti*, He manifests the three Viṣṇu forms: Kāraṇodakaśāyī, Garbhodakaśāyī, and Kṣīrodakaśāyī.

In His Kṛṣṇa form, He manifests all the spiritual affairs to the superlative degree. In His Baladeva *svarūpa* as *śeṣa-tattva*, He manifests *nitya-mukta-pārṣada-jīvas* (eternally liberated associates) who render eight types of service to Kṛṣṇa Himself, the origin of *śeṣa-tattva*. Again, as Saṅkarṣaṇa in Vaikuṇṭha, He manifests eight types of servants to render eight kinds of services as eternally liberated associates of Nārāyaṇa. Mahā-Viṣṇu, who is an expansion of Saṅkarṣaṇa, situates Himself in the heart of the *jīva-śakti*, and as Paramātmā, manifests the *jīvas* in the material world.

These *jīvas* are susceptible to the influence of *māyā*, and unless they attain the shelter of the *hlādinī-śakti* by Bhagavān's mercy, it is possible that they will be defeated by *māyā*. The countless conditioned *jīvas* who have been illusioned by *māyā* are under the control of the three modes of material nature.

Vrajanātha: You said earlier that the spiritual world is eternal, and so are the *jīvas*. If this is true, how can eternal entities possibly be created, manifested, or produced? If they are created at some point in time, they must have been non-existent before that; so how can we accept their eternality?

Śrī Raghunātha dāsa Bābājī: The time and space experienced in this material world are completely different from that of the spiritual world. Material time is divided into three aspects, namely past, present and future, whereas in the spiritual world there is only one undivided, eternally present time. Every event of the spiritual world is eternally present.

Whatever we say or describe in the material world is under the jurisdiction of material time and space. When we say, "The *jīvas* were created," "The spiritual world was manifested" or "There is no influence of *māyā* in creating the form of the *jīvas*," material time is bound to influence our language and statements. This is inevitable in our conditioned state, and therefore we cannot remove the influence of material time from our conceptions and descriptions of the atomic *jīva* and spiritual objects. We inevitably think and speak in terms of past, present, and future.

On the other hand, those who are dedicated to understanding the pure transcendental viewpoint can comprehend the application of the eternal present when they hear the descriptions of the spiritual world. Be very careful in this matter. Reject the unavoidable mundane aspect of the description, and perceive the spiritual reality.

The *jīva* is an eternal servant of Kṛṣṇa, his eternal nature is to serve Kṛṣṇa, and having forgotten that eternal nature, he has become bound by *māyā*. This understanding is shared by all types of Vaiṣṇavas, and all of them consider that there are two types of *jīva*: *nitya-mukta* and *nitya-baddha*. However, although all varieties of Vaiṣṇavas speak in this way, there are different types of understanding. The human intellect becomes overwhelmed by intoxication due to gross bodily identification, and therefore it cannot comprehend transcendental matters, whereas realized souls perceive the non-material truth through spiritual trance.

Our words always have some material limitation, so whatever we say will have material defects. My dear son, you should always endeavor to realize the pure truth. Logic and argument cannot help at all in this regard. It is futile to use them to try to understand inconceivable subject matters.

I am aware of the fact that you cannot immediately comprehend the depths of this line of spiritual thought. However, as your devotional practice and spiritual attachment increase, your power to discriminate between matter and spirit will be sharpened. In other words, the host of spiritual moods will spontaneously arise in your pure heart.

Your body is material and all the activities of your body are also material, but in reality you are non-material. You are an infinitesimal conscious entity. The more you know yourself, the more you will be able to realize how your real form is a truth superior to the world of *māyā*.

However, by my mere telling you this, you will not realize it; by hearing alone you will not attain it. Cultivate the practice of chanting *hari-nāma* as much as possible. As you go on chanting, the multitude of transcendental moods will naturally begin to manifest in your heart. To the degree that they do, you will be able to realize the transcendental world.

Both mind and speech have their origin in matter. They cannot touch the transcendental truth, even with the greatest endeavor. The Vedas say (*Taittirīya Upaniṣad* 2.9):

yato vāco nivartante aprāpya manasā saha

> Speech and mind return from their search for *brahma*, being unable to attain Him.

I advise you not to inquire about this philosophical subject from anyone else, but to realize it yourself. I have just given you an indication.

Vrajanātha: You have explained that the *jīva* is like a spark of a burning fire or like an atomic particle in the rays of the spiritual Sun. What is the role of *jīva-śakti* in this?

Śrī Raghunātha dāsa Bābājī: Lord Kṛṣṇa, who in these analogies is compared to the blazing fire or the Sun, is the self-manifesting Absolute

Truth. Thus, everything within the burning flames of that Sun is fully spiritual. The rays emanating from their source, the spiritual Sun, constitute the *jīva-śakti*, or *taṭasthā-śakti*, the subservient expansion of the *svarūpa-śakti*, and the atomic particles situated in the rays of this spiritual Sun are the *jīvas*.

The *svarūpa-śakti* has manifested the Sun planet, and the activities that take place outside the Sun globe are the activities of the *jīva-śakti*, the partial expansion of the *svarūpa-śakti*. Therefore, any activities pertaining to the *jīvas* are the action of *jīva-śakti* alone.

"*Parāsya śaktir vividhaiva śrūyate* – that inconceivable potency is called *parā-śakti*. Although it is one, this innate potency has manifold varieties" (*Śvetāśvatara Upaniṣad* 6.8). According to this scriptural aphorism, the *cit-śakti* is a manifestation of the *parā-śakti*, and it emanates from its own sphere, the spiritual realm. The *jīva-śakti*, in the marginal region between the spiritual and the material worlds, manifests innumerable, eternal *jīvas*, who are like atomic particles in the rays of the spiritual Sun.

Vrajanātha: The fire, the Sun, the burning sparks, and the atomic particles of sunshine – these are all material objects. Why has a comparison been made with these material objects in the discussion of spiritual truth?

Śrī Raghunātha dāsa Bābājī: As I have already said, inevitably there are material defects in any material statements we make about spiritual truth, but what alternative do we have? We are obliged to use these examples as guidelines because we are helpless without them. Therefore, those who know established truth try to explain spiritual substance (*cit-vastu*) by comparing it to fire or the Sun. In reality, the Sun of Lord Kṛṣṇa is far superior to the material Sun. His effulgence is far superior to the radiance of the Sun and His rays and the atoms in them – that is, the *jīva-śakti* and the *jīvas* – are far superior to the rays of the Sun and the atomic particles of the rays. Still, these examples have been used because there are similarities within them.

Examples can explain some spiritual qualities, but not all. The beauty of the Sun's light and the ability of its rays to illuminate other objects are both qualities that compare with spiritual reality, for it is the quality of spirit to reveal its own beauty and to illuminate other objects. However, the scorching heat in the sunrays have no counterpart in spiritual substance, nor does the fact that the rays are material. If we say, "This milk is like water," we are only considering the liquid quality of water in the comparison; otherwise, if all the qualities of water were present in milk, why would the milk not become water? Thus, examples can explain certain specific qualities and traits of an object, but not all.

Vrajanātha: The spiritual rays of the transcendental *kṛṣṇa*-sun and the spiritual atoms within those rays are non-different from the Sun; yet, at the same time they are eternally different from it. How can both these facts be true simultaneously?

Śrī Raghunātha dāsa Bābājī: In the material world, when one object is produced from another, the product is either completely different from its source, or else it remains a part of it. This is the nature of material objects. For example, an egg becomes separate from the mother bird once it is laid, whereas a person's nails and hair remain part of the body until they are cut, even though they are produced from his body.

The nature of spiritual reality is somewhat different. Whatever has manifested from the spiritual Sun, Śrī Kṛṣṇa, is simultaneously one with Him and different from Him. The rays of the Sun and the atomic particles in the rays are not separate from the Sun, even after they have emanated from it. Similarly, the rays of Kṛṣṇa's form and the atoms in those rays – *jīva-śakti* and the *jīvas* – are not separate from Him, even though they are produced from Him.

At the same time, although the *jīvas* are non-different from Him, they are also eternally different and separate from Him since they have their own minute particle of independent desires. Therefore, the *jīva's* difference and non-difference from Him is an eternal truth. This is the special feature of the transcendental realm.

The sages give a provincial analogy [an analogy that is not fully accurate but is like a place-holder until realization comes] from our experience of inert matter. Suppose you cut a small piece of gold from a large piece and use it to make a bangle. From the perspective of gold, the bangle is not different from the original piece of gold. However, from the perspective of the bangle, the two are different from each other. This example does not present a complete representation of transcendental truth, but it illustrates an important aspect.

From the point of view of qualitative spiritual reality, there is no difference between the Supreme Controller and the *jīva*, whereas from the perspective of status and quantity, these two are eternally different. God is complete spirit, whereas the *jīva* is atomic spirit. God is great, whereas the *jīva* is insignificant. Some people give the analogy of the sky in a pot and the unlimited sky in this regard, but this example is completely inconsistent with regard to the spiritual realm.

Vrajanātha: If transcendental entities and material objects belong to completely different categories, how can material objects be used as appropriate examples for understanding transcendental entities?

Śrī Raghunātha dāsa Bābājī: There are different categories of material objects, and the scholars of the school of mundane logic consider them eternal. However, there is no such categorical difference between the transcendental and material. I have already said that transcendence is the only reality and matter is simply its vitiated transformation. The transformation is different from the original source, but it is still similar to the pure, original object in many respects.

For example, ice is a transformation of water, and it becomes different from water through this transformation; but the two remain similar in many of their qualities, such as coldness. Hot and cold water do not both have the quality of coldness, but their quality of fluidity is the same. Therefore, the transformed object certainly retains some similarity to the pure, original object. According to this principle, the transcendental world can be understood to some extent with the help of material examples.

By adopting the logic of *arundhatī-darśana*[1], one can use material examples to understand something about the spiritual nature. By comparing the gross characteristics of matter with its opposite nature, spirit, we can surmise the esoteric truths of the spiritual nature, as certain characteristics inherent in the material nature are close to the spiritual truths.

Lord Kṛṣṇa's pastimes are completely spiritual, and there is not even the slightest scent of a material mood in them. The pastimes of Vraja described in *Śrīmad-Bhāgavatam* are transcendental, but when the descriptions are read in an assembly, the fruits of hearing them differ according to the respective qualifications of the listeners. Appreciating the ornamental figures of speech from the mundane perspective, those who are absorbed in material sense gratification hear these narrations as stories of an ordinary hero and heroine.

The intermediate devotees (*madhyama-adhikārīs*) take shelter of the logic of *arundhatī-darśana* and perceive the spiritual truth underlying the descriptions, and they experience sublime happiness because of their

1 Arundhatī is a very small star, situated close to the Vaśiṣṭha star in the Great Bear constellation. Its location is first determined by looking at a bigger star beside it, and then, if one looks carefully, one can see Arundhatī close by.

devotional mood. Finally, when the topmost devotees (*uttama-adhikārīs*) hear the descriptions of those pastimes, they become immersed in their pure transcendental relationship with the Lord, devoid of all mundane qualities, and thus relish spiritual *rasa*.

The Absolute Truth is beyond matter, so how can we educate the *jīvas* without taking help of the principles I have just described? Can the conditioned *jīva* understand a subject that renders the voice dumb and stops the working of the mind? There doesn't appear to be any method of explaining these subjects other than the principle of similarity – the logic of *arundhatī-darśana*.

Material objects can be either different or non-different from each other, so difference and non-difference are not visible in them at one and the same time; but this is not the case with transcendental truth. We have to accept that Śrī Kṛṣṇa is simultaneously different and non-different from His *jīva-śakti* and the *jīvas* in it. This simultaneous difference and oneness is said to be inconceivable, because it is beyond the limit of human intellect.

Vrajanātha: What is the difference between the Supreme Lord and the *jīva*?

Śrī Raghunātha dāsa Bābājī: First understand the non-difference, and then I will explain their eternal difference. The Supreme Lord is the embodiment of knowledge, the self-manifest supreme divinity, the illuminator of others, the knower of the fields of action (*kṣetrajña*), the self-determined, and the enjoyer.

The *jīva*, too, is an embodiment of knowledge, a knower, a thinker, and an enjoyer. He, too, is by nature self-effulgent and he illuminates others. He is the knower of the field of his own body and also acts as he desires. From this perspective, there is no difference between them.

However, God is omnipotent, and by dint of this omnipotence He is the basis of all these qualities, which are present in Him in full. These qualities are also present in the atomic *jīva*, but only to a minute degree. Thus, the nature and form of God and the *jīva* are eternally distinct from each other because one is full and all-encompassing and the other is extremely minute. Simultaneously, there is a lack of distinction between them, because their qualities are similar.

Through the absolute influence of His *svarūpa-śakti*, the Supreme Personality of Godhead is the Lord of *cit-śakti*, *jīva-śakti*, and *māyā-śakti*. These varieties of *śakti* are His maidservants, ready to execute His bidding alone, without individual prerogatives. He is the Lord of *śakti*, who acts in accord with His desire; this is the nature of the Lord. Though the qualities of the Supreme Lord are present in the *jīva* to a minute degree, the *jīva* is nonetheless under the control of *śakti*.

The word *māyā* has been used in *Daśa-mūla*[2], not only to indicate material *māyā*, but also to indicate *svarūpa-śakti*, which is also known as *yogamāyā*. "*Mīyate anayā iti māyā* – *māyā* is that by which things can be measured." The word *māyā* refers to the potency that illuminates Lord Kṛṣṇa's identity in all the three worlds, namely, the spiritual world, the material world, and the world of the marginal living entities. Kṛṣṇa is the controller of *māyā* and the *jīva* is under the control of *māyā*, as is said in the *Śvetāśvatara Upaniṣad* (4.9-10):

yasmān māyī sṛjate viśvam etat
tasmiṁś cānyo māyayā sanniruddhaḥ
māyāṁ tu prakṛtiṁ vidyān māyinaṁ tu maheśvaram
tasyāvayava-bhūtais tu vyāptaṁ sarvam idaṁ jagat

God is the Lord of *māyā*, and He has thoroughly bound up the host of *jīvas* within this world made of the five gross elements. It should be understood that *māyā* is His energy, and He is Maheśvara, the controller of *māyā*. This entire world is pervaded by the limbs of His Universal Form.

---

2 *Daśa-mūla* means 'ten roots'. In the *Ayurveda*, the science of herbal medicine, there are ten roots which, when combined together, produce a tonic which sustains life and counteracts disease. Similarly, there are ten ontological principles. When these are properly understood and realized, they destroy the disease of material existence and give life to the soul. The first of these principles is known as *pramāṇa*, the evidence which establishes the existence of the fundamental truths. The other nine principles are known as *prameya*, the truths which are to be established.

The *pramāṇa* refers to the Vedic literature and in particular to the *Śrīmad- Bhāgavatam*. The *Bhāgavatam* is the essence of all the Vedas; it reveals the most intimate loving feature of the Lord, as well as the soul's potential to unite with the Lord and His eternal associates in their play of divine loving exchange.

Of the nine *prameyas*, the first seven relate to *sambandha-jñāna*, knowledge of the inter-relationship between Śrī Bhagavān, His energies, and the living beings, both conditioned and liberated. The eighth *prameya* relates to *abhidheya-jñāna*, knowledge of the means by which the living entity can become established in an eternal loving relationship with Him. The ninth *prameya* relates to *prayojana*, the ultimate goal to be attained by pursuit of the transcendental path. That goal is known as *kṛṣṇa-prema*, and it takes on infinite varieties when manifest in the different *bhaktas* possessing variegated moods of divine love.

In this verse, the word *māyī* is used to indicate Kṛṣṇa, the controller of *māyā*, and *prakṛti* (energy) is used to indicate His complete potency or power. His great qualities and nature are His special characteristics. These are not present in the *jīva*, and the *jīva* cannot attain them even after liberation.

It is stated in the *Brahma-sūtra* (4.4.17): "*Jagat-vyāpāra-varjjam prakaraṇā sannihitatvāt* – the creation, maintenance, and control of the entire transcendental and inert world is the work of the Lord alone; no one else." Except for this activity in relation to the spiritual and material worlds, all other activities are possible for liberated *jīvas*. The Vedic scripture states: "*Yato vā imāni bhūtāni jāyante* – the Supreme Absolute Truth is the primal source of all the living entities, the sustainer of everything, and at the same time the destination into whom the total dissolution enters" (*Taittirīya Upaniṣad* 3.1).

These statements have only been made in relation to the Lord. They cannot be applied to the *jīva* by any amount of manipulation, because there is no reference to liberated *jīvas* here. Scripture states that it is only the Supreme Godhead, and not the liberated *jīva*, who performs activities of creation, maintenance, and annihilation.

One may suppose that the *jīva* can also perform these activities, but this gives rise to the philosophy of many Gods, which is defective. Therefore, the correct philosophical conclusion is that the *jīva* is not qualified for the above-mentioned activities, even when liberated. This establishes the eternal difference between the *jīva* and the Lord, and all learned persons support this.

This difference is not imaginary, but eternal; it does not disappear in any state of the *jīva's* existence. Consequently, the statement "*jīvera 'svarūpa' haya kṛṣṇera nitya-dāsa* – the *jīva* is an eternal servant of Kṛṣṇa" should be accepted as a *mahā-vākya*, a dictum whose import is all-encompassing and fundamental to a correct understanding of spiritual truth.

Vrajanātha: If the eternal difference between the Supreme Lord and the *jīva* is established, then how is nondifference accepted? Another point is that if there is undifferentiated oneness, does such a state as *nirvāṇa* actually exist? Does this have to be accepted?

Śrī Raghunātha dāsa Bābājī: No, not at all. The *jīva* is not one in all respects with Kṛṣṇa at any stage.

Vrajanātha: Then why do you speak of inconceivable oneness and difference?

Śrī Raghunātha dāsa Bābājī: From the point of view of spiritual quality there is no difference between the Supreme Lord and the *jīva*, but from the point of view of their constitutional nature (*svarūpa*), there is an eternal difference between them. Their oneness is eternal and their distinction is also eternal, but the aspect of eternal distinction between them is pre-eminent and conspicuous.

For example, let us say that the owner of a house is called Devadatta. His house is simultaneously separate from him, yet one with him because it is identified with him. Though from one point of view it is considered independent from him, still, people always know it as his.

Another example from the material world is the visible sky. It is inert matter and has a source, but in spite of its having oneness with its source – the general outer space – the visible sky is self-evident by its distinction from its source. In fact, its identity is discerned by this distinction from its source.

Thus, the eternal difference of the *jīva* from the Supreme Lord, in spite of His simultaneous eternal oneness with the Lord, actually bestows upon the *jīva* his eternal identity and is thus the most important aspect of their eternal relationship.

Vrajanātha: Kindly explain the eternal nature of the *jīva* more clearly.

Śrī Raghunātha dāsa Bābājī: The *jīva* is atomic consciousness, he is endowed with the quality of knowledge, and he is described by the word 'I.' He is the enjoyer, the thinker, and the knower. He has an eternal form which is very esoteric and subtle.

Just as the different parts of the gross body, namely the hands, legs, nose, eyes, and so on, combine to manifest a beautiful form when established in their respective places, the *jīva* has a very beautiful atomic spiritual body that is composed of different spiritual parts. This spiritual body is the eternal constitutional form of the *jīva*, but when the *jīva* is entangled in *māyā*, he is covered by two material designations, or false identities. One designation is called the subtle body and the other is called the gross body.

Although the subtle body is an artificial imposition upon the atomic spiritual body, from the beginning of the *jīva's* conditioned state until his liberation it cannot be relinquished. When the *jīva* transmigrates from one body to the next, the gross body changes but the subtle body does not.

Rather, as the soul leaves the gross body, the subtle body carries all his fruitive activities and desires to the next body. His change of body and transmigration are carried out through the science of *pañcāgni* (the five fires), which is delineated in the Vedas. The system of *pañcāgni*, such as the funeral fire, the fire of digestion, the fire which invokes rainfall, and so on[3] has been described in the *Chāndogya Upaniṣad* and *Brahma-sūtra*.

The *jīva's* conditioned nature in a new body is the result of the impressions (*saṁskāras*) made upon his subtle body from his previous births, and in accordance with this nature he takes birth within a particular status and caste (*varṇa*). After entering *varṇāśrama*[4], he becomes attached to fruitive activity again, and when he dies he repeats the same process. Thus, the first covering of the eternal spiritual form is the subtle body and the second is the gross body.

Vrajanātha: What is the difference between the eternal spiritual body and the subtle body?

Śrī Raghunātha dāsa Bābājī: The eternal body is the actual, original body, and it is atomic, spiritual, and faultless. It is the true entity, which should be spoken of as 'I,' the real ego. The subtle body arises from contact with matter, and it consists of three vitiated transformations, namely the mind, intelligence, and false ego.

Vrajanātha: Are mind, intelligence, and false ego material entities? If they are, how do they have the qualities of consciousness, knowledge, and activity?

Śrī Raghunātha dāsa Bābājī:

bhūmir āpo 'nalo vāyuḥ khaṁ mano buddhir eva ca
ahaṅkāra itīyaṁ me bhinnā prakṛtir aṣṭadhā
apareyam itas tv anyāṁ prakṛtiṁ viddhi me parām
jīva-bhūtāṁ mahā-bāho yayedaṁ dhāryate jagat
etadyonīni bhūtāni sarvāṇīty upadhāraya
ahaṁ kṛtsnasya jagataḥ prabhavaḥ pralayas tathā

Bhagavad-gītā (7.4–6)

My separated, eight-fold inferior energy consists of the five gross elements, namely earth, water, fire, air, and space; and the three subtle elements, namely mind, intelligence, and false ego.

---

[3] The word 'fire' refers metaphorically to one of the five components of *yajña*, which is used in Veda and Vedānta as a paradigm to explain all aspects of the cosmos – ed.

[4] *Varṇāśrama* is the Vedic social system, which organizes society into four occupational divisions (*varṇas*) and four stages of life (*āśramas*).

> Besides this, O mighty-armed Arjuna, I have a superior energy, which is in the form of conscious *jīvas*. All *jīvas*, who have manifested from this superior energy, make the inert world full of consciousness. The *jīva* is called *taṭasthā* because it is eligible for both worlds; the spiritual world, which is manifest from My internal energy; and the material world, which is manifest from My external energy.
>
> Since the entire spiritual and material worlds are manifest from these two energies of Mine, you should know that I, the Supreme Personality of Godhead, am the sole original cause of creation and destruction of all the worlds of the moving and non-moving beings.

These verses of *Gītopaniṣad* describe the two types of energy of the all-powerful Lord. One is called *parā-prakṛti* (the superior energy) and the other is called *aparā-prakṛti* (the inferior energy). They are also known as *jīva-śakti* and *māyā-śakti* respectively. The *jīva-śakti* is the superior energy because it is full of spiritual atomic particles. *Māyā-śakti* is inferior because it is inert.

The *jīva* is completely distinct from the inferior energy, which contains eight elements: the five gross elements, namely earth, water, fire, air, and space; and the three subtle elements, namely mind, intelligence, and false ego.

Regarding these last three material elements, the aspect of knowledge visible in them is material, not spiritual. The mind creates a false world by basing its knowledge of objects on the influences that it absorbs from the mundane realm. Although these three exhibit some form of consciousness and knowledge because of the presence of the *jīva* within them, it is not transcendental consciousness but mundane vitiated consciousness by the effect of the attachment of the *jīva* to the inferior *māyā-śakti*.

This array of knowledge has its root in dull matter, not in spirit. The faculty that relies on that knowledge to discriminate between the real and unreal is called intelligence, which also has its root in matter. The ego, or sense of 'I-ness,' that is produced by accepting the above knowledge is also material.

Together, these three faculties manifest the *jīva's* second form, which acts as the connection between the *jīva* and matter and is called the subtle body. As the false ego of the conditioned *jīva's* subtle body becomes stronger, it further covers the true ego of his eternal form.

The ego in the *jīva's* constitutional nature in relationship to the Spiritual Sun, Śrī Kṛṣṇa, is eternal and pure, and manifests in the liberated state. However, as long as the eternal body remains covered by the subtle body, the material conception arising from the gross and subtle body remains strong. Consequently, the self-conception of a relation with spirit is almost absent. The subtle body is very fine; thus the gross body covers it and through it performs its own functions.

In this way, identification with the caste and so on of the gross body arises in the subtle body. Although the three elements – mind, intelligence, and false ego – are material, the ego of having knowledge is inherent in them because they are vitiated, or perverted, transformations of the function of the soul.

Vrajanātha: I understand the eternal constitution of the *jīva* to be spiritual and atomic in nature, and that he has a beautiful and sublime body composed of spiritual limbs. In the conditioned state, that beautiful spiritual body remains covered by the subtle body and gross body. Being thus overshadowed, a corruption, or distortion, takes place regarding the constitutional nature of the *jīva*.

Now I desire to know if the *jīva* is completely flawless in his emancipated state.

Śrī Raghunātha dāsa Bābājī: The atomic spiritual form is free from defect, but because of its minute nature, it is inherently weak and vulnerable, and therefore called incomplete. The only defect in this state is that the *jīva's* spiritual form may be covered through association with the powerful material energy.

It is said in *Śrīmad-Bhāgavatam* (10.2.32):

ye 'nye 'ravindākṣa vimukta-māninas
tvayy asta-bhāvād aviśuddha-buddhayaḥ
āruhya kṛcchreṇa paraṁ padaṁ tataḥ
patanty adho 'nādṛta-yuṣmad-aṅghrayaḥ

O lotus-eyed Lord, apart from Your devotees, all others, such as impersonalists, *yogīs*, and renunciants falsely consider themselves fully liberated. However, because they lack devotion, their intelligence is not fully pure. They perform severe austerities and penances and achieve what they imagine to be the fully liberated position, but still they fall from there into a very low condition due to neglecting Your lotus feet.

Therefore, however elevated a position a liberated soul may attain, the incomplete nature of his constitution will always remain with him. That is the inherent nature of *jīva-tattva*. Thus it is said in the Vedas that the Supreme Lord is the controller of *māyā*, whereas the *jīva* remains potentially liable to her control in all circumstances.

Thus ends the Fifteenth Chapter of Jaiva-dharma,
entitled Jīva-tattva.

CHAPTER SIXTEEN
JĪVAS AND MĀYĀ

Having heard the illuminating description of *jīva-tattva* in *Daśa-mūla*, Vrajanātha returned home. Lying on his bed he was unable to sleep, and he began to reflect deeply, "I have received an answer to the question, 'Who am I?' Now I can understand myself to be an atom of light in the effulgent rays of the spiritual Sun, Śrī Kṛṣṇa. Although atomic by nature, I have my own inherent qualities, purpose of life, divine knowledge, and spiritual bliss.

"Even though my form is atomic, it is like Śrī Kṛṣṇa's human-like form. Presently I cannot see this form, and this is my misfortune. Only an extremely fortunate soul can realize it. It is important that I understand clearly why I am suffering in this unfortunate condition. Tomorrow I will inquire about this from Śrī Gurudeva."

Thinking thus, Vrajanatha finally fell asleep at around midnight. Before dawn, he dreamt he had left his family and accepted the dress of a Vaiṣṇava. When he awoke, he joyfully thought, "It appears that Lord Kṛṣṇa will soon pull me out of this material entanglement."

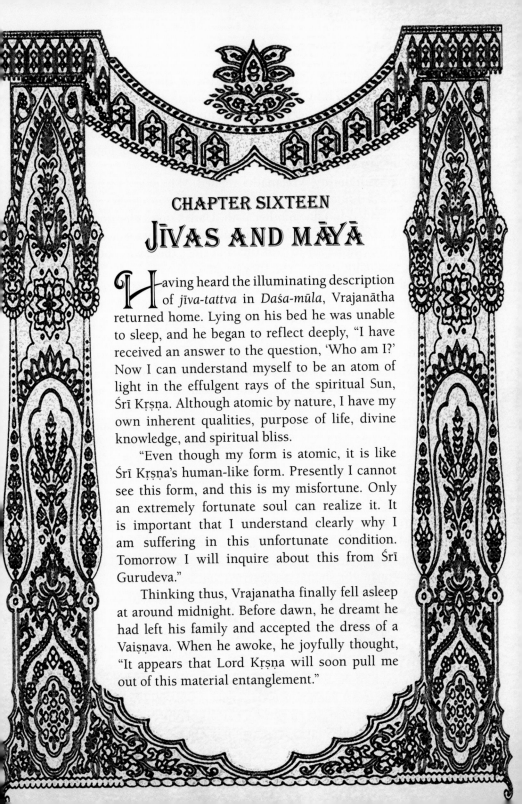

Later that morning, while he was sitting on the porch, some of his students approached him. Offering their respects, they said, "For a long time you have taught us very nicely, and under your guidance we have learned many profound subject matters pertaining to *nyāya* (logic). We hope that you will now instruct us on the famous book of logic, *Nyāya Kusumāñjali* (An Offering of the Flowers of Logic).

With great humility, Vrajanātha replied, "My dear brothers, I am unable to teach you anymore, for I cannot fix my mind on teaching at all. I have decided to take another path. Under these circumstances, I suggest that you study under the guidance of some other teacher." The students became unhappy to hear this, but since there was nothing they could do, gradually, one by one, they began to leave.

About that time, Śrī Caturbhuja Miśra Ghaṭaka came to Vrajanātha's house to present a proposal to his paternal grandmother for his marriage. He said, "I am sure you know Vijayanātha Bhaṭṭācārya. His family is good, and quite well off; it will be a suitable match for you. Most importantly, this girl is as qualified as she is beautiful. On his part, Bhaṭṭācārya will make no conditions regarding the marriage of his daughter with Vrajanātha. He is ready to marry her in whichever way you desire."

Hearing this proposal Vrajanātha's grandmother became exhilarated, but Vrajanātha felt dissatisfied within his heart. "Alas!" he thought, "My grandmother is arranging my marriage while I am planning to leave my family and the world. How can I feel happy to discuss marriage at this time?"

Later, there was an intense struggle of arguments and counter-arguments in their home regarding marriage. Vrajanātha's mother, grandmother, and the other elderly ladies were on one side, while on the other, completely alone, was Vrajanātha. The ladies insisted in various ways that Vrajanātha should get married, but he did not agree.

The discussion continued for the entire day. Around evening time it began to rain heavily. It continued pouring throughout the night, and therefore Vrajanātha could not go to Māyāpura. Then, on the next day, because of the heated arguments about marriage, he could not even eat his meals properly.

In the evening he went to Bābājī's cottage. He paid obeisances and sat down close to Śrī Raghunātha dāsa Bābājī, who told him, "Yesterday night it was raining quite heavily. That's probably why you couldn't come. Seeing you today gives me much happiness."

Vrajanātha said, "Master, I am facing a problem which I will tell you about later. First, please explain to me, if the *jīva* is a pure spiritual entity, how did he become entangled in this miserable world?"

Śrī Raghunātha dāsa Bābājī smiled and said:

> *svarūpārthair hīnān nija-sukha-parān kṛṣṇa-vimukhān*
> *harer māyā-dandyān guṇa-nigaḍa-jālaiḥ kalayati*
> *tathā sthūlair lingair dvi-vidhāvaraṇaiḥ kleśa-nikarair*
> *mahākarmālānair nayati patitān svarga-nirayau*
>
> (*Daśa-mūla*, Verse 6)

By their original nature, the *jīvas* are eternal servants of Kṛṣṇa; it is their constitutional nature to render Him service. The Lord's illusory potency, *māyā*, punishes those *jīvas* who have abandoned their eternal occupational duty, who are averse to Kṛṣṇa, and who are absorbed with their own happiness. *Māyā* binds them with the shackles of the three modes of material nature – goodness, passion, and ignorance – covers their constitutional forms with gross and subtle bodies, and throws them into the miserable bondage of fruitive action and reaction. She thus repeatedly causes them to experience happiness and distress in heaven and hell.

Innumerable *nitya-parsada jīvas* (eternally liberated associates) manifest from Śrī Baladeva Prabhu to serve Vṛndāvana-vihārī Śrī Kṛṣṇa as His eternal associates in Goloka Vṛndāvana, and others manifest from Śrī Saṅkarṣaṇa to serve the Lord of Vaikuṇṭha, Śrī Nārāyaṇa, in the spiritual world. Forever relishing *rasa*, engaged in the service of their worshipable Lord, they always remain fixed in their constitutional position. They always strive to please the Lord and are always attentive to Him.

Having the shelter of *cit-śakti*, they are always strong. They have no connection with the material energy. In fact, they do not know whether there is a bewildering energy called *māyā* or not. Since they reside in the spiritual world, *māyā* is very far away from them and does not affect them at all. Always absorbed in the bliss of serving their worshipable Lord, they are eternally liberated and are free from material happiness and distress. Their life is love alone, and they are not at all conscious of misery, death or fear.

There are also innumerable atomic conscious *jīvas* who emanate from Kāraṇodakaśāyī Māhā-Viṣṇu's glance upon His *māyā-śakti*. Since these *jīvas* are situated next to *māyā*, they perceive her wonderful workings. Although they have all the qualities of the *jīvas* I have already described, because of their minute and marginal nature, they sometimes look to the spiritual world, and sometimes to the material world.

In this marginal condition, the *jīva* is very weak because up to this point in time he has not attained spiritual strength by the mercy of his worshipful Lord. Among these unlimited *jīvas*, those who want to enjoy *māyā* become engrossed in mundane sense gratification and enter a state of perpetual slavery to her.

On the other hand, the *jīvas* who endeavor to serve the Lord receive spiritual power by His mercy and enter the spiritual world. It is our great misfortune that we have forgotten our service to Śrī Kṛṣṇa and have become bound in the shackles of *māyā*. Being thus bereft of the true purpose for our very existence, we are now in this deplorable condition.

Vrajanātha: Master, I understand that this marginal position is situated at the junction of the spiritual and material worlds. Why is it that some *jīvas* go from there to the material world, while others go to the spiritual world?

Śrī Raghunātha dāsa Bābājī: Kṛṣṇa's qualities are also present in the *jīvas*, but only in a minute quantity. Kṛṣṇa is supremely independent, so the desire to be independent is eternally present in the *jīvas* as well. When the *jīva* uses his independence correctly, he remains properly inclined to the service of Śrī Kṛṣṇa, but when he misuses it, he becomes indifferent to Him. It is just this indifference that gives rise to the desire in the *jīva's* heart to enjoy *māyā*.

Because of the desire to enjoy *māyā*, the *jīva* develops the contemptible false ego that he can enjoy material sense gratification. At that time, the five types of ignorance – *tamaḥ* (not knowing anything about the spirit soul), *moha* (the illusion of the bodily concept of life), *mahā-moha* (madness for material enjoyment), *tāmisra* (forgetfulness of one's constitutional position due to anger or envy) and *andha-tāmisra* (considering death to be the ultimate end) – cover his pure, atomic nature. Our liberation or subjugation simply depends on whether or not we use our minute independence properly.

Vrajanātha: Lord Kṛṣṇa is overflowing with mercy, so why did He make the *jīva* so weak that he became entangled in *māyā*?

Śrī Raghunātha dāsa Bābājī: It is true that He is overflowing with mercy, but He is also overflowing with desire to perform pastimes. With the view that the *jīva* could become an active partner for His various spiritual pastimes, the Supreme Lord has made him versatile and capable of rising from his humble position as a marginal being to the stage of the *gopis'* love for Kṛṣṇa, called *mahā-bhāva*, the highest spiritual consciousness, which is unlimited and transcendental. To facilitate the *jīva's* progressing practically and steadfastly towards becoming qualified for His service, He has also created the lower levels of material existence, beginning from the lowest inert matter up to false ego.

Should the *jīva* choose the path of material progress, the inert matter presents practically insurmountable obstacles in his search for supreme happiness. Divorced from his constitutional position, the *jīva* who is entangled in *māyā* is inimical to Kṛṣṇa and engrossed in personal sense gratification. However, because Śrī Kṛṣṇa is the reservoir of mercy, the more the *jīva* becomes depraved, the more Kṛṣṇa provides him with opportunities to attain the highest spiritual perfection. He brings this about by appearing before him along with His spiritual abode and eternal associates. Those *jīvas* who take advantage of this merciful opportunity and sincerely endeavor to attain the higher position gradually reach the spiritual world and attain a state similar to that of the Lord's eternal associates.

Vrajanātha: Why must some *jīvas* suffer for the sake of the Lord's pastimes?

Śrī Raghunātha dāsa Bābājī: The *jīvas* possess some independence, and this is actually a sign of the Lord's special mercy upon them. Inert objects are very insignificant and worthless because they have no such independent desire. The *jīva* has attained sovereignty over the inert world only because of this independent desire.

Misery and happiness are conditions of the mind. Thus, what we may consider misery is happiness for one engrossed in it. Since all varieties of material sense gratification finally result in nothing but misery, a materialistic person only achieves suffering. When that suffering becomes excessive, it gives rise to a search for unalloyed and endless happiness. From that desire discrimination arises, and from discrimination, the tendency for inquiry about the ultimate reality is born. As a result of this, one attains the association of saintly devotees, whereupon *śraddhā* (faith in serving Kṛṣṇa) develops. When *śraddhā* is born, the *jīva* gradually ascends upon the lofty path leading to devotional service to the Lord.

Gold is purified in a fire by heating and hammering. Being indifferent to Kṛṣṇa, the *jīva* has become impure through illusory sense gratification and aversion towards Him. Therefore, he must be purified by being beaten with the hammers of misery on the anvil of this material world. By this process, the misery of the *jīvas* averse to Kṛṣṇa finally culminates in happiness. Suffering is therefore just a sign of God's mercy. That is why persons endowed with divine vision perceive the suffering of *jīvas* in Lord Kṛṣṇa's pastimes within His material creation as auspicious, though those who lack such vision abhor it as only suffering.

Vrajanātha: The *jīva's* suffering in his conditioned state is ultimately auspicious, but at the same time it is very painful. Since Kṛṣṇa is omnipotent, could He not think of a less troublesome path?

Śrī Raghunātha dāsa Bābājī: Lord Kṛṣṇa's pastimes are extremely astonishing and of many varieties; and this is also one of them. If the independent Lord performs all kinds of pastimes, why should this be the only pastime that He neglects? No pastime can be rejected if there is to be full variety. Whatever the pastime, the participants assisting the Lord may have to accept many hardships and pain.

Srī Kṛṣṇa is the Supreme Enjoyer as well as Creator. All the participants and paraphernalia are fully under His control and they are His working tools. In fully surrendering oneself to the sweet will of the Supreme Lord, it is only natural that one may have to accept adversities. If finally this material adversity turns into an auspicious state that is far from miserable, then why, ultimately, should one call it adversity?

On the transcendental platform, the tribulations of the *jīva* trying to satisfy the Lord in His pastimes are by all means pleasurable. The so-called suffering he undergoes in order to nourish and support Kṛṣṇa's pastimes is actually the source of supreme delight.

The *jīva's* independent desire has caused him to abandon the pleasure of serving Kṛṣṇa. Denying himself the exultation one experiences while directly assisting Śrī Kṛṣṇa in His transcendental pastimes, intead he embraces *māyā*, who gives him only harassment. This is the *jīva's* fault, not Kṛṣṇa's.

Vrajanātha: What harm would there have been if the *jīva* had not been given independent desire? Kṛṣṇa is omniscient, and He gave this independence to the *jīvas* even though He knew that they would suffer on account of it. So isn't He responsible for the *jīva's* suffering?

Śrī Raghunātha dāsa Bābājī: Independence is a precious jewel, in the absence of which inert objects are insignificant and worthless. If the *jīva* had not received independence, he would also have become as insignificant and worthless as the material objects.

The *jīva* is an atomic spiritual entity, so he must certainly have all the qualities of spiritual entities. He is part and parcel of the Complete Spiritual Entity (*cit-vastu*); hence he possesses the same qualities as the Absolute Whole, but in minute measure. The only difference between him and the ultimate spiritual substance, Śrī Kṛṣṇa, is that the complete spiritual entity possesses all these qualities in full, whereas the *jīva* only possesses them to a very minute degree.

Independence is a distinctive quality of the spiritual entity, and an entity's inherent quality cannot be separated from him. Consequently, the *jīva* also has this quality of independence, but only to a very minute degree because he is atomic. It is only because of this independence that the *jīva* is the most exalted of all entities within the material world, and is its lord and master in the material sense.

Endowed with minute independence, the *jīva* is a beloved servant of Kṛṣṇa. Seeing the *jīva's* misfortune as he misuses his independence and becomes attached to *māyā*, Kṛṣṇa chases after him, weeping, and He appears in the material world to deliver him. Śrī Kṛṣṇa, the ocean of compassion, His heart melting with mercy for the *jīva*, manifests His inconceivable pastimes in the material world, considering that His appearance will enable the *jīva* to see those nectarean pastimes.

However, even after being showered by so much mercy, the *jīva* does not understand the truth of Kṛṣṇa's pastimes. Lord Kṛṣṇa then descends in Śrī Navadvīpa in the form of *guru*. He personally describes the supreme process of chanting His name and glorifying His form, qualities, and pastimes. He personally instructs and inspires the *jīva* to take to this path by practicing it Himself. How can you accuse Kṛṣṇa of being at fault in any way, when He is so merciful? His mercy is unlimited, but our misfortune is lamentable.

Vrajanātha: Is *māyā-śakti* the cause of our misfortune then? Would the *jīvas* have had to suffer like this if the omnipotent and omniscient Śrī Kṛṣṇa had kept *māyā* away from them?

Śrī Raghunātha dāsa Bābājī: *Māyā* is a shadow and vitiated transformation of Kṛṣṇa's internal potency, *svarūpa-śakti*, and she is like a fiery furnace where the *jīvas* who are not qualified for Kṛṣṇa's service are chastized and then made fit for the spiritual world. *Māyā* is Kṛṣṇa's maidservant. In order to purify the *jīvas* who have turned against Him, she punishes them and gives them appropriate therapy to purify them.

The infinitesimal *jīva* has forgotten that he is an eternal servant of Kṛṣṇa. For this offense, *māyā*, taking the form of a witch, punishes him. This material world is like a prison, and *māyā* is the jailer who imprisons the estranged *jīvas* and punishes them. A king constructs a prison for the benefit of his subjects, and in the same way, God has shown His immense mercy towards the *jīvas* by making this prison-like material world and appointing *māyā* as its custodian.

Vrajanātha: If this material world is a prison, it also requires some suitable shackles. What are they?

Śrī Raghunātha dāsa Bābājī: *Māyā* incarcerates the offensive *jīvas* with three types of shackles: those made of mundane goodness, those made of passion, and those made of ignorance. These fetters bind the *jīva*, whether his inclination is in the mode of ignorance, passion, or even goodness. Shackles may be made of different metals – such as gold, silver, or iron – but that makes no difference to the pain of being bound by them.

Vrajanātha: If we accept that the *jīva* is spiritual, how can the chains of *māyā* hold him in bondage?

Śrī Raghunātha dāsa Bābājī: Objects of this material world cannot touch spiritual objects. However, as soon as the *jīva* develops the conception that he is an enjoyer of *māyā*, his atomic, spiritual form is covered by the subtle body made of false ego. That is how the shackles of *māyā* bind his legs.

The *jīvas* with a false ego in the mode of material goodness reside in the higher planets and are called demigods. Their legs are bound by shackles in that mode, which are made of gold. *Jīvas* under the mode of passion have a mixture of the propensities of the demigods and of the human beings, and they are confined by the shackles in that mode, which are made of silver. The *jīvas* under the mode of ignorance, who are mad to taste bliss derived from dull matter, are bound in iron shackles of ignorance. Once the *jīvas* are bound in these shackles, they cannot leave the prison. Suffering various types of miseries, they remain in captivity.

Vrajanātha: What sort of activities do the *jīvas* perform while confined in *māyā's* prison?

Śrī Raghunātha dāsa Bābājī: Initially, the *jīva* performs activities to provide himself with his desired sense pleasure in accordance with his material propensities. After that, he performs activities to try and dispel the miseries that result from being bound by the shackles of *māyā*.

Vrajanātha: Please explain the first type of fruitive activity in detail.

Śrī Raghunātha dāsa Bābājī: The covering of the gross material body has six stages, namely birth, existence, growth, creation of by-products, decline, and death. These six transformations are the inherent attributes of the gross body. Additionally, the body undergoes hunger, thirst, and other discomforting needs. The *jīva* who is situated in the material body is controlled by eating, sleeping, and sensual activities, as his material sense desires dictate. In order to enjoy material comforts, he engages in a variety of activities that are born of his material desires.

To acquire such desired objectives, he may take the option of material piety. Thus, from his birth to his last breath he may perform the ten Vedic ritualistic pious activities (*saṁskāras*) to maintain himself and acquire his material goals. His intention is to accumulate pious credits through these activities so that he can enjoy material pleasures by taking birth in a brahminical or other high-class family in this world, and thereafter have godly pleasures in the higher planets. Thus, he undertakes the path of fruitive activity.

In contrast, impious conditioned *jīvas* take shelter of irreligiosity, and they enjoy sensual pleasures sacrilegiously by performing many types of sinful activities.

Jīvas in the first category attain the higher planets and enjoy celestial pleasures as a result of their pious activities. When this period of enjoyment ends, as it must, they again take birth on the eartly planets as human beings or in other life-forms. *Jīvas* in the second category go to hell because of their sinful activities, and after suffering a variety of miseries there, they take birth on Earth again.

Thus the *jīva*, bound in *māyā* and entangled in the cycle of fruitive activity and its fruits, wanders here and there, seeking to enjoy sense gratification. Intermittently, he enjoys some temporary pleasures as a result of pious activities and suffers miseries because of his sins.

Vrajanātha: Please clearly describe the second type of fruitive action as well.

Śrī Raghunātha dāsa Bābājī: The *jīva* situated in the gross body undergoes immense suffering due to being caught within the entangling web of its deficiencies, and he performs various types of activity in an attempt to minimize these miseries. He collects various foods and drinks to assuage his hunger and thirst, and he toils arduously to earn money so that he can buy food easily. He collects warm clothes to protect himself from the cold, marries to satisfy his desire for sensual pleasures, and works hard to maintain and nurture his family and children and to fulfill their needs. He takes medicines to cure diseases of the gross body, fights with others, and goes to courts of law to protect his material assets.

Because he is controlled by the six foes, namely lust, anger, intoxication, illusion, envy, and fear, he also indulges in various sinful activities such as fighting, enviousness, stealing, and other misdemeanors. All these activities of the bewildered *jīva* are performed to alleviate his sufferings, and thus his entire life is wasted in trying to fulfill his desires and avoid suffering.

Vrajanātha: Wouldn't *māyā's* purpose have been served if she had covered the *jīva* with only the subtle body?

Śrī Raghunātha dāsa Bābājī: The gross body is also necessary, because the subtle body cannot perform work. Desires develop in the subtle body because of the activities the *jīva* performs in his gross body, and he receives another gross body that is suitable to fulfil those desires.

Vrajanātha: What is the connection between *karma* (fruitive or reward-seeking activity) and its fruits? According to the Mīmāṁsā school of thought, there is no Supreme Controller, or God, who awards the fruits of activity. God is only an imaginary entity. The followers of this school say that there is an unprecedented and ever-changing principle, known as *karma*, which is generated from previously performed activity, and this principle awards the result of all activity. Is this true?

Śrī Raghunātha dāsa Bābājī: The followers of the Mīmāṁsā school are not acquainted with the actual principles taught in the Vedas. Seeing that there is a general recommendation within the Vedas for various kinds of *karma*, headed by the practice of *yajña*, they have with much difficulty fabricated a philosophy based on this. But their doctrine is not found anywhere in the Vedas. On the contrary, the Vedas state very clearly that the Lord awards all the fruits of material activity. For example, *Śvetāśvatara Upaniṣad* (4.6) and *Mundaka Upaniṣad* (3.1.1) state:

dvā suparṇā sayujā sakhāyā
samānaṁ vṛkṣaṁ pariṣaṣvajāte
tayor anyaḥ pippalaṁ svādv atty
anaśnann anyo 'bhicākaśīti

> Kṣīrodakaśāyī Viṣṇu and the *jīva* reside in this temporary body, like two friendly birds in a *pippala* tree. Of these two birds, one – the *jīva* – tastes the fruits of the tree according to the results of his past *karma*. The other – Paramātmā – does not taste the fruits, but simply observes as a witness.

The meaning of the above-mentioned verse is that this transitory material body is like a *pippala* tree in which two birds are perched. One of these is the conditioned *jīva*, and the other is his friend, the Supreme Lord in His form as Paramātmā, the Supersoul. The first bird tastes the fruits of the tree, while the other bird does not enjoy those fruits but simply watches the first bird. This means that the *jīva* who is bound by *māyā* performs *karma* and enjoys the fruits. God, the Lord of *māyā*, awards the results of those actions.

This pastime of the Supreme Lord continues until the *jīva* turns towards Him. In other words, as long as the *jīva* is unable to attain a direct audience with the Lord, the Lord continues to perform pastimes with the *jīva* appropriate to his situation. Now, where is the relevance of the Mīmāṁsā followers' 'destiny caused by the resultant actions of remote *karma*'? Think about this yourself. Godless doctrines can never be complete and perfect in all respects.

Vrajanātha: Why have you said that *karma* is beginningless?

Śrī Raghunātha dāsa Bābājī: The root of all material activity is the desire to perform it, and the root cause of this desire is *avidyā*, ignorance. *Avidyā* is forgetfulness of the truth: "I am an eternal servant of Kṛṣṇa," and it does not have its origin in mundane time. Rather, it originates in the *taṭastha* region, at the junction of the spiritual and material worlds. That is why *karma* does not have its beginning in mundane time and is therefore called beginningless.

Vrajanātha: What is the difference between *māyā* and *avidyā*?

Śrī Raghunātha dāsa Bābājī: *Māyā* is a potency of Kṛṣṇa. Śrī Kṛṣṇa has created the material universe through her, and has instigated her to purify the *jīvas* who are averse to Him. *Māyā* has two functions: *avidyā*, ignorance, and *pradhāna*, the condition of material nature immediately prior to its manifestation. *Avidyā* is related to the *jīvas* whereas *pradhāna* is related to inert matter. The entire inert, mundane world has originated from *pradhāna*, whereas the *jīva's* desire to perform material activity originates in *avidyā*.

There are also two other divisions of *māyā*, namely *vidyā* (knowledge) and *avidyā* (ignorance), both of which are related to the conditioned *jīva*. *Avidyā* binds the *jīva* whereas *vidyā* liberates him.The function of *avidyā* keeps working as long as the imprisoned *jīva* continues to forget Kṛṣṇa, but when he becomes favorable to Kṛṣṇa, *avidyā* is replaced by the function of *vidyā*. *Brahma-jñāna* (knowledge concerning the Supreme Spirit, the minute spirit souls, and their inter-relationship) is the specific function of *vidyā*.

Manifesting within the spiritually awakening consciousness of the *jīva*, *vidyā* has two phases. In her first phase, *vidyā* prompts pious deeds and a positive spiritual endeavour, and in her second, mature phase bestows realization of the Supreme Truth. When discrimination first develops, the *jīva* tries to engage in auspicious activities, and when discrimination has matured, spiritual knowledge manifests. *Avidyā* covers the *jīva*, and *vidyā* removes that covering.

Vrajanātha: What is the function of the *pradhāna*?

Śrī Raghunātha dāsa Bābājī: The condition of material nature immediately previous to its manifestation is called *pradhāna*. When the Supreme Lord engages the Time factor to stimulate His potency of *māyā*, *māyā* first creates the aggregate of the material elements (*mahat-tattva*), which is itself produced from the unmanifest *pradhāna*. Thus, when the *pradhāna* is stirred into motion by Time, matter comes into existence.

False ego is born from a transformation of the *mahat-tattva*, and space (ether) is created from a transformation of the false ego in the mode of ignorance. Air is created from a transformation of space, and fire is created from a transformation of air. Water is then created by the transformation of fire, and earth is created by the transformation of water. This is how the material elements are created. They are called the five gross elements.

Now hear how the five sense objects are created. Time stimulates the faculty of material energy called ignorance (*avidyā*) and creates the tendencies within the *mahat-tattva* for fruitive activity (*karma*) and material knowledge (*jñāna*). When the propensity or tendency of the *mahat-tattva* is transformed, it creates knowledge and activities from the modes of goodness and passion respectively. *Mahat-tattva* is also transformed to become false ego, and intelligence is then created from a transformation of ego. Sound, which is the property of space, is created from the transformation of intelligence. The property of touch is created from the transformation of sound, and it includes both touch, the quality of air, and sound, the quality of space. Life-air, energy, and strength are created from this quality of touch. From a transformation of touch, form and color in illuminating objects is generated, which is the property of fire. Fire has three qualities, namely, form, touch and sound. When this quality is transformed by Time, it becomes water, which has four qualities, namely taste, form, touch, and sound. When these are further transformed, the result is the five qualities in earth, which are smell, taste, form, touch and sound. All the activities of transformation take place by the assistance and support of the Supreme Personality of Godhead.

There are three kinds of false ego, namely goodness, passion, and ignorance. The material elements are born from false ego in the mode of ignorance, and the ten senses are born from false ego in passion. There are two types of senses: knowledge-acquiring senses and working senses. The eyes, ears, nose, tongue and skin are the five senses for acquiring knowledge; and voice, hands, feet, anus, and genitals are the five working senses.

Even if the five gross elements combine with the subtle elements, there is still no activity unless the atomic conscious *jīva* enters into them. As soon as the *jīva*, who is a localized particle within the ray of the Lord's glance, enters into the body made of gross and subtle matter, all the activities are set in motion. In this way, the senses manifested by the modes of material goodness and passion encounter the sense-objects that the *pradhāna* has manifested through the mode of ignorance. All these elements amalgamate and interact to form a suitable field for the material action of the *jīva*. *Avidyā* and *pradhāna* work in this way.

Thus there are twenty-four elements within this world of *māyā*: the five gross elements, namely, earth, water, fire, air, and space; the five sense-objects, namely smell, taste, form, touch, and sound; the five senses for acquiring knowledge; the five working senses; mind; intelligence; contaminated consciousness; and false ego. These are the twenty-four elements of material nature. The atomic conscious *jīva* who enters into the body made of twenty-four elements is the twenty-fifth principle, and Paramātmā, is the twenty-sixth.

Vrajanātha: Please tell me, how much of the entire human body, which is three and a half spans of a person's combined arm and hand, is occupied by the subtle body, and how much by the gross body; and in which part of the body does the conscious *jīva* reside?

Śrī Raghunātha dāsa Bābājī: The five gross elements, the five sense-objects, and the ten senses altogether comprise the gross body. The four subtle elements, namely intelligence, contaminated consciousness, mind, and false ego, form the subtle body. One who falsely identifies with the body and makes claims in relationship to the body, thus living under the false concepts of 'I' and 'mine,' is the *jīva* who is thus deprived of his true intrinsic nature.

The *jīva* is extremely subtle, beyond mundane space, time, and qualities, but in spite of being very minute, he pervades the entire body. Just as the pleasurable effect of a minute drop of sandalwood paste spreads all over the body when it is applied to one part, so the atomic *jīva* is the knower of the entire body and the experiencer of its pains and pleasures.

Vrajanātha: If it is the *jīva* who performs *karma* and experiences the consequent pains and pleasures, where is the question of the Supreme Lord's active involvement?

Śrī Raghunātha dāsa Bābājī: *Jīva* is the initiator, and when he performs material activity, the Lord arranges for the fruits which the *jīva* is eligible to enjoy. The Lord also arranges for the future activity for which the *jīva* has become eligible. In short, the Supreme Lord awards the fruits, while the *jīva* 'enjoys' them.

Vrajanātha: How many types of conditioned souls are there?

Śrī Raghunātha dāsa Bābājī: There are five kinds, namely, those whose consciousness is completely covered; those whose consciousness is stunted or contracted; those whose consciousness is budding slightly; those with developed consciousness; and those with fully developed consciousness.

Vrajanātha: Which *jīvas* have completely covered consciousness?

Śrī Raghunātha dāsa Bābājī: These are *jīvas* with the bodies of trees, creepers, grass, stone, and so on, who have totally forgotten their service to Kṛṣṇa and are so engrossed in the material qualities of *māyā* that they have no trace of their sentient nature. There is only a slight indication of their sentience through the six transformations.

This is the lowest stage of the *jīva's* fall, and this fact is corroborated by the epic stories of *Ahalyā*, *Yamalārjuna*, and *Sapta-tāla*. One only reaches this stage because of some grave offense, and one can only be delivered from it by Kṛṣṇa's mercy.

Vrajanātha: Which *jīvas* have stunted consciousness?

Śrī Raghunātha dāsa Bābājī: Beasts, birds, snakes, fish, aquatics, mosquitoes, and various similar creatures have stunted or contracted consciousness. The consciousness of these *jīvas* is apparent to some degree, unlike that of *jīvas* in the previous group, whose consciousness is completely covered. For example, these *jīvas* perform activities such as eating, sleeping, coming and going at will, and quarrelling with others for things that they consider their property. They also show fear, and they become angry when they see injustice. However, they have no knowledge of the spiritual world.

Even monkeys have some scientific understanding in their mischievous minds, for they have some idea of what will or will not happen in the future, and they also have the quality of being grateful. Some animals have good knowledge about various objects, too. However, despite all these attributes, they do not have a propensity for inquiring about God. Thus, their consciousness is contracted.

It is said in scripture that Mahārāja Bharata had knowledge of the names of the Lord even while he was in the body of a deer, but this is unusual; this only happens in special cases. Bharata and King Nṛga had to take birth as animals because of their offenses, and they were delivered when their offenses were nullified by the Lord's mercy.

Vrajanātha: Which *jīvas* have slightly budding consciousness?

Śrī Raghunātha dāsa Bābājī: Conditioned *jīvas* with human bodies fall into three categories: those with slightly budding consciousness, those with developed consciousness, and those with fully developed consciousness. Generally, the human race can be divided into five groups: (1) immoral atheists, (2) moral atheists, (3) moral theists, who have both morals and faith in God, (4) those who are engaged in *sādhana-bhakti*, devotional service performed with the aim of attaining *bhāva*, or spiritual emotions for Kṛṣṇa, and (5) those who are engaged in *bhāva-bhakti*, devotion performed by those who have attained spiritual emotions; pure devotees, whose devotion to the Lord is spontaneous.

Those who are knowingly or unknowingly atheists are either immoral or moral atheists. When a moral person develops a little faith in God, he is called a moral theist. Those who develop interest in *sādhana-bhakti* according to the tenets of scripture are called *sādhana-bhaktas*, and those who have developed some unalloyed love for God are called *bhāva-bhaktas*. Both immoral and moral atheists have slightly budding consciousness; moral theists and *sādhana-bhaktas* have developed consciousness; and the *bhāva-bhaktas* have fully developed consciousness.

Vrajanātha: How long do the *bhāva-bhaktas* stay bound in *māyā*?

Śrī Raghunātha dāsa Bābājī: I will answer that question when I explain the seventh verse of *Daśa-mūla*. Now it's quite late, so it's best that you return home.

Vrajanātha then returned home, contemplating all the truths he had heard.

Thus ends the Sixteenth Chapter of Jaiva-dharma,
entitled "Jīvas Possessed by Māyā"

CHAPTER SEVENTEEN

LIBERATION OF THE JĪVA FROM MĀYĀ

Vrajanātha's grandmother completed all the arrangements for his marriage, and in the evening she explained to him the details. Vrajanātha simply took his meal, in silence, and made no reply that day. He lay awake on his bed late that night, deep in thought about the state of the pure spirit soul. Meanwhile, his elderly grandmother was busy trying to find ways of convincing him to agree to the marriage.

At that time, Vrajanātha's maternal cousin, Veṇī-mādhava, arrived. The girl Vrajanātha was supposed to marry was Veṇī-mādhava's paternal cousin, and Vijaya-vidyāratna had sent him to finalize the arrangements.

Veṇī-mādhava inquired, "What's the matter, Grandmother? Why are you delaying in arranging brother Vraja's marriage?"

Vrajanātha's grandmother replied in a rather anxious voice, "My son, you are an intelligent boy. Perhaps he will change his mind if you speak to him. All my efforts have been in vain."

Veṇī-mādhava's character was clearly pro-claimed by his short stature, small neck, black complexion, and his eyes which blinked frequently. He liked to pry into everything that was going on rather than taking care of his own business, and his involvement in others' affairs was never particularly useful. After listening to the old lady, he frowned slightly and then boasted, "This is no problem. I just need your permission. Veṇī-mādhava can accomplish anything. You know me quite well; I can make money just by counting the waves. Let me discuss this with him just once. And if I succeed, you'll treat me to a nice feast with *pūrīs* and *kacorīs*?"

"Vrajanātha has taken his meal, and he's asleep now," said Grandmother.

"All right, I'll come in the morning and put things in order," replied Veṇī-mādhava, and then he returned home.

The next day he returned early in the morning, carrying a waterpot in his hand, and completed his morning ablutions. Somewhat surprised to see him, Vrajanātha said, "Brother why have you come so early in the morning?"

Veṇī-mādhava answered, "Elder brother, you have been studying and teaching *nyāya-śāstra* for a long time now. You are the son of the Paṇḍita Harinātha Cūḍāmaṇi, and you have become famous all over the country. You are the only surviving male member of the house, and if you don't have any heirs, who do you suppose will take care of this big house of yours? We have a request. Please get married."

Vrajanātha replied, "Brother, don't give me unnecessary trouble. Nowadays I'm accepting the shelter of Śrī Gaurasundara's devotees, and I don't have any desire to get involved in worldly affairs. I feel real peace in the company of the Vaiṣṇavas in Māyāpura, and I don't find any attraction for this world. I will either accept *sannyāsa* or spend my life in the shelter of the Vaiṣṇavas' lotus feet. I have expressed my heart to you because I know that you are my close friend, but don't disclose this to anyone else."

Veṇī-mādhava understood that nothing but trickery could change Vrajanātha's mind, so he cleverly curbed his feelings. In order to create a particular impression, he said, "I have always remained your assistant in whatever you have done. I used to carry your books when you were studying in the Sanskrit school, so I will carry your staff and waterpot when you accept *sannyāsa*."

It is difficult to understand the minds of wicked people. They have two tongues, saying one thing with one, and exactly the opposite with the other. They are bandits in the garb of saints, carrying the name of Śrī Rāma in the mouth and a dagger under the armpit.

Warming to Veṇī-mādhava's sweet words, Vrajanātha said, "Brother, I have always regarded you as my dear friend. Being an old woman, Grandmother doesn't understand serious matters. She is very enthusiastic to drown me in this ocean of worldly affairs by getting me married to some girl. It will be a relief if you can change her mind and somehow dissuade her. I will always be indebted to you."

Veṇī-mādhava replied, "No one will dare to oppose your desire as long as Sharmarāma is living. Elder brother, you will see what I am capable of. But just let me know one thing; why have you developed such an aversion towards this world? Who is advising you to embrace such feelings of renunciation?"

Vrajanātha described all the events which had led up to his feelings of detachment. He said, "There is an elderly and experienced *bābājī* in Māyāpura named Śrī Raghunātha dāsa Bābājī. He is my spiritual preceptor. I go every day after dusk to the shelter of his feet, where I find relief from the burning fire of this material world. He is very merciful to me."

The evil Veṇī-mādhava began conspiring within himself, "Now I understand brother Vraja's weakness. He has to be brought back to the right track by deception and skill." Outwardly he said, "Brother, don't worry. I am going home now, but I will gradually change Grandmother's mind."

Veṇī-mādhava pretended to take the road that led to his home, but instead he took another way and reached Śrīvāsāṅgana in Māyāpura. There he sat on the raised platform under the *bakula* tree and began to admire the opulences of the Vaiṣṇavas. "These Vaiṣṇavas are the actual enjoyers of this world," He said to himself. "What beautiful cottages and lovely groves! What a nice dias in a wonderful courtyard!

"In each of the cottages, a Vaiṣṇava sits chanting *hari-nāma* on his beads, and each one seems quite content, like the bulls of religion. Of their own accord, the women of the neighboring villages who come to bathe in the Gaṅgā supply these Vaiṣṇavas with fruits, roots, water, ghee, spices, and other tasty ingredients.

"The *brāhmaṇas* practice *karma-kāṇḍa* activities (fruitive activites as described in the Vedas for elevation to the heavenly planets and resultant high birth and material enjoyment) just to receive these facilities, but these groups of *bābājīs* are enjoying the cream instead!

"All glories to Kali-yuga, the age of quarrel and hypocracy! These disciples of Kali are blessed with good fortune, and my birth in a high *brāhmaṇa* family is useless! Alas! Nowadays no one even inquires about anything from us, what to speak of offering us fruits and water! The Vaiṣṇavas condemn the scholarly *brāhmaṇa* logicians, accusing us of using word jugglery simply for the discussion of material objects, and calling us fools. Moreover, even after having studied this science of logic thoroughly and becoming a well-educated man, my elder brother Vrajanātha has begun to accept the words of these sly loin-cloth people. I, Veṇī-mādhava, will reform Vrajanātha and give a sound beating to these *bābājīs* as well!"

Thinking like this, Veṇī-mādhava entered one of the cottages, which happened to be the one in which Śrī Raghunātha dāsa Bābājī was sitting on a mat made of banana leaves, chanting *hari-nāma.*

A person's character is evident from his face, and the elderly Bābājī could understand that Kali personified had entered in the form of this son of a *brāhmaṇa.* Vaiṣṇavas consider themselves lower than a blade of grass. They offer respect to those who insult them, and they pray for the well-being of an opponent, even if he tortures them. Without any desire for personal honor, they give honor to all others. Accordingly, Bābājī Mahārāja respectfully offered Veṇī-mādhava a seat. Veṇī-mādhava had no Vaiṣṇava qualities at all, so after sitting down, he offered his blessings to Bābājī Mahārāja, considering himself to be above all Vaiṣṇava etiquette.

"Bābā, what is your name? What brings you here?" inquired Śrī Bābājī Mahāśaya informally. Veṇī-mādhava became furious by being addressed with the informal usage of the word 'you' instead of the formal one. Thus, with a face twisted by contempt he said, "O Bābājī, can you become equal to the *brāhmaṇas* just by wearing a loincloth? Never mind! Just tell me, do you know Vrajanātha Nyāya-pañcānana?"

Śrī Raghunātha dāsa Bābājī: (understanding the reason for his annoyance) Please excuse this old man; don't become offended by my words. Yes, Vrajanātha comes here sometimes, by his mercy.

Veṇī-mādhava: Don't think that he's a simpleton. He comes here with ulterior motives. He is being polite at first, to gain your confidence. The *brāhmaṇas* of Belpukura are extremely annoyed at your behavior, and they have consulted with each other and decided to send Vrajanātha to you. You are an old man. Just be careful. I will keep coming from time to time, to inform you how their conspiracy progresses. Don't tell him about me; otherwise you will run into even deeper trouble. I will take leave for today.

So saying, Veṇī-mādhava got up and returned to his home; and later, just after completing his midday meal, he visited Vrajanātha. While Vrajanātha was sitting on his verandah, Veṇī-mādhava suddenly appeared as if from nowhere, sat next to him, and struck up a conversation.

"Brother, I went to Māyāpura for some business today," he began. "There I saw an old man, maybe the same Raghunātha dāsa Bābājī with whom you spoke. We were talking about things in general, and then the conversation turned to you. The things he said about you! I have never heard such repulsive things being spoken about any *brāhmaṇa*. In the end he said, 'I will bring him down from his high *brahminical* status by feeding him leftovers from many low-caste people.' Fie on him! It is not proper for a learned man like you to associate with such a person. You will ruin the high prestige of the *brāhmaṇas* if you act like this."

Vrajanātha was astounded to hear Veṇī-mādhava say all this. For some unknown reason, his faith and respect for the Vaiṣṇavas and Śrī Raghunātha dāsa Bābājī Mahārāja only doubled, and he said gravely, "Brother, I am busy at present. You go now; I will hear everything from you tomorrow, and then I will make a decision."

Veṇī-mādhava went away, and Vrajanātha was now fully aware of Veṇī-mādhava's two-tongued nature. Although He was well versed in the *nyāya-śāstra* and had a natural dislike for wickedness, the thought that Veṇī-mādhava would help him on the path to *sannyāsa* had induced him to be friendly.

Now, however, Vrajanatha understood that all Veṇī-mādhava's sweet words had been for a particular motive. After further thought, he realized that Veṇī-mādhava was acting deceitfully because he was involved in the marriage proposal. He realized that that must have been why Veṇī-mādhava had gone to Māyāpura – to sow the seed of some secret plot. He prayed in his mind, "O Lord! Let my faith in the lotus feet of my Gurudeva and the Vaiṣṇavas remain firm. May it never be reduced by the disturbance of such impure people." He remained absorbed in these thoughts until evening. He then started for Śrīvāsāṅgana, the courtyard of Śrīvasa Ṭhākura's house, and arrived there deep in anxiety.

Back in Māyāpura, after Veṇī-mādhava had left, Bābājī thought, "This man is certainly a *brahma-rākṣasa*. '*Rākṣasāḥ kalim āśritya jāyante brahma-yoniṣu* – taking shelter of Kali-yuga, *rākṣasas* (demons) take birth in *brāhmaṇa* families.' This statement of scripture certainly holds true for that person. His face clearly shows his pride in his high caste, his false ego, his envy of Vaiṣṇavas, and his religious hypocrisy. His short neck, his eyes, and his deceptive way of talking actually represent his internal state of mind. Ah, this man is a complete atheistic demon by nature, whereas Vrajanātha is such a sweet-natured person. O Kṛṣṇa! O Gaurāṅga! Never give me association of such a person. I must warn Vrajanātha today."

As soon as Vrajanātha reached the cottage, Bābājī called out to him affectionately, "Come, come!" and embraced him. Vrajanātha's throat choked with emotion, and tears began flowing from his eyes as he fell down at Śrī Raghunātha dāsa Bābājī's feet. Śrī Bābājī Mahārāja picked him up very affectionately and said gently, "A black-complexioned *brāhmaṇa* came here this morning. He said some agitating things and then went away again. Do you know him?"

Vrajanātha: Prabhu, your good self told me earlier that there are different kinds of *jīvas* in this world. Some of them are so envious that without any cause they find satisfaction in troubling others. Our brother, Veṇī-mādhava, is one of the leaders in that category. I will be glad if we don't discuss him further. It is his very nature to criticize you to me and me to you, and to cause disputes between us by manufacturing false accusations. I hope you didn't pay any attention to what he said.

Śrī Raghunātha dāsa Bābājī: O Kṛṣṇa! O Gaurāṅga! I have been serving the Vaiṣṇavas for many days now, and by their mercy, I have received the power to tell the difference between a Vaiṣṇava and a non-Vaiṣṇava. So, I am aware of everything in this regard. You don't need to say anything to me about this.

Vrajanātha: Yes, let us forget all this. Please tell me how the conditioned soul can become free from *māyā's* clutches .

Śrī Raghunātha dāsa Bābājī: You will get your answer in the seventh verse of *Daśa-mūla*:

yadā bhrāmaṁ bhrāmaṁ hari-rasa-galad-vaiṣṇava-janaṁ
kadācit saṁpaśyan tad-anugamane syād ruci-yutaḥ
tadā kṛṣṇāvṛttyā tyajati śanakair māyika-daśāṁ
svarūpaṁ bibhrāṇo vimala-rasa-bhogaṁ sa kurute

When, in the course of wandering among higher and lower species in the cycle of repeated birth and death, a *jīva* bound by *māyā-śakti* beholds a Vaiṣṇava intoxicated by the mellows of devotion to Śrī Hari, and a taste arises in his heart for following the Vaiṣṇava path. By regularly chanting Śrī Kṛṣṇa's names, he gradually becomes fully aloof from all effects of his illusory conditioning. Step by step, he then realises his constitutional spiritual form and becomes qualified to relish the unalloyed mellows of direct service to Śrī Śrī Rādhā-Kṛṣṇa.

Vrajanātha: I would like to hear some evidence from the Vedas to verify this.

Śrī Raghunātha dāsa Bābājī: Both the *Muṇḍaka Upaniṣad* (3.1.2) and *Svetāśvatara Upaniṣad* (4.7) repeat the same *śloka*:

samāne vṛkṣe puruṣo nimagno
'nīśayā śocati muhyamānaḥ
juṣṭaṁ yadā paśyaty anyam īśam
asya mahimānam eti vīta-śokaḥ

The *jīva* is situated in the material body like a bird is situated on a tree. Being illusioned by the Lord's deluding potency, he falls into bodily identification and tries to enjoy eating the fruits of that tree. Thus he laments repeatedly, feeling himself bereft of shelter. However, when he perceives within the tree of his body another bird, the Supreme Lord, who is the proper object of his service, he then becomes free of all lamentation and attains his own glory in the form of service to Śrī Kṛṣṇa."

Vrajanātha: This verse states that when the *jīva* sees the worshipable Lord, he becomes free forever from all anxieties and directly perceives His Lord's magnificence. Does this imply liberation?

Śrī Raghunātha dāsa Bābājī: The termination of the *jīva's* captivity within *māyā* is called *mukti*, which is attainable by the person who associates with pure devotees. Most importantly, one should consider the details of the status which the *jīva* attains after *mukti*. The *Śrīmad-Bhāgavatam* (2.10.6) declares:

muktir hitvānyathā-rūpaṁ svarūpeṇa vyavasthitiḥ

Mukti is the permanent situation of the living entity in his constitutional transcendental form, having been attained after giving up the changeable gross and subtle material bodies.

This verse explains that liberation means to abandon these other forms and to be situated in one's original spiritual form. Attaining one's constitutional position is the fundamental necessity for the *jīva*. The work of liberation is complete the moment the *jīva* is released from the clutches of *māyā*. Then, so many activities begin once he attains his natural, constitutional position. *Mukti* can also be defined as *atyanta-duḥkha-nivrtti*, which means 'release from endless suffering.' However, after attaining this liberation, there is the stage of positive spiritual happiness. That state is described in the *Chāndogya Upaniṣad* (8.12.3):

evam evaiṣa samprasādo 'smāc charīrāt samutthaya
paraṁ jyoti-rūpa-sampadya svena rūpenābhiniṣpadyate
sa uttama-puruṣaḥ sa tatra paryeti jakṣan krīḍan ramamāṇaḥ

The liberated *jīva* transcends the confines of his gross and subtle material bodies and acquires a spiritual form luminescent with transcendental lustre. This is his intrinsic, supramundane identity. He is a perfect being and resides in the spiritual world, relishing sublime activities and divine bliss at every moment.

Vrajanātha: What are the symptoms of those who are liberated from *māyā*?

Śrī Raghunātha dāsa Bābājī: They have eight symptoms, which the *Chāndogya Upaniṣad* (8.7.1) describes as follows:

ya ātmāpahata-pāpmā vijaro vimṛtyur viśoko 'vijighatso
'pipāsaḥ satya-kāmaḥ satya-saṅkalpaḥ so 'nveṣṭavyaḥ

One should earnestly seek the association of a liberated soul, who possesses the following eight qualities: (1) *apahata-pāpmā* – he is freed from all sin, that is to say he is free from any connection with addiction to sinful activities that arises from the nescience of *māyā*; (2) *vijara* – he is not subject to the miseries of old age; that is, since he has no tendency to decay, he always remains young and fresh; (3) *vimṛtyu* – he does not die; he never falls under the influence of death; (4) *viśoka* – he is never morose; (5) *vijighatsa* – he has no desire for personal enjoyment; (6) *apipāsa* – he has a natural inclination towards serving his most beloved Kṛṣṇa, with no other desires; (7) *satya-kāma* – his desires are just suitable for the service of Śrī Kṛṣṇa, and conversely, his desires are free from fault (since they are only for the pleasure of the Supreme Absolute Truth); and (8) *satya-saṅkalpaḥ* – all of his desires become fulfilled. These eight qualities are absent in the *jīvas* bound by *māyā*.

Vrajanātha: It is said in the *Daśa-mūla* verse, "The good fortune of the *jīva* who is wandering aimlessly in the material world arises when he meets a *rasika* Vaiṣṇava, that pure devotee who relishes the nectar of Hari." One might raise the objection that one could eventually attain devotion to Lord Kṛṣṇa by performing pious activities, such as *aṣṭāṅga-yoga* (the eight-fold *yoga* system) and the cultivation of knowledge of the impersonal feature of the Lord.

Śrī Raghunātha dāsa Bābājī: These are Śrī Kṛṣṇa's own words:

na rodhayati māṁ yogo na sāṅkhyaṁ dharma eva ca
na svādhyāyas tapas tyāgo neṣṭā-pūrttaṁ na dakṣiṇā
vratāni yajñāś chandāṁsi tīrthāni niyamā yamāḥ
yathāvarundhe sat-saṅgaḥ sarva-saṅgāpaho hi mām

(*Śrīmad-Bhāgavatam* 11.12.1–2)

The Supreme Personality of Godhead said, "My dear Uddhava, by associating with My pure devotees one can destroy one's attachment for all objects of material sense gratification. The devotion developed in such purifying association brings Me under the control of My devotee. One may perform the *aṣṭāṅga-yoga* system, engage in philosophical analysis of the elements of material nature, practice non-violence and other ordinary principles of piety, chant the Vedas, perform penances, take to the renounced order of life, execute sacrificial performances and dig wells, plant trees and perform other public welfare activities, give in charity, carry out severe vows, worship the *devas*, chant confidential *mantras*, visit holy places or accept major and minor disciplinary injunctions, but even by performing all such activities one does not bring Me under his control."

It is also stated in *Hari-bhakti-sudhodhaya* (8.51):

yasya yat-saṅgatiḥ puṁso maṇi-vat syāt sa tad-guṇaḥ
sva-kularddhyaitato dhīmān sva-yūthāny eva saṁśrayet

Just as a jewel or crystal reflects the color of the object with which it is in contact, so a person develops qualities according to the company he keeps. Therefore, by keeping association with pure unalloyed devotees, one can also become a pure devotee.

Thus, the association of such devotees is the root cause of all good fortune.

In the scriptures, the word *niḥsaṅga* means 'to live in solitude.' This implies that we should only live in the association of devotees. *Niḥsaṅga* means to leave all other association and take the association of a pure devotee. Even unintentional association with saintly people brings good fortune for the *jīva*.

saṅgo yaḥ saṁsṛter hetur asatsu vihito 'dhiyā
sa eva sādhuṣu kṛto niḥsaṅgatvāya kalpate

(*Śrīmad-Bhāgavatam* 3.23.55)

The association of materialists causes bondage in the material world, even though one may not know that this is so. Similarly, association with saintly people, even if it happens by chance or unknowingly, is called *niḥsaṅga*.

It is said in *Śrīmad-Bhāgavatam* (7.5.32):

naiṣāṁ matis tāvad urukramāṅghriṁ
spṛśaty anarthāpagamo yad-arthaḥ
mahīyasāṁ pāda-rajo-'bhiṣekaṁ
niṣkiñcanānāṁ na vṛṇīta yāvat

The lotus feet of the Lord, who is glorified for His uncommon activities, destroy all *anarthas* in the heart. However, those who are very materialistic cannot be attached to His lotus feet until they smear their bodies with the dust from the lotus feet of great souls who are absorbed in His loving service and who are completely freed from material attachments.

Śrīmad-Bhāgavatam (10.48.31) states:

na hy am-mayāni tīrthāni na devā mṛc-chilā-mayāḥ
te punanty uru-kālena darśanād eva sādhavaḥ

Only after a long period of worshiping Gaṅgā-devī, the holy places of pilgrimage, and the earthen and marble deity forms of the demigods, is the soul of such a worshiper sanctified, whereas an unalloyed devotee of the Lord purifies any person simply by giving a moment's association through his mere presence.'

Śrīmad-Bhāgavatam (10.51.53) states further:

bhavāpavargo bhramato yadā bhavej
janasya tarhy acyuta sat-samāgamaḥ
sat-saṅgamo yarhi tadaiva sad-gatau
parāvareśe tvayi jāyate matiḥ

O infallible Lord! The *jīva* has been wandering in this world of birth and death since time without beginning. When the time comes for him to leave this cycle of birth and death, he receives association with Your self-realized pure devotees. From the moment he achieves this association, his mind becomes firmly fixed on You who are the sole and supreme shelter of the surrendered devotees, the controller of all, and the cause of all causes.

Since time without beginning, the *jīva* who is eternally bound by *māyā* has been moving throughout the universe, taking birth according to his past fruitive actions; sometimes as a demigod and sometimes in the various animal species. From the time he attains the association of saintly people by dint of of his past pious activities (*sukṛti*), he fixes his mind very firmly on Kṛṣṇa, the controller of all.

Vrajanātha: You have said that *sādhu-saṅga* is achieved by *sukṛti*. What is *sukṛti*? Is it part of fruitive activity or the cultivation of knowledge?

Śrī Raghunātha dāsa Bābājī: The scriptures assign the term *sukṛti* to auspicious activity. There are two kinds of *sukṛti*. One (*bhakti-sukṛti*) causes the appearance of *bhakti*, and the other (*sādhāraṇa-sukṛti*) produces various inferior transitory results. Another meaning of *karma* is 'prescribed duties.' Such duties are of two types: Those compulsory every day (*nitya*), and those that are compulsory for particular occasions (*naimittika*), like *piṇḍa*. Performance of pious activities (those prescribes for daily execution and those prescribed for particular occasions) and the cultivation of knowledge leading to impersonal liberation give inferior results. The auspicious activities that generate devotion to Lord Kṛṣṇa as an end result are the association of pure devotees, and contact with sanctified places, auspicious times, and sanctified items.

When enough of such *sukṛti* has been accumulated, it gives rise to *kṛṣṇa-bhakti*. The other type of *sukṛti*, however, is consumed after one enjoys its results, so it does not accumulate to give any permanent result. Charity and all other pious deeds in the world result only in achieving the objects of sense gratification. The *sukṛti* of impersonal speculation results in impersonal liberation. Neither of these kinds of *sukṛti* can give devotional service to the Supreme Lord.

Activities such as *sādhu-saṅga* and observing holy days like Ekādaśī, Janmāṣṭamī, and Gaura-pūrṇimā all help to develop one's saintly qualities. Tulasī, the remnants of the Lord's foodstuffs called *mahā-prasādam*, the Lord's temples, holy places, and articles used by *sādhus* are all auspicious and give rise to *bhakti*.

Vrajanātha: Can a person obtain *bhakti* if he is tormented by material problems and intelligently takes shelter of Śrī Hari's lotus feet to become relieved of his problems?

Śrī Raghunātha dāsa Bābājī: The *jīva* who is harassed by the afflictions of the goddess of illusion may somehow understand through discriminating intelligence that worldly activities are simply troublesome, and that his only solace is the lotus feet of Kṛṣṇa and His pure devotees. Knowing this, he runs to take shelter of Śrī Kṛṣṇa's lotus feet, the first step in this process being the acceptance of the shelter of *bhagavad-bhaktas*. Such acceptance is the principal *bhakti*-bestowing *sukṛti*, through which he obtains the lotus feet of the Supreme Lord.

The *jīva's* initial mood of renunciation and state of awakening consciousness play an indirect, secondary role as stepping stones towards his ultimate devotional goal. However, *sādhu-saṅga*, an indispensable need, is the principal means to attain *śuddha-bhakti* at the lotus feet of Śrī Kṛṣṇa.

Vrajanātha: If *karma*, *jñāna*, renunciation, and discrimination are indirect ways of achieving *bhakti*, what is the objection to refer to them as *bhakti*-bestowing *sukṛti*?

Śrī Raghunātha dāsa Bābājī: There is a strong objection: they bind one to inferior, temporary results. The performance of fruitive activity has no permanent result; rather it binds the *jīva* to the objects of sense gratification and thus renders him complacent. Renunciation and empirical knowledge immerse the *jīva* in knowledge of the impersonal Supreme and cause him to become indifferent to the Lord. This principle prevents him from attaining the Supreme Lord's lotus feet.

It is true that these processes very rarely take one to *bhakti*, but that is the exception, not the rule. On the other hand, association of pure devotees does not award any inferior benefit, but surely brings the *jīva* towards *prema*. It is explained in *Śrīmad-Bhāgavatam* (3.25.25):

satāṁ prasaṅgān mama vīrya-samvido
bhavanti hṛt-karṇa-rasāyanāḥ kathāḥ
taj-joṣaṇād āśv apavarga-vartmani
śraddhā ratir bhaktir anukramiṣyati

In the association of pure devotees, the recitation and discussion of My glorious activities and pastimes are pleasing to both the heart and the ears. By engaging in devotional service in this way, one becomes established on that path whereby all ignorance is nullified, and one progressively attains *śraddhā*, then *bhāva*, and finally *prema-bhakti*.

Vrajanātha: I understand that *sādhu-saṅga* is the only *sukṛti* that causes devotional service to expand and develop. One has to listen to the *hari-kathā* flowing from the mouths of *sādhus*, and thereafter one obtains *bhakti*. Is this the proper sequence to progress in *bhakti*?

Śrī Raghunātha dāsa Bābājī: I will explain the proper way of progressing in devotion; please listen with deep contemplation. Only by good fortune does the *jīva* who is wandering throughout the universe achieve the *sukṛti* that gives rise to *bhakti*.

Any one of the many limbs of pure *bhakti* may touch a *jīva's* life. For example, he may fast on Ekādaśī, or see or touch the holy places of the Lord's pastimes, or serve a guest there who happens to be a pure devotee, or have the chance to hear *hari-nāma* or *hari-kathā* flowing from the lotus mouth of a devotee who has no other possession than Kṛṣṇa.

If someone desires material benefits or impersonal liberation from such activities, the result does not lead to devotional service. In contrast, if these activities are performed even by a person who has no knowledge of the scientific spiritual truths of *bhakti* but has no objective to attain impersonal liberation or sense gratification, and they are performed either because of accidental association with *sādhus* or for some mundane reason such as to please one's relatives etc. these activities lead to the accumulation of *sukṛti* that gives rise to *bhakti*.

After accumulating such *sukṛti* for many births, it becomes concentrated enough to give faith in unalloyed *bhakti*, and when faith in such *bhakti* develops further, one develops greed to associate with pure devotees. By association with *sādhus* one gradually becomes engaged in performing *sādhana* (devotional activities that regulate and purify the tendency for sense gratification) and *bhajana* (chanting, hearing and remembering Lord Kṛṣṇa). This leads to the removal of *anarthas* (unwanted habits and activities which distract one from pure devotion) in proportion to the purity of the devotee's chanting.

When *anarthas* are removed, the previous faith is purified still further from contaminants and transforms into *niṣṭhā* (firm faith). This *niṣṭhā* is also gradually purified and transforms into *ruci* (spiritual taste), and by the influence of the enchanting beauty of *bhakti*, this *ruci* is strengthened and becomes transformed into *āśakti* (transcendental attachment). *Aśakti* then gradually matures into the great gift of the fully perfected state of *rati* or *bhāva* (spiritual emotions). Then, when *rati* combines with the appropriate ingredients, it becomes *rasa* (a transcendental relationship in pure divine love for Kṛṣṇa). This is the step-by-step progression in the development of *kṛṣṇa-prema*.

The principal idea is that when people with sufficient *sukṛti* encounter pure *sādhus*, an inclination is born in their hearts to proceed on the path of *bhakti*. First of all one associates with a pure devotee by chance, and this leads to initial *śraddhā*, whereupon one gets the association of such devotees a second time. The result of the first association is *śraddhā*, which can also be termed 'acceptance of the path of surrender.' The initial *sādhu-saṅga* is brought about by contact with holy places, auspicious times and paraphernalia, and recipients of Śrī Hari's grace, all of which are beloved by Him. These lead to faith in His shelter. The symptoms of the development of such faith are described in the *Bhagavad-gītā* (18.66):

> *sarva-dharmān parityajya mām ekaṁ śaraṇaṁ vraja*
> *ahaṁ tvāṁ sarva-pāpebhyo mokṣayiṣyāmi mā śucaḥ*

Here the words *sarva-dharmān* imply worldly religious duties, *aṣṭāṅga-yoga*, *sāṅkhya-yoga*, *jñāna*[1], and renunciation. The *jīva* can never achieve his ultimate spiritual goal by practicing all these worldly religions, which is why the instruction here is to give them up. Śrī Kṛṣṇa says, "My form of condensed eternity, knowledge and bliss, appearing as the performer of wonderful pastimes in Vraja, is the only shelter for the *jīvas*. When one understands this, he gives up all desire for material sense enjoyment and impersonal liberation, and takes shelter of Me with undivided attention." Such *śraddhā* is the sole means whereby the process of *bhakti* can dynamically advance. When such faith dawns in

[1] See glossary for the definitions of *aṣṭāṅga-yoga*, *sāṅkhya-yoga* and *jñāna*.

the *jīva's* heart, with tears in his eyes he resolves to become a follower of a Vaiṣṇava *sādhu*. The Vaiṣṇava of whom he takes shelter is known as *śrī-guru*.

Vrajanātha: How many different kinds of *anarthas* (unwanted habits and mentalities) are there?

Śrī Raghunātha dāsa Bābājī: There are four types of *anarthas*: (1) *svarūpa aprāpti*, inability to realize one's constitutional form; (2) *asat-tṛṣṇā*, hankering for the impermanent; (3) *aparādha*, offenses; and (4) *hṛdaya-daurbalya*, weakness of heart.

When the *jīva* forgets that he is a minute particle of spirit and a servant of Kṛṣṇa, he is carried very far from his original, spiritual position as Kṛṣṇa's servant and begins superimposing his conception of 'I' and 'mine' upon inert matter. *Asat-tṛṣṇā* arises in the form of three desires to enjoy transitory sensual pleasure; the desire for offspring, wealth, and the pleasures of heaven. There are ten types of *aparadha*, offenses, which I will discuss later. Then on account of *hṛdaya-daurbalya*, weakness of heart, lamentation arises. These four types of *anarthas* develop due to the material conditioned nature of the *jīvas* bound by ignorance, and they are removed gradually by cultivating pure Kṛṣṇa consciousness in the association of pure devotees.

The path of *yoga* consists of the four parts: (1) *pratyāhāra*, withdrawal from sense-objects; (2) *yama*, fundamental principles such as abstinence from licencious sexlife, consumption of meat, fish etc, intoxication, gambling, and other frivolous activities; (3) *niyama*, secondary regulations such as rising early, bathing etc; and (4) *vairāgya*, renunciation. This path is not a means to free oneself from material anxiety, for it cannot award ultimate perfection and is filled with problems and the danger of falldown and failure. Ultimately, purification by this path [without being in conjunction with *bhakti*] is only a most distant possibility.

The only one process which is free from disturbance is the cultivation of pure Kṛṣṇa consciousness in the association of pure devotees. The *jīva* is thus freed from *māyā's* stranglehold, and his constitutional position is revealed to the extent that *anarthas* are removed from his heart.

Vrajanātha: Can people with no trace of *anarthas* be termed liberated people?

Śrī Raghunātha dāsa Bābājī: Please consider the following *śloka*:

rajobhiḥ sama-saṅkhyātāḥ pārthivair iha jantavaḥ
teṣāṁ ye kecanehante śreyo vai manujādayaḥ
prāyo mumukṣavas teṣāṁ kecanaiva dvijottama
mumukṣūṇāṁ sahasreṣu kaścin mucyate sidhyati
muktānām api siddhānāṁ nārāyaṇa-parāyaṇaḥ
sudurlabhaḥ praśāntātmā koṭiṣv api mahā-mune

(*Śrīmad-Bhāgavatam* 6.14.3–5)

O Lord! There are as many *jīvas* in this material world as there are grains of sand. Only a few of these are human beings, among whom only a few strive for any form of spiritual auspiciousness. (Most of the *jīvas* are sense gratifiers who are intoxicated by insignificant sense enjoyment). One may actually achieve liberation, in the sense of giving up material attachment to society, friendship, love, country, home, wife and children; but among many thousands of such liberated persons, one who can understand the true meaning of liberation is very rare. Among hundreds of millions of such liberated or perfected beings, it is very rare to find a great soul whose mind is fully peaceful and is a devotee of Lord Nārāyaṇa. Therefore a devotee of Nārāyaṇa is very rare.

A person free from all *anarthas* is known as a pure devotee. Such devotees are very rare; indeed, even among millions of liberated persons, one can hardly find a single devotee of Śrī Kṛṣṇa. Therefore, no association in this world is rarer than the association of Kṛṣṇa's devotees.

Vrajanātha: Does the word Vaiṣṇava imply a *bhakta* who has renounced family life?

Śrī Raghunātha dāsa Bābājī: A pure devotee of Kṛṣṇa is a Vaiṣṇava whether he is a householder or *sannyāsī* (renunciant), a *brāhmaṇa* or a *caṇḍāla* (dog-eater), rich or poor. To the degree that he has pure devotion for Kṛṣṇa, he should be known as a *kṛṣṇa-bhakta*.

Vrajanātha: You have already said that there are five types of *jīvas* who are bound by *māyā*. You have also included devotees performing *sādhana-bhakti* and *bhāva-bhakti* in that category. At what stage are devotees liberated from *māyā*?

Śrī Raghunātha dāsa Bābājī: One is freed from the clutches of *māyā* from the very beginning of his devotional service, but complete liberation from the two material bodies (gross and subtle), is only obtained when one reaches the stage of full maturity in *bhakti-sādhana*. Before this, a person is liberated to the extent that he is aware of his constitutional position. The *jīva* achieves complete freedom from *māyā* only when he is completely disassociated from the gross and subtle bodies.

The stage of *bhāva-bhakti* dawns in the *jīva's* heart as a result of practicing *sādhana-bhakti*. When the *jīva* is firmly established in *bhāva-bhakti*, he gives up his gross body and after that his subtle body and becomes established in his pure spiritual body. Consequently, he is not fully free from *māyā's* control even in the beginning stage of *bhāva-bhakti*, because a trace of the conditioning of *māyā* always remains as long as he is performing *sādhana-bhakti*.

The authorities in our line have carefully considered *sādhana-bhakti* and *bhāva-bhakti*, and have included devotees practicing both these stages amongst the five stages of conditioned souls. The materialists and impersonalists are definitely included amongst the five categories of conditioned souls.

The only path of deliverance from the clutches of *māyā* is pure devotion for Śrī Hari. The imprisonment of the *jīva* began when he forgot his position as the eternal servant of Śrī Kṛṣṇa. This forgetfulness is his original offence and root of all his subsequent offences. Only the mercy of Śrī Kṛṣṇa can forgive all these offences and nothing else. Therefore, the mercy of Śrī Kṛṣṇa is alone the indispensable instrument that can fully release the *jīva* from the captivity of *māyā*.

The impersonalists believe that only by cultivating impersonal knowledge can one gain liberation from *māyā*, but this belief has no basis. There is no possibility of becoming free from *māyā* without Kṛṣṇa's mercy. This is explained in *Śrīmad-Bhāgavatam* (10.2.32–33):

ye 'nye 'ravindākṣa vimukta-māninas
tvayy asta-bhāvād aviśuddha-buddhayaḥ
āruhya kṛcchreṇa paraṁ padaṁ tataḥ
patanty adho 'nādṛta-yuṣmad-aṅghrayaḥ

O lotus-eyed Lord! Those who proudly think that they are liberated but do not render devotional service unto You, certainly have impure intelligence. Although they perform severe austerities and penances and rise up to the spiritual position of impersonal realization of *brahma*, they fall down again because they have no respect for devotional service to Your lotus feet.

tathā na te mādhava tāvakāḥ kvacid
bhraśyanti mārgāt tvayi baddha-sauhṛdāḥ
tvayābhiguptā vicaranti nirbhayā
vināyakānīkapa-mūrddhasu prabho

O Mādhava, Your dearmost *bhaktas*, who have true love for Your lotus feet, are not like those proud *jñānīs*, for they never fall down from the path of devotional service. Since You protect them, they move about fearlessly, stepping on the very heads of those who obstruct their path so that no obstacle can check their progress.

Vrajanātha: How many different types of *jīvas* are liberated from *māyā*?

Śrī Raghunātha dāsa Bābājī: Two kinds of *jīvas* are free from *māyā's* control: (1) *nitya-mukta*, the *jīvas* who were never under *māyā's* control; and (2) *baddha-mukta*, those who were once under *māyā's* control but are now free.

The *nitya-mukta-jīvas* are divided again into two categories: (1) those who are attracted by the Supreme Lord's feature of opulence and majesty (*aiśvarya-gata*); and (2) those who are attracted by His feature of sweetness (*mādhurya-gata*).

Those *jīvas* who are attracted by Kṛṣṇa's opulence and majesty are personal associates of Śrī Nārāyaṇa, the Master of Vaikuṇṭha. They are particles of spiritual effulgence emanating from Śrī Mūla-Saṅkarṣana who resides in Vaikuṇṭha. Those *jīvas* who are attracted by the Lord's sweet, human-like pastimes are personal associates of Śrī Kṛṣṇa, the Master of Goloka Vṛndāvana. They are particles of spiritual effulgence manifesting from Śrī Baladeva, who resides in Goloka Vṛndāvana.

There are three kinds of *baddha-mukta-jīvas*: (1) *aiśvarya-gata*, those who are attracted to the Lord's features of opulence and majesty; (2) *mādhurya-gata*, those who are attracted to His feature of sweetness; and (3) *brahma-jyoti-gata*, those who are attracted to His impersonal effulgence.

Those who are attracted to His opulence during their period of spiritual practice become eternal associates of Śrī Nārāyaṇa, the master of the spiritual sky, and they achieve *sālokya-mukti* (the opulence of residing on His planet). *Jīvas* who are attracted to Śrī Kṛṣṇa's sweetness during their period of devotional practice attain direct service to Him when they are liberated in the eternal abodes of Vṛndāvana and other similar abodes. *Jīvas* who attempt to merge into the impersonal effulgence during their period of practice attain *sāyujya-mukti* when they are liberated. They merge into His effulgence and are thus completely destroyed.

Vrajanātha: What is the ultimate destination of the unalloyed devotees of Śrī Gaura-Kiśora (Caitanya Mahāprabhu)?

Śrī Raghunātha dāsa Bābājī: Śrī Kṛṣṇa and Śrī Gaura-Kiśora are not a separate reality. They are both the abodes of *madhura-rasa* (the mood of sweetness) However, there is a slight difference between Them because *madhura-rasa* has two chambers. One is the mood of *mādhurya* (sweetness), and the other is the mood of *audārya* (magnanimity). Wherever the mood of *mādhurya-rasa* is prominent Śrī Kṛṣṇa's form becomes gracefully manifest, and Śrī Gaurāṅga's form is radiantly manifest where *audārya* is prominent. Similarly, the original Vṛndāvana also has two divisions: Śrī Kṛṣṇa's abode and Śrī Gaura's abode.

In Śrī Kṛṣṇa's abode, His *nitya-siddha* and *nitya-mukta* associates have a mood of *audārya*, but there is a predominance of *mādhurya-rasa*, whereas in Śrī Gaura's abode His associates have sweetness, yet that *mādhurya-rasa* is predominated and covered over by an overwhelming mood of munificence. Some associates reside in both abodes simultaneously by expansions of the self (*svarūpa-vyūha*), while others reside in one spiritual form in only one abode, and not in the other.

Those who only worship Śrī Gaura during their period of *sādhana* only serve in the abode of Śrī Gaura when they achieve perfection, while those who only serve Śrī Kṛṣṇa during their period of *sādhana* serve in Śrī Kṛṣṇa's abode on achieving perfection. However, those who worship the forms of both Śrī Kṛṣṇa and Śrī Gaura during.their period of *sādhana* manifest two forms when they attain perfection, and reside in both abodes simultaneously. This truth of the simultaneous oneness and difference of Śrī Gaura and Śrī Kṛṣṇa is a supremely confidential secret.

When Vrajanātha heard all these teachings about the state of the *jīvas* who are liberated from *māyā*, he could no longer keep his composure. Brimming with emotion, he fell down at the elderly Vaiṣṇava's lotus feet, and Bābājī Mahāśaya, crying profusely, lifted him up and embraced him.

It was already quite late in the night. Vrajanātha took leave of Śrī Bābājī Mahāśaya and went home, totally engrossed in meditating on his instructions.

When Vrajanātha reached home he took his meal, and while doing so he warned his grandmother sternly, "Grandmother, if you people want to see me here, stop all this talk about my marriage and do not keep any sort of contact with Veṇī-mādhava. He is my greatest enemy, and from tomorrow I will never speak with him again. You should also neglect him."

Vrajanātha's grandmother was very intelligent. Thus, understanding Vrajanātha's mood, she decided to postpone any question of marriage. "From the kind of sentiments he's displaying," she thought, "It seems that if he is forced too much, he might leave for Vṛndāvana or Vārāṇasī. Let God decide as He wills."

Thus ends the Seventeenth Chapter of Jaiva-dharma, entitled "Prameya: The Jīvas Free from Māyā"

Part Three

ŚRĪLA PRABHUPĀDA'S LEGACY

FROM THE JUNCTION

In order to help his audiences understand the essential and complex subject of *jīva-tattva*, and especially to increase their faith in Śrī Kṛṣṇa's abode as the *jīva's* eternal shelter, Śrīla Nārāyaṇa Gosvāmī Mahārāja often requests them to seek guidance from his *śikṣā-guru* Śrīla Prabhupāda Bhaktivedānta Svāmī Mahārāja.

On Śrīla Nārāyaṇa Gosvāmī Mahārāja's request, in this chapter the editors introduce and quote from Śrīla Prabhupāda's translations, purports, lectures, and letters. Unless otherwise mentioned, the indented quotes in Part Three are cited directly from his Bhaktivedanta Book Trust Vedabase folio, the comprehensive database of all of his spoken and written words.

From the Borderline

The following quotes confirm that the *jīvas* in this world emanate from the region called *taṭasthā-śakti*, which is located on the borderline between the spiritual and material worlds.

The Supreme Personality of Godhead has three primary energies, or potencies. The first is called *antaraṅga-śakti*, or the internal potency. The second is called *taṭasthā-śakti*, or the marginal potency. The third is called *bahiraṅga-śakti*, or the external potency. The living entities constitute the marginal potency, and they are situated between the internal and external potencies.

(*Nectar of Instruction*, Verse 2, purport)

According to *Viṣṇu Purāṇa*, *Bhagavad-gītā*, and all other Vedic literatures, the living entities are generated from the *taṭasthā* energy of the Lord, and thus they are always the energy of the Lord and are not the energetic.

(*Śrīmad-Bhāgavatam* 3.7.9, purport)

The *jīva* has access to two places, both of which he may seek, this material world and the spiritual realm. He is situated in *svapna-sthanam*, the dream-like third state, on the margin of these two worlds. From that junction he is able to see both the material and the spiritual worlds.

(*Bṛhad-āraṇyaka Upaniṣad* 4.3.9)

The symptoms of the marginal existence are like those of a huge aquatic who is capable of living on both the eastern and western sides of the river at his own will. Similarly, the *jīva* soul, situated within the waters of the Causal Ocean, which lies between the material and spiritual worlds, is able to reside in both the dream-world of matter and the spiritual world of divine wakefulness.

(*Bṛhad-āraṇyaka Upaniṣad* 4.3.18)

The borderline between water and land is called *taṭa*. Yet, the water is contiguous to the land; where then is the *taṭa*, the margin? The *taṭa* is merely the demarcation that separates the water from land. This *taṭa* is a very subtle state; it cannot be perceived through mundane vision. From this allegory, we take the water as the spiritual world and the land as the material world. Thus, the fine line that divides the two worlds is the *taṭa*, the subtle demarcation exactly whereupon the *jīva* soul is located.

(*Jaiva-dharma*, Chapter 15)

Our First Time in Kṛṣṇa's Abode

The following quotes explain that we, the conditioned souls, have not yet been to our eternal home, the Lord's spiritual abode.

> The mature devotees, who have completely executed Kṛṣṇa consciousness, are immediately transferred to the universe where Kṛṣṇa is appearing. In that universe the devotees get their first opportunity to associate with Kṛṣṇa personally and directly.
>
> (*Kṛṣṇa, The Supreme Personality of Godhead*, Chapter 28)

> In further reference to your question about the form of the spirit soul of the conditioned living entity: there is a spiritual form always, but it develops fully only when the living entity goes to Vaikuṇṭha. This form develops according to the desire of the living entity. Until this perfectional stage is reached, the form is lying dormant as the form of the tree is lying dormant in the seed.
>
> (Letter to Rūpānuga. Los Angeles, August 8, 1969)

> The sole potency of Kṛṣṇa, which is spiritual, functioning as Kṛṣṇa's own proper power, has manifested His pastimes of Goloka or Gokula. By Her grace [the grace of Śrīmatī Rādhikā, who is the personification of Kṛṣṇa's sole potency], individual souls, who are constituents of the marginal potency, can have admission into even those pastimes.
>
> (*Brahma-saṁhitā*, Verse 6, purport)

> An unlimited number of atomic conscious particles emerge from the spiritual rays of Paramātmā as the aggregate of the living entities. These innumerable *jīvas* have no relation with the mundane world when they come to know themselves to be the eternal servants of the Supreme Lord. At that time, they are incorporated into the realm of Vaikuṇṭha.
>
> (*Brahma-saṁhitā*, Verse 16, purport)

No Māyā in the Spiritual World

In the following quotes, Śrīla Prabhupāda confirms that residents of the spiritual world never fall into the material world.

The eternally liberated living beings are in the Vaikuṇṭha-jagat, the spiritual world, and they never fall into the material world.

(*Śrīmad-Bhāgavatam* 5.11.12, purport)

From authoritative sources it can be discerned that associates of Lord Viṣṇu who descend from Vaikuṇṭha do not actually fall. They come with the purpose of fulfilling the desire of the Lord, and their descent to this material world is comparable to that of the Lord. The Lord comes to this material world through the agency of His internal potency, and similarly, when a devotee or associate of the Lord descends to this material world, he does so through the action of the spiritual energy. Any pastime conducted by the Supreme Personality of Godhead is an arrangement by *yogamāyā*, not *mahāmāyā*. Therefore it is to be understood that when Jaya and Vijaya descended to this material world, they came because there was something to be done for the Supreme Personality of Godhead. Otherwise it is a fact that no one falls from Vaikuṇṭha… From authoritative sources it is learned that Jaya and Vijaya were sent to this material world to fulfill the Lord's desire to fight… Otherwise, as Mahārāja Yudhiṣṭhira says, *aśraddheya ivābhāti*: the statement that a servant of the Lord could fall from Vaikuṇṭha seems unbelievable.

(*Śrīmad-Bhāgavatam* 7.1.35, purport)

Sometimes it is asked how the living entity falls down from the spiritual world to the material world. Here is the answer. Unless one is elevated to the Vaikuṇṭha planets, directly in touch with the Supreme Personality of Godhead, he is prone to fall down, either from the impersonal Brahman realization or from an ecstatic trance of meditation.

(*Śrīmad-Bhāgavatam* 3.25.29, purport)

The conclusion is that no one falls from the spiritual world, or Vaikuṇṭha planet, for it is the eternal abode.

(*Śrīmad-Bhāgavatam* 3.16.26, purport)

The Lord is the soul of all living beings, and He desires always to have all the living beings in their *svarūpa*, in their constitutional position, to participate in transcendental life in His association. His attractive features and sweet smiles go deep into the heart of everyone, and once it is so done the living being is admitted into the kingdom of God, from which no one returns. This is confirmed in the *Bhagavad-gītā*.

(*Śrīmad-Bhāgavatam* 1.10.27, purport)

The spiritual relation with the Lord is so enlivening and resourceful that no one can leave the company of the Lord, once having taken shelter of Him.

(*Śrīmad-Bhāgavatam* 1.11.33 purport)

The Perfect Abode, Vaikuṇṭha

The following statements confirm that because in Vaikuṇṭha there is no *māyā* – no ignorance, passion, or even materially contaminated goodness – no one ever makes the wrong decision to leave.

Kāraṇābdhi-pāre. Just on the other side of the Causal Ocean, this material energy is situated. *Virajāra pāre paravyome nāhi gati*. And this material energy has no entrance in the spiritual kingdom.

(Lecture on *Śrī Caitanya-caritāmṛta*, *Madhya-līlā* 20.255–281. New York, 1966)

At that time, Śrī Bhagavān, being pleased with Brahmā's penance, showed him His abode. Vaikuṇṭha is devoid of all distress (*kleśa*) and free from illusion or fear generated by that distress. No place is superior to that abode, and pious, self-realized souls always desire to go there. It is devoid of material passion and ignorance, and even of material goodness, which is mixed with passion and ignorance. Only pure goodness is present and there is no effect of the force of time. What to speak of anger, envy, and so forth, even *māyā*, the illusory potency, the root cause of material happiness and sorrow, does not exist there. It is the permanent residence of Bhagavān's eternal associates, who are worshiped both by demigods and demons.

(*Śrīmad Bhāgavatam* 2.9.9–10)

The Lord has His internal energy also, which has another creation known to be the Vaikuṇṭha *lokas*, where there is no ignorance, no passion, no illusion, and no past and present.

(*Śrīmad-Bhāgavatam* 2.9.10, purport)

> The inhabitants of those planets are liberated from birth, death, old age, and diseases, and have full knowledge of everything; they are all godly and free from all sorts of material hankerings. They have nothing to do there except to render transcendental loving service to the Supreme Lord Nārāyaṇa, who is the predominating Deity of such Vaikuṇṭha planets.
>
> (*Śrīmad-Bhāgavatam* 2.6.18, purport)

> All the residents of Vaikuṇṭha-loka know perfectly well that their master is Nārāyaṇa, or Kṛṣṇa, and that they are all His servants. They are all self-realized souls who are *nitya-mukta*, everlastingly liberated. Although they could conceivably declare themselves Nārāyaṇa or Viṣṇu, they never do so; they always remain Kṛṣṇa conscious and serve the Lord faithfully. Such is the atmosphere of Vaikuṇṭha-loka.
>
> (*Śrīmad-Bhāgavatam* 6.1.34–6, purport)

In the following conversation, Śrīla Prabhupāda reveals that the emotions and feelings of this world are reflections of the spiritual world, but they are full of imperfections and inebriety. In contrast, all the emotions and feelings of the residents of the Lord's spiritual abode, the real world, are perfect and beautiful.

> **Question**: Svāmīji, if all things here are a reflection of what is perfect in the spiritual world, then shouldn't hate and frustration and despair and prejudice also appear in the spiritual world?
> **Prabhupāda**: Yes.
> **Question**: Does it?
> **Prabhupāda**: Yes.
> **Question**: Then isn't that... aren't they bad?
> **Prabhupāda**: But that frustration has no disappointment. That is the beauty. Just like Lord Caitanya is manifesting that spiritual frustration: "Oh Kṛṣṇa, I could not see You." He's jumping in the sea in frustration, but that frustration is the highest perfection of love. Yes, everything is there, but without inebriety. There is frustration, but not this material frustration. That spiritual frustration enriches one's eagerness of love for Kṛṣṇa.
>
> Now, see Viṣṇu. Of course, in Vaikuṇṭha-jagat there is no violence. But Viṣṇu is taking the symbol of violence. Otherwise what is the meaning of this disc and club? So when He wants to be

violent, He comes here as Nṛsiṁha-mūrti. And, He sends some of His devotees to play violence. That is Hiraṇyakaśipu.

There, the devotees are so much in accord with Kṛṣṇa and Viṣṇu that there is no question of disagreement. But violence is when there is disagreement, by the atheist. Therefore, sometimes a devotee is deputed in this world to play as atheist, and Kṛṣṇa comes to kill him – to teach these people that, "If you become atheist, here is My disc and club for you." But this is not possible to be displayed in Vaikuṇṭha. Just like there is sometimes mock fight. A father is fighting in mock with a small child, and he has become defeated; but there is pleasure.

(Room Conversation. New York, April 11, 1969)

Therefore, the conclusion is that the inhabitants of the Vaikuṇṭha planets are all *brahma-bhūta* (self-realized) living entities, as distinguished from the mundane creatures, who are all compact in hankering and lamentation. When one is not in the modes of ignorance and passion, one is supposed to be situated in the mode of goodness in the material world. Goodness in the material world also at times becomes contaminated by touches of the modes of passion and ignorance. In the Vaikuṇṭha-loka, it is unalloyed goodness only. The whole situation there is one of freedom from the illusory manifestation of the external energy.

(*Śrīmad-Bhāgavatam* 2.9.10, purport)

The Most Perfect Abode, Vṛndāvana

In the following passages, Śrīla Prabhupāda glorifies Vṛndāvana, which is higher than the Vaikuṇṭha planets, as the highest destination. Vṛndāvana is nondifferent from Kṛṣṇa, and thus it is as worshipable as He is. As there is no *māyā* in Him, there is none in His abode. We can have faith in that abode.

Śrīla Viśvanātha Cakravartī Ṭhākura said that the mission of Lord Caitanya is *ārādhyo bhagavān vrajeśa-tanaya*: "Kṛṣṇa, the Supreme Personality of Godhead, is *ārādhya*." *Ārādhya* means 'He is worshipable.' He's the only worshipable personality. *Ārādhyo bhagavān vrajeśa-tanaya tad-dhāmaṁ vṛndāvanam*: "And, as Lord

Kṛṣṇa is worshipable, similarly His place of pastimes, Vṛndāvana-dhāma, is also worshipable."

(Lecture on *Śrī Caitanya-caritāmṛta, Madhya-līlā* 20.124–125. New York, November 26, 1966)

The holy place known as Mathurā is spiritually superior to Vaikuṇṭha, the transcendental world, because the Lord appeared there. Superior to Mathurā-Purī is the transcendental forest of Vṛndāvana because of Kṛṣṇa's *rāsa-līlā* pastimes. And superior to the forest of Vṛndāvana is Govardhana Hill, for it was raised by the divine hand of Śrī Kṛṣṇa and was the site of His various loving pastimes. And, above all, the superexcellent Śrī Rādhā-kuṇḍa stands supreme, for it is overflooded with the ambrosial nectarean prema of the Lord of Gokula, Śrī Kṛṣṇa. Where, then, is that intelligent person who is unwilling to serve this divine Rādhā-kuṇḍa, which is situated at the foot of Govardhana Hill?

(*Nectar of Instruction*, Verse 9)

I worship that transcendental seat, known as Śvetadvīpa where, as loving consorts, the Lakṣmīs in their unalloyed spiritual essence practice the amorous service of the Supreme Lord Kṛṣṇa as their only lover; where every tree is a transcendental purpose tree; where the soil is the purpose gem, all water is nectar, every word is a song, every gait is a dance, the flute is the favorite attendant, effulgence is full of transcendental bliss and the supreme spiritual entities are all enjoyable and tasty, where numberless milk cows always emit transcendental oceans of milk; where there is eternal existence of transcendental time, which is ever present and without past or future and hence is not subject to the quality of passing away even for the space of half a moment. That realm is known as Goloka only to a very few self-realized souls in this world.

(*Brahma-saṁhitā* 5.56)

God's Mercy - The Soul's Free Will

These conversations clarify why the Supreme Lord has endowed the *jīva* with free will.

Prabhupāda: That potentiality is eternal. God is eternal. We are eternal. Our relationship is eternal. Everything is eternal. But because we are small, minute fragments, sometimes we fall down.

Question: They say, "God should have created us so that we..."

Prabhupāda: Why should you dictate to God? God has created perfectly. He has given you independence. You fall down; it is your fault. If you misuse your independence, you fall down. Just like the government gives everyone an opportunity. Why do you become criminal and go to the jail? That is your fault.

Question: They say that God should have created us so that we...

Prabhupāda: Why 'should have created'? He has already created perfectly. Because you are perfect, therefore you have got the independence to misuse. You are not a dead stone. That is perfection.

Ye yathā māṁ prapadyante (*Bhagavad-gītā* 4.11). You can go anywhere – Svarga. You can go to the Vaikuṇṭha. *Yānti deva-vratā devān* (*Bhagavad-gītā* 9.25). You can go to the higher planets. You can go to hell. When you go to hell, it is your choice. God has given you all perfection. *Pūrṇam idaṁ, pūrṇam adaḥ, pūrṇāt pūrṇam udacyate* (*Śrī Īśopaniṣad*, Invocation). Everything is complete, perfect, and because you are perfect, you have got independence. But, misusing that independence, you are imperfect. Again, reviving your proper use of independence, you can become perfect although you are imperfect now. That is the Kṛṣṇa consciousness movement…

Because they have become imperfect, therefore they are blaming God. "God is good" – they forget this. That is their imperfection. On one side they say, "God is good." Still, they're blaming God. What is this nonsense? If He's God and God is good, how can you blame Him? God is good; in all circumstances He's good. That is the meaning of good. Good does not mean that one time you are good and next time you are bad…

God has made everything. Just like here [pointing to a material object]. It is made not to move. Stay. But we are better than this. Is it not? It cannot move. So God has made this also. But because we can move, we are better than this. And they say, "Why has God made me to commit mistake?" This rascal does not understand that that is freedom. Why don't you take the right path? God says, "This is right." *Sarva-dharmān parityajya mām ekaṁ śaraṇaṁ vraja* (*Bhagavad-gītā* 18.66). Why don't you take it? How can you say God is bad? What is the argument?

Question: Well, the argument is that if God is so all-powerful, why does He even let me fall?… Why doesn't He save me from my own foolishness? Why doesn't He...?
Prabhupāda: Yes, He's saving you, but you don't carry out His order… Just like I say, "Chant sixteen rounds." If you do not do it, what can I do? That is your fault.
Question: If God were to force us, there'd be no love.
Prabhupāda: No, no. Force is not good. Force is there. Force is there. The *māyā* is another force.

(Morning Walk. Los Angeles, December 6, 1973)

The references above mercifully share with us that, under the guidance of Śrī Śrī Rādhā-Kṛṣṇa's pure devotees, we spirit souls can learn to properly use our jewel-like independence. With full faith in the Lord's perfect spiritual realm, we can gradually become qualified to enter and perpetually enjoy our loving services to the Lord.

THE SAME MESSAGE

We present this chapter to further the understanding that Śrī Kṛṣṇa's abode, as well as its residents, are eternally perfect.

Another aim of this chapter is to further establish that the teachings of Śrīla Bhaktivedānta Svāmī Prabhupāda, Śrīla Bhaktivedānta Nārāyaṇa Gosvāmī Mahārāja, and all of our predecessor *ācāryas* are one; their message is the same. By this understanding, we may be blessed with their combined mercy.

Introduction: No Contradiction

In these quotes, Śrīla Prabhupāda explains that the same message is given in all scriptures and by all pure devotees, *gurus*, and *ācāryas*.

> Vedic literature means there is no contradiction. Either you read this Veda or that Veda. People who are foolish, who cannot understand, sometimes see contradiction. No. There is no contradiction. Same one law.
>
> (Lecture on *Śrīmad-Bhāgavatam* 7.9.30. Māyāpur, 1976)

So there is a link between one Vedic literature to another. There is no contradiction. But different things are there for different classes of men.

(Lecture on *Bhagavad-gītā* 4.1. Montreal, August 24, 1968)

What five thousand years ago Vyāsadeva instructed or Kṛṣṇa instructed, the same thing we are also instructing. Therefore there is no difference between instructions. Therefore *guru* is one. Although hundreds and thousands of *ācāryas* have come and gone, but the message is one. Therefore *guru* cannot be two. Real *guru* will not talk differently.

Guru must come from the *paramparā* system by disciplic succession. Five thousand years or five millions of years, what was spoken by the supreme God or *guru*, the present *guru* also will say the same thing. That is *guru*. That is bona fide *guru*. Otherwise, he's not *guru*. Simple definition. *Guru* cannot change any word of the predecessor.

(Lecture: *What is a Guru?* London, August 22, 1973)

The above statements affirm that Śrīla Prabhupāda's teaching regarding the origination of the soul is without contradiction. That teaching may be expressed in different ways according to the capacity of a particular audience to understand, but the essence is the same.

We now offer to our respected reader some passages from Śrīla Prabhupāda's books, letters, and other writings that are sometimes misunderstood to mean that the souls of this world fell here from Goloka Vṛndāvana or Vaikuṇṭha. As Śrīla Nārāyaṇa Gosvāmī Mahārāja explains in his lectures in Part One of *Journey of the Soul*, misconstruing such passages weakens the spiritual seeker's faith in Kṛṣṇa's abode and invariably weakens his desire and enthusiasm to attain it.

Therefore, in this Part Three of *Journey of the Soul*, we will explain those same passages in the light of clarifying quotes from Śrīla Prabhupāda, in the light of Śrīla Nārāyaṇa Gosvāmī's discourses in Part One, and also in the light of the three chapters of *Jaiva-dharma* found in Part Two.

Please forgive us for any shortcomings in our presentation.

The Editors.

We Have Not Seen Kṛṣṇa' Yet

As a pure follower of the disciplic succession of self-realized *gurus*, Śrīla Prabhupāda teaches that when the conditioned soul becomes self-realized, he will see God for the first time. The souls of this world have never directly seen Him before.

> Regarding your second question, have the conditioned souls ever seen Kṛṣṇa? Were they with the Lord before being conditioned by the desire to lord it over material nature? Yes, the conditioned souls are parts and parcels of the Lord and thus they were with Kṛṣṇa before being conditioned.
>
> Just as the child must have seen his father because the father places the child in the womb of the mother, similarly each soul has seen Kṛṣṇa or the Supreme Father. But at that time, the conditioned souls are resting in the condition called *suṣupti*, which is exactly deep sleep without dream, or anesthetized state. Therefore they do not remember being with Kṛṣṇa when they wake up in the material world and become engaged in material affairs.
>
> (Letter to Jagadīśa. Los Angeles, March 25, 1970)

Initially, the above letter may seem to state that conditioned souls were previously with Śrī Kṛṣṇa in His transcendental abode, Goloka Vṛndāvana. But careful study reveals a different history.

Śrīla Prabhupāda states that Kṛṣṇa is like a father who injects the child into the womb of the mother. Although the child is part and parcel of the father and was within the body of the father before entering the womb of the mother, he was in seed-form at that time. He had never associated with his father.

Similarly, in the Lord's form as Mahā-Viṣṇu, He is the seed-giving father who injects the seeds of the living entities into the womb of material nature. The living entity in this world has yet to personally associate with Kṛṣṇa in His abode.

How Were We in Kṛṣṇa's Līlā?

In 1972, in response to a letter from his Australian disciples, Śrīla Prabhupāda dictated a brief essay entitled "Crow and Tala-fruit Logic." The following statements are excerpts from that essay.

> We never had any occasion when we were separated from Kṛṣṇa.

Śrīla Prabhupāda will reveal later that we were never separated from Kṛṣṇa because we have always been with His energies, which are non-different from Him. In fact, we are one of His energies; as stated in *Śrīmad-Bhāgavatam* (3.5.6): "He expands Himself into many living entities, which are manifested as different species of life." In addition, His expansion as the Supersoul in the hearts of all beings has been with us since the beginning of time. In these ways we have never been separated from Him.

The essay continues:

> Just like one man is dreaming and he forgets himself. In dream he creates himself in different forms: "Now I am the King," discussing like that. This creation of himself is as seer and the subject matter as seen, two things. But as soon as the dream is over, the 'seen' disappears, but the seer remains. Now he is in his original position.
>
> Our separation from Kṛṣṇa is like that. We dream of this body and of so many relationships with other things. First the attachment comes to enjoy sense gratification. Even with Kṛṣṇa, desire for sense gratification is there.

Here, Śrīla Prabhupāda teaches that Kṛṣṇa is everywhere because Kṛṣṇa's various energies are everywhere. His statement, "even with Kṛṣṇa, desire for sense-gratification is there" means that even though Kṛṣṇa is in our hearts as Supersoul, and even though we are with Him now in the sense that this world has no separate existence from Him, still we turn away from Him and desire to enjoy separate from Him. The meaning of 'original position' will be discussed soon.

His essay continues:

> There is a dormant attitude for forgetting Kṛṣṇa and creating an atmosphere for enjoying independently. Just like at the edge of the beach, sometimes the water covers, sometimes there is dry sand, coming and going. Our position is like that, sometimes covered, sometimes free, just like at the edge of the tide. As soon as we forget, immediately the illusion is there. Just like as soon as we sleep, dream is there. We cannot say, therefore, that we are not with Kṛṣṇa.

When Śrīla Prabhupāda says, "We cannot say, therefore, that we are not with Kṛṣṇa," he is confirming that his previous statement, "Even with Kṛṣṇa, desire for sense gratification is there" does not necessarily mean we were in His abode. Kṛṣṇa is everywhere. He is therefore also present in this *taṭasthā* region, where spirit souls are connected with Him as His parts and parcels. He also resides with the souls in the material world, where He is situated within the hearts of the conditioned souls as Supersoul. Also, in this material world, the material elements themselves are emanations of His energy. In this way Śrīla Prabhupāda writes, "We cannot say, therefore, that we are not with Kṛṣṇa."

He writes about the analogy of the edge of the beach. He discusses the imaginary line between the open land and the water called *taṭa*. The *jīva* originates in this area between the spiritual and material worlds, known in spiritual philosophy as *taṭasthā*.

The essay continues:

> As soon as we try to become the Lord, immediately we are covered by *māyā*. Formerly we were with Kṛṣṇa in His *līlā* [pastimes] or sport. But this covering of *māyā* may be of very, very, very, very long duration; therefore many creations are coming and going.

In the material world, since time immemorial, we have been serving in Kṛṣṇa's *līlā* (pastimes). The creation, maintenance, and destruction of this material world are also the Lord's pastimes. This cycle is referred to in *Śrīmad-Bhāgavatam* (2.4.12) as *sad-udbhava-sthāna-nirodha-līlayā* and in *Caitanya-caritāmṛta* (*Adi-līlā* 5.9) as *srsti-līlā*. We have been, and still are, serving in Kṛṣṇa's *līlā* here in the material world. Directly or indirectly, all living entities are serving the Lord. It is for this reason that Śrīla Prabhupāda states, "We cannot say, therefore, that we are not with Kṛṣṇa."

The essay continues:

> Due to this long period of time it is sometimes said that we are ever-conditioned. But this long duration of time becomes very insignificant when one actually comes to Kṛṣṇa consciousness. Just like in a dream we are thinking very long time, but as soon as we awaken we look at our watch and see it has been a moment only.

> The real position is servant of Kṛṣṇa, and servant of Kṛṣṇa means in *kṛṣṇa-līlā*. Directly or indirectly, always we are serving Kṛṣṇa's *līlā*. Even in dream. Just like we cannot go out of the sun when it is daytime, so where is the chance of going out of *kṛṣṇa-līlā*?

Śrīla Prabhupāda confirms here that even now we are in Kṛṣṇa's *līlā*. The creation of both *taṭasthā-śakti* and the material world is also a feature of His pastimes.

The essay continues:

> The cloud may be there, it may become very gray and dim, but still the sunlight is there, everywhere, during the daytime. Because I am part and parcel of Kṛṣṇa, I am always connected. My finger, even though it may be diseased, remains part and parcel of my body. Therefore, we try to treat it, cure it, because it is part and parcel. So Kṛṣṇa comes Himself when we forget Him, or He sends His representative.

A disciple once asked Śrīla Prabhupāda, "If we've never been with Kṛṣṇa, if we've never been in Kṛṣṇa-loka, then how is it that we start 'remembering' His pastimes and His form?" Śrīla Prabhupāda replied, "You remember Kṛṣṇa's pastimes by hearing *Śrīmad-Bhāgavatam*. You can hear Kṛṣṇa's pastimes. That you can remember." The disciple then asked, "But how can we 'remember' if we've never known them before?" Prabhupāda replied, "You can know by hearing from *Śrīmad-Bhāgavatam*. Why are we citing so many scriptures like *Śrīmad-Bhāgavatam* and *Bhagavad-gītā*? Just to remember" (Room Conversation. Boston, April 27, 1969). In this 1969 conversation, Prabhupāda confirmed that words like 'remember' and 'forget' are mere indications.

The essay continues:

> Awakening or dreaming, I am the same man. As soon as I awaken and see myself, I see Kṛṣṇa. Cause and effect are both Kṛṣṇa. Just like cotton becomes thread and thread becomes cloth, still, the original cause is cotton. Therefore, everything is Kṛṣṇa in the ultimate sense. When we cannot contact Kṛṣṇa personally, we contact His energies. So there is no chance to be outside Kṛṣṇa's *līlā*.

Here, Śrīla Prabhupāda verifies that his previous referral to the conditioned souls having formally been in Kṛṣṇa's *līlā* refers to His *līlā* of material creation. As stated in *Jaiva-dharma*, Chapter Sixteen, some souls are in His *līlā* in the spiritual world and some are in His *līlā* in the material world.

In the following conversation, Śrīla Prabhupāda further establishes that in this world we are always with Kṛṣṇa and have always been with Him. In this way we can further reconcile his statement: "Formerly we were with Kṛṣṇa in His *līlā*." In other words we were in His *līlā*, and we are in His *līlā*, while in the *taṭasthā* region and while in the material world.

Yaśomatīnandana: Is [the *jīva*] allowed to associate with Kṛṣṇa in the beginning?
Prabhupāda: He's always with Kṛṣṇa. Simply he has forgotten. Have you not been with Kṛṣṇa? We are standing on this sand. The sand is Kṛṣṇa, Kṛṣṇa's energy. We are standing by the water. This is Kṛṣṇa's energy. *Bhūmir āpo 'nalo vāyuḥ* (*Bhagavad-gītā* 7.4). Don't you read that? So is it different from Kṛṣṇa?
Yaśomatīnandana: No, but it is...
Prabhupāda: My body is also Kṛṣṇa's energy. I am also Kṛṣṇa's energy. I am always with Kṛṣṇa. Simply I have forgotten it.
Yaśomatīnandana: But this is Kṛṣṇa's inferior energy, right?
Prabhupāda: That may be. That is a comparative study, inferior or superior. But it is energy.
Yaśomatīnandana: Yes.
Prabhupāda: As energy, it is not different from Kṛṣṇa.
Yaśomatīnandana: *Vāsudevaḥ sarvam iti* (*Bhagavad-gītā* 7.19).
Prabhupāda: Yes. As energy, how can you differentiate from Kṛṣṇa?
(Morning walk. Los Angeles, December 5, 1973)

We Are With Kṛṣṇa as Supersoul

Prabhupāda explains below that the activities of Paramātmā, the Supersoul in the hearts of all created beings, are also considered to be Kṛṣṇa's pastimes. The conditioned soul has formerly associated with Kṛṣṇa in the form of the Supersoul, and is also associating with Him now.

So we are also associated with Kṛṣṇa, as Paramātmā within the heart...
(Lecture on *Bhagavad-gītā* 4.5. Bombay, March 25, 1975)

We Have Not Been Home Yet

In the verses below, Paramātmā, in the form of a *brāhmaṇa*, appears to His devotee and converses with her. These verses are sometimes mistaken to mean that the spirit soul has left his original home, Goloka Vṛndāvana.

> The *brāhmaṇa* inquired as follows: Who are you? Whose wife or daughter are you? Who is the man lying here? It appears you are lamenting for this dead body. Don't you recognize Me? I am your eternal friend. You may remember that many times in the past you have consulted Me.
>
> The *brāhmaṇa* continued: My dear friend, even though you cannot immediately recognize Me, can't you remember that in the past you had a very intimate friend? Unfortunately, you gave up My company and accepted a position as enjoyer of this material world.
>
> My dear gentle friend, both you and I are exactly like two swans. We live together in the same heart, which is just like the Mānasa Lake. Although we have been living together for many thousands of years, we are still far away from our original home.
>
> (*Śrīmad-Bhāgavatam* 4.28.52–54)

Paramātmā has been traveling with us since time immemorial, from one body to another. However, as Śrīla Prabhupāda explains in the following purport, Paramātmā is not Śrī Kṛṣṇa of Goloka Vṛndāvana:

> In His Paramātmā feature, Kṛṣṇa is the old friend of everyone. The Supreme Personality of Godhead, Paramātmā, appeared before the Queen as a *brāhmaṇa*, but why didn't He appear in His original form as Śrī Kṛṣṇa? Śrīla Viśvanātha Cakravartī Ṭhākura remarks that unless one is very highly elevated in loving the Supreme Personality of Godhead, one cannot see Him as He is.
>
> (*Śrīmad-Bhāgavatam* 4.28.51, purport)

Paramātmā is neither Śrī Kṛṣṇa in Vṛndāvana nor Lord Nārāyaṇa in Vaikuṇṭha. Paramātmā has never resided in Vṛndāvana or Vaikuṇṭha, the original home of all existence, nor will He ever reside there. This is explained in the following purport excerpt:

> The Paramātmā manifestation is also a temporary, all-pervasive aspect of the Kṣīrodakaśāyī Viṣṇu. The Paramātmā manifestation

> is not eternal in the spiritual world. Therefore the factual Absolute Truth is the Supreme Personality of Godhead Kṛṣṇa. He is the complete energetic person, and He possesses different separated and internal energies.
>
> (*Bhagavad-gītā* 7.4, purport)

Although Lord Paramātmā utters the words 'our original home,' He has never been there, nor have the conditioned souls of this world been there. The discernment that the souls of this world have not fallen from the spiritual world is explained in the next section.

No Going Back and Forth

> The original home of the living entity and the Supreme Personality of Godhead is the spiritual world. In the spiritual world both the Lord and the living entities live together very peacefully. Since the living entity remains engaged in the service of the Lord, they both share a blissful life in the spiritual world. However, when the living entity wants to enjoy himself, he falls down into the material world. Even while in that position, the Lord remains with him as the Supersoul, his intimate friend.
>
> (*Śrīmad-Bhāgavatam* 4.28.54, purport)

It is certainly true that the constitutional home of the living entity is in the spiritual world, but it is not that the same living entity goes back and forth between the spiritual and material worlds. In his translations, purports, and lecture below, Śrīla Prabhupāda states that there are two categories of living entities:

> The living entities, the *jīvas*, are divided into two categories. Some are *nitya-mukta*, eternally liberated, and others are eternally conditioned.
>
> (*Śrī Caitanya-caritāmṛta, Madhya-līlā* 22.10)

The first category is that of the eternally liberated living entities, those who are in the spiritual world, and they are never overwhelmed by *māyā*. They never desire to gratify their own senses; they only desire Kṛṣṇa's happiness.

> Those who are eternally liberated are always awake to Kṛṣṇa consciousness, and they render transcendental loving service at

the feet of Lord Kṛṣṇa. They are to be considered eternal associates of Kṛṣṇa, and they are eternally enjoying the transcendental bliss of serving Kṛṣṇa.

(*Śrī Caitanya-caritāmṛta, Madhya-līlā* 22.11)

The second category is that of the perpetually conditioned souls of this world, who have yet to become pure devotees and join the eternally liberated souls in the kingdom of God.

Apart from the ever-liberated devotees, there are the conditioned souls, who always turn away from the service of the Lord. They are perpetually conditioned in this material world and are subjected to the material tribulations brought about by different bodily forms in hellish conditions.

(*Śrī Caitanya-caritāmṛta, Madhya-līlā* 22.12)

The *nitya-baddhas* are always conditioned by the external energy, and the *nitya-muktas* never come in contact with the external energy. Sometimes, an ever-liberated personal associate of the Supreme Personality of Godhead descends into this universe just as the Lord descends. Although working for the liberation of conditioned souls, the messenger of the Supreme Lord remains untouched by the material energy. Generally, ever-liberated personalities live in the spiritual world as associates of Lord Kṛṣṇa, and they are known as *kṛṣṇa-pāriṣada*, associates of the Lord. Their only business is enjoying Lord Kṛṣṇa's company, and even though such eternally liberated persons come within this material world to serve the Lord's purpose, they enjoy Lord Kṛṣṇa's company without stoppage. The ever-liberated person, who works on Kṛṣṇa's behalf, enjoys Lord Kṛṣṇa's company through his engagement.

(*Śrī Caitanya-caritāmṛta, Madhya-līlā* 22.14–15, purport)

svāṁśa-vibhinnāṁśa-rūpe hañā vistāra
ananta vaikuṇṭha-brahmāṇḍe karena vihāra

So Kṛṣṇa is both in the spiritual world and the material world. Because we represent Kṛṣṇa, we are in this *brahmāṇḍa* – conditioned. But there are many living entities who are eternally liberated. They never come to this [world]. Just like the ocean and the rivers. In the river you will find fishes and in the ocean you will find fishes. Sometimes it may be that the fishes of the river may go to the ocean, but the fishes of the ocean never come to the river – never come to the river. There is no place for them.

sei vibhinnāṁśa jīva-dui ta' prakāra
eka-'nitya-mukta', eka-'nitya saṁsāra'

Now, this energy manifested as the living entities; they are also two kinds. What are they? *Eka-nitya-mukta.* One class of living entities, they are eternally liberated. Just like the fishes in the ocean. Take the ocean as the place of liberation. That individuality is there. And that individuality is reciprocated between Kṛṣṇa and the individual souls. They are called *nitya-mukta*, eternally liberated. And the other class, who are just like in the river fishes, they are called *nitya-baddha*. Their, I mean to say, limited sphere is in the river or in the pond or in the well.

(Lecture on *Śrī Caitanya-caritāmṛta, Madhya-līlā* 22.6.
New York, January 8, 1967)

In this way, Śrīla Prabhupāda clarifies that eternally liberated souls never become conditioned, and the souls in this world were never previously residents of the spiritual world. It is by great fortune that by the process of *bhakti-yoga* under proper guidance, conditioned souls also can join the Supreme Lord.

We've Not Yet Spoken with Our Supreme Father

It may appear from the statement below that the conditioned souls have previously conversed with Kṛṣṇa directly:

> We are very proud of our senses. But these senses are given just like a boy is given some plaything by the father; similarly, we wanted to enjoy this material world. Therefore our material senses are awarded: "All right, you enjoy. You just have experience of this material world, and when you get experience that 'I am not happy,' then you shall come back again to Me."
>
> (Lecture on *Bhagavad-gītā* 2.55–58. New York, April 15, 1966)

Directly hearing from the Lord or directly discussing with the Lord is only possible for the great devotees – those who are free from the propensity to enjoy the material senses. Why, then, does Prabhupāda seem to say that Kṛṣṇa is speaking directly to a conditioned soul who has turned away from Him?

This is another example of *śākhā-candra-nyāya*, the logic of the moon on the branch. Śrīla Prabhupāda writes in one of his purports from the *Caitanya-caritāmṛta*: "First a child is shown the branches of a tree, and then he is shown the moon through the branches. This is called *śākhā-candra-nyāya*. The idea is that first one must be given a simpler example. Then the more difficult background is explained" (*Śrī Caitanya-caritāmṛta*, *Madhya-līlā* 21.31, purport).

Because *Jīva-tattva* cannot be truly understood by one who thinks, "I am a lady" or "I am a lad," therefore, having mercifully descended to this world of materialistic persons who were fully absorbed in the concepts of "I am this body and everything in relation to this body is mine," Prabhupāda is giving an indication here – God is our father, He loves us, and He wants us to seek His shelter and become happy.

Factually, when we, conditioned souls, reach perfection in our devotional life, we will meet Śrī Kṛṣṇa in His abode for the first time. This is explained below, in Prabhupāda's *Kṛṣṇa, The Supreme Personality of Godhead*:

> The mature devotees, who have completely executed Kṛṣṇa consciousness, are immediately transferred to the universe where Kṛṣṇa is appearing. In that universe the devotees get their first opportunity to associate with Kṛṣṇa personally and directly.
>
> (*Kṛṣṇa, The Supreme Personality of Godhead*, Chapter 28)

This conclusive quote confirms that when the conditioned soul becomes free from *māyā's* clutches, he will attain the spiritual abode of the Lord and associate with Him for the first time.

Back Home, Back to Godhead

> The material creation by the Lord of creatures (Viṣṇu) is a chance offered to the conditioned souls to come back home, back to Godhead.
>
> (*Bhagavad-gītā* 3.10, purport)

Śrīla Prabhupāda has made the phrase "Back Home, Back to Godhead" quite well-known throughout the world. This phrase may seem to mean that the souls of this world were previously in Goloka Vṛndāvana, they left there, and now they must return there. We hope that the discussion below helps to clarify the meaning of 'returning home, Back to Godhead':

In Vṛndāvana, in 1993, a senior disciple of Śrīla Prabhupāda asked Śrīla Nārāyaṇa Gosvāmī Mahārāja, "What did Śrīla Prabhupāda mean when he said, 'Back to home, back to Godhead?'"

Using that disciple's own life as an analogy, Śrīla Nārāyaṇa Gosvāmī Mahārāja explained that although her son was born and raised in Vṛndāvana, India, he considers himself American – because his mother is American. When the school holidays begin, he tells his friends and classmates at the Vṛndāvana Gurukula, "I am going home."

Similarly, Śrīla Prabhupāda's famous phrase "Back Home, Back to Godhead" helps the conditioned souls to think of the Supreme Lord as their father, and wherever their father resides is home. This phrase helps us to understand that Kṛṣṇa is not impersonal, and that His home is our rightful home. This is explained in the excerpt below:

> Back to Godhead means God is a person, a person like you and me. Just like your father is a person. That is practical knowledge. Your father's father is also a person. His father is also a person. His

> father is also a person. Immediately you can understand. Therefore the supreme father must be a person.
>
> (Lecture on *Śrīmad-Bhāgavatam* 6.1.11. New York, July 25, 1971)

> The Lord does not want His sons, the living beings, to suffer the threefold miseries of life. He desires that all of them come to Him and live with Him, but going back to Godhead means that one must purify himself from material infections.
>
> (*Śrīmad-Bhāgavatam* 1.5.35, purport)

> Back to Godhead means one must be completely pure. A slight impurity will not be allowed.
>
> (Lecture on *Śrīmad-Bhāgavatam* 6.1.34–39. Surat, December 19, 1970)

In two of the three quotes above, the concept of purity is mentioned along with going back home. This means that in the Lord's abode there is no impurity, no impure desire to enjoy separately from Kṛṣṇa. *Māyā* cannot enter the spiritual world.

For Newcomers

The following quote from Śrīla Prabhupāda's lecture may seem controversial in its contrast to the previous statements regarding the origin of the living entities, and may even seem to contradict the previous *ācāryas*, but in fact it does not.

> ...because we have also come down from Vaikuṇṭha some millions and millions of years ago. *Anādi karama-phale. Anādi* means 'before the creation.' We living entities, we are eternal. Even the creation is annihilated after millions and trillions of years, the living entities, are not annihilated.
>
> (Lecture on *Bhagavad-gītā* 2.6. London, August 6, 1973)

There is no contradiction between Śrīla Prabhupāda and his *guru* or *parātpara-guru*. Being a pure follower of his *parātpara-guru*, Śrīla Bhaktivinoda Ṭhākura, he is a pure follower of his statement in *Jaiva-dharma*: "Inasmuch as they reside in the spiritual world, *māyā* stays far from them and does not affect them at all." And of course he himself has written, "There are Vaikuṇṭha planets in the spiritual world, and the devotees there are all liberated. These devotees are *akṣara*, which means they do not fall down into the material world. They remain in the spiritual world of the Vaikuṇṭhas" (*Śrīmad-Bhāgavatam* 7.1.35, purport).

So why, on rare occasions does Prabhupāda speak in such a way in the above-mentioned London lecture? He answers this himself in his 1968 lecture that is quoted at the beginning of this article: "There is no contradiction, but different things are there for different classes of men." As explained above, he sometimes simplified the concepts of eternality and "Back Home, Back to Godhead" for a particular audience, for those new to the Kṛṣṇa conscious path. In this way, we could gradually come to understand the inconceivable *jīva-tattva*.

Śrīla Nārāyaṇa Gosvāmī Mahārāja has explained that our *ācāryas* sometimes give 'baby-food to babies.' In other words, they give explanation that are easy for aspiring devotees to accept and understand according to those devotees' level of advancement. We have seen that on very rare occasions Śrīla Nārāyaṇa Gosvāmī Mahārāja personally gives this 'baby-food' to his new audiences. For example, at a *darśana* in Miami, in 2008, he told a first-time guest, "By chance you have been thrown to this world from Goloka Vṛndāvana. The guard of that Goloka planet, Yogamāyā-devī, threw us into this world. You are actually a male or female servant of Śrī Śrī Rādhā-Kṛṣṇa, but you wanted to enjoy sense gratification and have forgotten your true heritage."

Vaikuṇṭha Residents Do Not Take the Chance

It is true that *jīvas* always have independence, even in Vaikuṇṭha...

> Constitutionally, every living entity, even if he is in the Vaikuṇṭha-loka, has the chance of falling down.
>
> (Letter to Upendra. Tittenhurst, October 27, 1969)

But those in Vaikuṇṭha never choose to misuse that independence and forget Kṛṣṇa. Śrīla Prabhupāda's consistency of philosophical thought is confirmed below:

> **Question**: When the souls that were never conditioned at all..., do they also have the independence?

Prabhupāda: Yes, but they have not misused. They know that "I am meant for Kṛṣṇa's service," and they are happy in Kṛṣṇa's service.
Question: Could they ever misuse it?
Prabhupāda: Yes, they can misuse it also. That power is there. Yes?
Question: Well, I believe you once said that once a conditioned soul becomes perfected and gets out of the material world and he goes to Kṛṣṇa-loka, there's no possibility of falling back.
Prabhupāda: No, there is possibility, but he does not come. Just like after putting your hand in the fire, you never put it again if you are really intelligent. So those who are going back to Godhead, they become intelligent.

(Lecture on *Śrī Caitanya-caritāmṛta, Ādi-līlā* 7.108.
San Francisco, 1967)

There are Vaikuṇṭha planets in the spiritual world, and the devotees there are all liberated. These devotees are *akṣara*, which means they do not fall down into the material world. They remain in the spiritual world of the Vaikuṇṭhas. They are also persons like us, but they are eternal persons, complete with full knowledge and bliss. That is the difference between them and us. That is *tattva-jñāna*. In other words, these associates of the Lord, Jaya and Vijaya, descended to the material world to serve the Lord by fulfilling His desire to fight. Otherwise, as Mahārāja Yudhiṣṭhira says, *aśraddheya ivābhāti*: the statement that a servant of the Lord could fall from Vaikuṇṭha seems unbelievable.

(*Śrīmad-Bhāgavatam* 7.1.35, purport)

No Wrong in Vaikuṇṭha Devotees

The previous purport tells us that Yudhiṣṭhira Mahārāja said, "The statement that a servant of the Lord could fall from Vaikuṇṭha seems unbelievable." The purport states that all the residents of Vaikuṇṭha are eternal, and full of bliss and knowledge. Although the following purport is not contradictory, it may initially appear to contradict Yudhiṣṭhira's words.

In the *Bhakti-sandarbha* by Śrīla Jīva Gosvāmī, there is a quotation from the *Skanda Purāṇa* admonishing that a person who eats grains on Ekādaśī becomes a murderer of his mother, father, brother, and spiritual master, and even if he is elevated to a Vaikuṇṭha planet, he falls down.

(*Śrī Caitanya Caritāmṛta, Ādi-līlā* 15.9, purport)

In effect, Prabhupāda is saying, "Even if one thinks himself a perfect transcendentalist, qualified to be a resident of Vaikuṇṭha, he should not neglect Ekādaśī." Prabhupāda implies that no one should be so proud as to think that one need not follow Ekādaśī, which is Kṛṣṇa Himself, manifest in the form of a time period. Śrīla Prabhupāda wrote this statement as a warning to aspiring devotees about the gravity of following the Ekādaśī fast – not that pure devotees, once having attained Vaikuṇṭha, fall down.

Even in This World, True Devotees Do Not Fall

True devotees remain in their sublime position, even in this world, what to speak of the spiritual world. In a cursory first reading of the following passages from the *Caitanya-caritāmṛta*, the contrary seems to be presented, but we will soon see that there is no contradiction.

There, Śrī Caitanya Mahāprabhu's associate Svarūpa Dāmodara Gosvāmī, a pure devotee, seems to imply that even *he* may fall from his position by hearing impersonalist (Māyāvāda) philosophy. Bhagavān Ācārya had requested Svarūpa Dāmodara Gosvāmī to hear a commentary upon Vedānta from his Māyāvādī brother, Gopāla. Somewhat angry, Svarūpa Dāmodara Gosvāmī replied as follows. "When a Vaiṣṇava listens to the *Śārīraka-bhāṣya*, the Māyāvāda commentary upon *Vedānta-sūtra*, he gives up the Kṛṣṇa conscious attitude that the Lord is the master and the living entity is His servant. Instead, he considers himself the Supreme Lord.

maha-bhagavata yei, kṛṣṇa prana-dhana yara
māyāvāda-sravane citta avasya phire tanra.

The Māyāvāda philosophy presents such a jugglery of words that even a highly elevated devotee who has accepted Kṛṣṇa as his life and soul changes his decision when he reads the Māyāvāda commentary on *Vedānta-sūtra*.

Svarūpa Dāmodara Gosvāmī is the most beloved follower of Mahāprabhu, and in *kṛṣṇa-līlā* he is none other than Śrīmatī Rādhārāṇī's dearmost *sakhī*, Lalitā-devī. When such an exalted Vaiṣṇava refers to the possibility that even *he* may fall down, he does so out of humility, or joke, or warning to others. Svarūpa Dāmodara Gosvāmī is cautioning the neophyte Vaiṣṇava, who may artificially believe himself to be advanced and invulnerable. If that neophyte hears Māyāvāda philosophy, he may lose his tenuous faith in Kṛṣṇa as the Supreme Person.

Further on, Svarūpa Dāmodara Gosvāmī reveals his true, underlying reason for not wanting to listen to Māyāvāda philosophy: his heart breaks when he hears any offense to his beloved Lord Kṛṣṇa.

The conversation continues in the following passage:

> In spite of Svarūpa Dāmodara's protest, Bhagavān Ācārya continued, "We are all fixed at the lotus feet of Kṛṣṇa with our hearts and souls. Therefore the *Śārīraka-bhāṣya* cannot change our minds."
>
> Svarūpa Dāmodara replied, "Nevertheless, when we hear the Māyāvāda philosophy, we hear that Brahman is knowledge and that the universe of *māyā* is false, but we gain no spiritual understanding. The Māyāvādī philosopher tries to establish that the living entity is only imaginary and that the Supreme Personality of Godhead is under the influence of *māyā*. Hearing this kind of commentary breaks the heart and life of a devotee."
>
> (*Śrī Caitanya-caritāmṛta*, *Antya-līlā* 2.96–99)

Brahmā and Śiva Also Do Not Fall

> These are examples. Brahmā became attracted with his daughter. Lord Śiva became attracted with the beauty of Mohinī-mūrti, even in the presence of his wife. So this sex life can be controlled only by becoming Kṛṣṇa conscious.
>
> (Room Conversation. Bombay, January 7, 1977)

The above passage may seem to imply that even Lord Brahmā and Lord Śiva, who are both pure devotees, can become bewildered by *māyā*. However, the pastimes of Brahmā and Śiva wherein they appear to be attracted by *māyā* are only meant to instruct conditioned souls.

Brahmā and Śiva occupy the highest posts in the universe – as the creator and the destroyer respectively – and conditioned souls sometimes desire such high posts. In the following conversation, Śrīla Prabhupāda cautions his audience about desiring any exalted position in this world, for all material situations are fraught with the miseries offered by *māyā*. Śrīla Prabhupāda encourages his audience to desire only pure devotion to Lord Kṛṣṇa.

> **Devotee:** It says here that a pure devotee like Haridāsa Ṭhākura would not fall victim to Māyādevī's temptations, but even Lord Brahmā, Lord Śiva, might fall victim. I always thought that they were pure devotees of the Lord.
>
> **Prabhupāda:** No. They are pure devotees, but they are *guṇāvatāra* (presiding deities of the modes of nature). Just like Lord Brahmā is the supreme personality within this material universe. He's the father of all living entities. So they are pure devotees. Of course, if we very scrutinizingly study, Haridāsa Ṭhākura is, in devotional service, in a greater position than Brahmā, although he is considered the incarnation of Brahmā – Brahmā Haridāsa.
>
> So we should not be disturbed when we see Lord Brahmā and Lord Śiva are captivated in that way. We should take this instruction, that is, "Lord Brahmā or Lord Śiva become victim of *māyā* sometimes, what to speak of us? Therefore we shall be very, very careful. There is chance of fall-down even in the status of Brahmā and Śiva, what to speak of ordinary persons. Therefore we should be very strongly inclined to Kṛṣṇa consciousness like Haridāsa Ṭhākura. Then we shall be able very easily to overcome the allurement of *māyā*." That is to be understood. Not that "Brahmā showed weakness. He is weak or he is less." No. That is for our instruction.
>
> (Lecture on *Bhagavad-gītā* 2.62–72.
> Los Angeles, December 16, 1968)

These quotes show that Brahmā and Śiva, as pure devotees of Kṛṣṇa, assist the Lord in giving His instructions to the souls of this universe.

> The sages like Marīci were not in the wrong in submitting their protests against the acts of their great father [Brahmā]. They knew very well that even though their father committed a mistake, there must have been some great purpose behind the show; otherwise such a great personality could not have committed such a mistake. It might be that Brahmā wanted to warn his subordinates about human frailties in their dealings with women.
>
> (*Śrīmad-Bhāgavatam* 3.12.29)

> The illusory, material energy is represented by Durgādevī, who is the wife of Girīśa, or Lord Śiva. Durgādevī could not captivate Lord Śiva's mind, but now that Lord Śiva wanted to see Lord Viṣṇu's feminine form, Lord Viṣṇu, by His mystic power, would assume a form that would captivate even Lord Śiva. Therefore Lord Viṣṇu was grave and at the same time was smiling.
>
> (*Śrīmad-Bhāgavatam* 8.12.14)

> The Supreme Personality of Godhead knew that because Lord Śiva is not an ordinary person, he cannot be bewildered even by the most beautiful woman. Cupid himself tried to invoke Lord Śiva's lusty desires in the presence of Pārvatī, but Lord Śiva was never agitated. Rather, the blazing fire from Lord Śiva's eyes turned Cupid to ashes. Therefore, Lord Viṣṇu had to think twice about what kind of beautiful form would bewilder even Lord Śiva.
>
> (*Śrīmad-Bhāgavatam* 8.12.15)

Brahmā and Śiva are not ordinary souls and are not subjected to temptation. They remain free from the lure of *māyā*; rather they are under the influence of *yogamāyā* – so what to speak of the residents of the spiritual abodes of the Lord. In fact, Brahmā and Śiva worship the residents of the Lord's abodes, especially the residents of Vṛndāvana.

Other Examples

There are innumerable other examples of personalities in scriptural history whom conditioned souls like us cannot understand without the help of pure devotees like Śrīla Prabhupāda and his disciplic succession. For example, *Śrīmad-Bhāgavatam* relates the history of Śrī Kṛṣṇa's associates and personal family members who, just before the Lord's disappearance, fought with and killed eachother after having become intoxicated by drinking rice-wine. In this regard Śrīla Visvanātha Cakravārti Thākura, whose commentaries are often quoted by Śrīla Prabhupāda, states that this was just like a magic show performed by the greatest magician, Śrī Kṛṣṇa Himself, in order to return them to their abodes.

Another example is the history of the 'demon' Śiśupāla, Kṛṣṇa's cousin, who tried to kill Kṛṣṇa and who was finally beheaded by him. How is it possible that Kṛṣṇa's cousin could become a demon? In this regard, Prabhupāda's *Śrīmad-Bhāgavatam* translations and purports reveal that by entering Kṛṣṇa's body after being 'killed' by Him, Śiśupāla 're-entered' Vaikuṇṭha as one of the Lord's two associates, Jaya and Vijaya. Moreover, Jaya and Vijaya had never left Vaikuṇṭha. According to our *ācāryas*, their original forms remained in Vaikuṇṭha and, in order to fulfill the Lord's desire for chivalrous fighting, their expansions played the role of demons in this world.

Another example is the history of Choṭa Haridāsa, which is mercifully translated by Prabhupāda in his *Śrī Caitanya-caritāmrta*. In that history Śrī Caitanya Mahāprabhu chastised and rejected His associate, Choṭa Haridāsa, who was in the renounced order and at the same time looked lustfully at a lady. How is it possible that Mahāprabhu's dear associate could fall into lust? Śrīla Prabhupāda quotes the version of his Guru Mahārāja, Śrīla Bhaktisiddhānta Sarasvatī Ṭhākura, who said that Śrī Caitanya Mahāprabhu, the ocean of mercy, chastised Choṭa Haridāsa, although Choṭa Haridāsa was His dear devotee, in order to establish that one in the devotional line should not be a hypocrite. Choṭa Haridāsa did not actually fall.

Another example is the history of Kālā Kṛṣṇadāsa, who was assigned by Mahāprabhu's devotees to carry His waterpot and other belongings while He travelled through South India. During these travels Kālā Kṛṣṇadāsa was influenced and allured by gypsies who enticed him with women. Mahāprabhu' saved Kālā Kṛṣṇadāsa from this plight but later, despite Kālā Kṛṣṇadāsa's tears, He rejected him from His company. However, even though the Lord rejected him, His confidential devotees mercifully gave him another chance. They considered, "We want a person to go to Bengal just to inform Śacīmātā about Śrī Caitanya Mahāprabhu's arrival at Jagannātha Purī." Thus they engaged him as an instrument in pleasing the Lord's pure devotees.

Did Kālā Kṛṣṇadāsa fall from the spiritual world and was then reinstated? In the spiritual world are no gypsies to allure the eternal, liberated associates of Śrī Kṛṣṇa. Prabhupāda writes in *Śrī Caitanya-caritāmṛta, Madhya-līlā* 7.39:

> This Kṛṣṇadāsa, known as Kālā Kṛṣṇadāsa, is not the Kālā Kṛṣṇadāsa mentioned in the Eleventh Chapter, verse 37, of the *Ādi-līlā*. The Kālā Kṛṣṇadāsa mentioned in the Eleventh Chapter is one of the twelve *gopālas* (cowherd boys) who appeared to substantiate the pastimes of Lord Caitanya Mahāprabhu. He is known as a great devotee of Lord Nityānanda Prabhu. The *brāhmaṇa* named Kālā Kṛṣṇadāsa who went with Śrī Caitanya to South India and later

to Bengal is mentioned in the *Madhya-līlā*, Tenth Chapter, verses 62–79. One should not take these two to be the same person.

In this world there are many fortunate souls who come in contact with Śrī Caitanya Mahāprabhu during His manifest pastimes here, and they all benefit tremendously. They get further purified by contact with the Lord and His associates, and then attain perfection. Still, they are in this world because they originally desired to enjoy sense gratification. That is the teaching in this pastime.

One may inquire why his name is mentioned in *Śrī Caitanya-caritāmṛta*, *Ādi-līlā* 10.145 as being a branch of *prema-kalpataru*, Śrī Caitanya Mahāprabhu. The answer is given by Śrīla Prabhupāda's *guru*, Śrīla Bhaktisiddhānta Sarasvatī Ṭhākura, in his lecture delivered in 1933 and which is published in *Gauḍīya*, Eleventh Year, Issue Forty-one, pages 646-648. This was a very important discussion about Choṭa Haridāsa, and Jagāi and Mādhāi, wherein he also shed light on the topic of Kālā Kṛṣṇadāsa.

He states that Śrīman Mahāprabhu had rejected Kālā Kṛṣṇadāsa at first, but by the mercy of Śrīman Nityānanda Prabhu and his own genuine repentence he was again reinstated as servant of Mahāprabhu. It was due to Nityānanda prabhu's mercy alone that he was later added as a branch of Mahāprabhu's *prema-kalpataru*. It is not that he was previously an eternal associate.

By this pastime Mahāprabhu taught that one has to be extremely careful while practicing devotional process because until we have reached perfection we may become allured by Mahāprabhu's illusory *māyā*. In *Śrī Caitanya-caritāmṛta*, *Madhya-līlā* 17.14 Mahāprabhu told His associates:

> "Such a person must be a new man, and he must have a peaceful mind. If I can obtain such a man, I shall agree to take him with Me."

Śrīla Prabhupāda writes in his purport:

> Formerly, when Śrī Caitanya Mahāprabhu went to South India, a *brāhmaṇa* named Kālā Kṛṣṇadāsa went with Him. Kālā Kṛṣṇadāsa fell victim to a woman, and Śrī Caitanya Mahāprabhu had to take the trouble to free him from the clutches of the gypsies. Therefore the Lord here says that He wants a new man who is peaceful in mind. One whose mind is not peaceful is agitated by certain drives,

especially sex desire, even though he be in the company of Caitanya Mahāprabhu… *Māyā* is so strong that unless one is determined not to fall victim, even the Supreme Personality of Godhead cannot give protection.

The Supreme Lord and His representative always want to give protection, but a person must take advantage of their personal contact. If one thinks that the Supreme Personality of Godhead or His representative is an ordinary man, he will certainly fall down. Thus Śrī Caitanya Mahāprabhu did not want a person like Kālā Kṛṣṇadāsa to accompany Him. He wanted someone who was determined, who had a peaceful mind, and who was not agitated by ulterior motives.

In his lecture of May 3, 2001, Śrīla Nārāyaṇa Gosvāmī Mahārāja supports the version of Śrīla Kṛṣṇadāsa Kavirāja and Śrīla Prabhupāda thus:

> Śrī Caitanya Mahāprabhu's personal servant, Kālā Kṛṣṇadāsa, went with Him to South India for about four months. He did not have a taste for chanting, remembering or hearing *hari-katha*, but he was helping Mahāprabhu. He was very lucky to serve, but he had no taste. Mahāprabhu was chanting, "Hare Kṛṣṇa, Hare Kṛṣṇa" in all the temples and making everyone Vaiṣṇavas, but what became of His servant?
>
> This fellow had no taste. He had never said to Mahāprabhu, "O, I want to hear *hari-katha*." He never questioned Him and he never heard His teachings. What became of him? He was attracted by the Bhaṭṭathāris, gypsy girls, who were so beautiful that in a moment he gave up Caitanya Mahāprabhu, the Supreme Personality of Godhead Kṛṣṇa Himself.

And in addition, on November 20, 2001 he said in a discourse:

> It was amazing, however, that although Kālā Kṛṣṇadāsa was traveling with the Lord, Śrī Caitanya Mahāprabhu, Mahāprabhu was not able to help him. This is because Kālā Kṛṣṇadāsa was only engaged in Mahāprabhu's external service. He did not inquire from Him about *bhakti*, neither did he have taste for His *hari-katha*, neither did he have a taste for chanting. In other words, he could not adopt Mahāprabhu's inner mood.

The Perfect Remain Perfect

The following quotes show the infallible position of self-realized devotees who are here in this world. The pure devotees in this world don't fall from their position despite the all-pervading lure of *māyā* here. What to speak, then, of those devotees in their forms as residents of the spiritual world. We can have faith in them, and faith in the world from which they come.

> Pure devotional service is so spiritually relishable that a devotee becomes automatically uninterested in material enjoyment. That is the sign of perfection in progressive devotional service. A pure devotee continuously remembers the lotus feet of Lord Śrī Kṛṣṇa and does not forget Him even for a moment, not even in exchange for all the opulence of the three worlds.
>
> (*Śrīmad-Bhāgavatam* 1.5.19, purport)

> When Uddhava was fully absorbed in the transcendental ecstasy of love of God, he actually forgot all about the external world. The pure devotee lives constantly in the abode of the Supreme Lord, even in the present body, which apparently belongs to this world. The pure devotee is not exactly on the bodily plane, since he is absorbed in the transcendental thought of the Supreme.
>
> (*Śrīmad-Bhāgavatam* .3.2.6 purport)

> **Question**: Prabhupāda, a devotee, very often, after chanting, they develop very, very high. I see a lot of devotees; they fall down back to the *māyā*. What is the reason?
>
> **Prabhupāda**: He is not a devotee. He is pretending to be a devotee. One who is a devotee never falls down. There are so many false devotees. He falls down.
>
> (Morning Walk. Toronto, June 21, 1971)

> **Question**: Often the devotee thinks that he's more unhappy than the *karmīs*, because he knows he's unhappy.
>
> **Prabhupāda**: Then that means he is not a devotee.
>
> **Question**: He's not a devotee.
>
> **Prabhupāda**: Yes. He's not a devotee. Devotee means, the first sign will be that he is happy. *Brahma-bhūtaḥ prasannātmā* (*Bhagavad-gītā* 18.54). If he's not *prasannātmā*, he's a rascal. He has not even entered devotional life. He's outside. That is the test. Just like

Dhruva Mahārāja. When he saw Viṣṇu, he said, "Everything is all right. I don't want anything. *Svāmin kṛtārtho 'smi.*" That is Vaiṣṇava. And if he is still in want or unhappiness, that means he has no spiritual life at all. He is simply making a show.

(Morning Walk. Melbourne, April 24, 1976)

The link connecting these four quotes is this concept of 'higher taste'. Śrīla Prabhupāda explains that perfect devotees experience the higher taste of service to Śrī Kṛṣṇa, and therefore the allure of *māyā* simply does not attract them. Those who have not actually reached that relishable higher taste will still have a taste for material enjoyment. *Māyā* still has the power to attract the aspiring devotee away from the path of devotion.

> The third-class person in Kṛṣṇa consciousness may fall down, but when one is in the second class he does not fall down, and for the first-class person in Kṛṣṇa consciousness there is no chance of falling down.
>
> (*Bhagavad-gītā* 9.3, purport)

> There is no possibility that a first-class devotee will fall down, even though he may mix with non-devotees to preach.
>
> (*Śrī Caitanya-caritāmṛta, Madhya-līlā* 22.71, purport)

A false *guru* will fall prey to *māyā*, whereas a bona fide *guru*, the true devotee, never forgets Kṛṣṇa for even a moment. Such a *guru* can bring his disciples, followers, and audiences to his own level of perfection.

Śrīla Prabhupāda has written in the conclusion of his purport to Nectar of Instruction, Verse Five: "One should not become a spiritual master unless he has attained the platform of *uttama-adhikārī* [first-class devotee]. A neophyte Vaiṣṇava or a Vaiṣṇava situated on the intermediate platform can also accept disciples, but such disciples must be on the same platform, and it should be understood that they cannot advance very well toward the ultimate goal of life under his insufficient guidance. Therefore a disciple should be careful to accept an *uttama-adhikārī* as a spiritual master."

"Devarsi Narada is an example of the topmost *uttama-bhāgavata.* Sukadeva Gosvāmī belongs to the intermediate stage of *uttama-bhāgavatas* (*nirdhuta-kasaya*). Śrī Narada in his previous birth as the son of a maidservant is an example of the preliminary stage of *uttama-bhāgavatas* (*mūrcchita-kāśayā*). The association and mercy of these three kinds of *maha-bhāgavatas* is the cause of the manifestation of *śraddhā*" (*Śrī Bhakti-rasāmṛta-sindhu-bindu*, Verse 3, *Śrī Bindu-vikāśinī-vṛtti*, comment).

Our Original Position

To illustrate the conditioned souls' turning away from their inherent love and service to Kṛṣṇa, Śrīla Prabhupāda gives the analogy of sparks falling out of a fire. This analogy refers to the *jīvas* in the *taṭasthā* region who turn away from their inherent nature.

> It is stated in several places that the living entities are like sparks of a fire, and the Supreme Personality of Godhead is like the fire itself. If the sparks somehow or other fall out of the fire, they lose their natural illumination; thus it is ascertained that the living entities come into this material world exactly as sparks fall from a great fire. The living entity wants to imitate Kṛṣṇa and tries to lord it over material nature in order to enjoy sense gratification; thus he forgets his original position, and his illuminating power, his spiritual identity, is extinguished.
>
> (*Kṛṣṇa, The Supreme Personality of Godhead*, Chapter 87)

The Supreme Lord is infinitely greater than fire, and therefore the above-mentioned analogy is not fully accurate; still, mundane analogies give us at least an initial glimmer of understanding. In this connection, the phrases 'fall out of the fire,' 'lose their natural illumination,' 'forgets his original position,' and 'his spiritual identity is extinguished' do not mean to say that the soul fell to this world from Vaikuṇṭha or Goloka Vṛndāvana. Rather, the phrases are further examples of the moon-on-the-branch logic.

In the *Kṛṣṇa-book* quote above, the words 'forgets his original position' imply that love of Kṛṣṇa, pure Kṛṣṇa consciousness, is inherent, or latent, in our soul, just as the almond oil is inherent in the almond, the ghee is inherent in the milk, and the tree is inherent in its seed. Śrīla Prabhupāda confirms this conclusion in the following letter:

> Regarding your question – "What does it mean: 'We are all originally Kṛṣṇa conscious entities?' We are always with Kṛṣṇa. Where is Kṛṣṇa not present? So how can you say that we were not before? You are always with Kṛṣṇa, and when we forget this fact we

are far, far away from Him. In the *Īśopaniṣad* it is clearly stated, *tad dure tad vantike* – He is very far away, but He is very near as well.

(Letter to Upendra. Los Angeles, July 15, 1970)

So this forgetfulness is our fall-down. It can take place at any moment, and we can counteract this forgetfulness immediately by rising to the platform of Kṛṣṇa consciousness.

(Letter to Upendra. Los Angeles, July 15, 1970)

The following excerpt also includes the words 'forget' and 'original,' and it further establishes their meaning in the context of *jīva-tattva*, the truth of the soul:

You are Christian; you can change your faith tomorrow. The Sanskrit word religion does not mean faith. Religion means the original characteristic. That is called religion. So the original characteristic means that it cannot be changed. That quality, that characteristic, is always with us. The Vedic version is that the living entity is an eternal servant of God. When he forgets this relationship, that he is the eternal servant of God, this means that his material existence begins.

(Lecture at St. Pascal's Franciscan Seminary. Melbourne, June 28, 1974)

As Prabhupāda explains above, in discussing *jīva-tattva* the word 'original' means 'unchangeable' or 'that which is inherent or dormant in us.' This is further confirmed in the following statement:

Since Kṛṣṇa consciousness is inherent in every living entity, everyone should be given a chance to hear about Kṛṣṇa. Simply by hearing and chanting – *śravaṇaṁ kīrtanam* – one's heart is directly purified, and one's original Kṛṣṇa consciousness is immediately awakened.

(*Nectar of Instruction*, Verse 4, purport)

Our Natural Position

In the quotes below, Śrīla Prabhupāda uses the phrase 'natural position' to explain the soul's inherent nature to be Kṛṣṇa conscious, just as ghee is inherent in milk or almond oil is inherent in the almond.

> Eternally conditioned means... We cannot be eternally conditioned, because we are part and parcel of Kṛṣṇa. Our natural position is ever liberated, eternally liberated. But because we wanted to imitate Kṛṣṇa, we wanted to become Kṛṣṇa as the Māyāvādīs want to do, therefore [we are conditioned.] In the spiritual world, Kṛṣṇa is the only enjoyer.
>
> (Lecture on *Śrīmad-Bhāgavatam* 1.10.5. Māyāpur, June 20, 1973)

The word 'regaining' below has the same meaning as 'reviving.' In connection with *jīva-tattva*, 'to revive' means to awaken what is inherent, as the tree is inherent within the seed.

Below, Śrīla Prabhupāda explains how the soul's natural position, his inherent and dormant potency for Kṛṣṇa consciousness, is eternally present within.

> There are certain prescribed methods for employing our senses and mind in such a way that our dormant consciousness for loving Kṛṣṇa will be invoked, as much as the child, with a little practice, can begin to walk. One who has no basic walking capacity cannot walk by practice. Similarly, Kṛṣṇa consciousness cannot be aroused simply by practice. Actually there is no such practice. When we wish to develop our innate capacity for devotional service, there are certain processes which, by our accepting and executing them, will cause that dormant capacity to be invoked. Such practice is called *sādhana-bhakti*.
>
> (*Nectar of Devotion*, Chapter 2)

Here is another analogy showing how 'natural' means that something is present in a latent stage, but has not yet developed. Prabhupāda explains this as follows:

> *Prema* is not something you have to get outside. It is already there. Just like a young boy, young girl. As soon as they meet, there is natural attraction. That is already there. It is not that he has brought this attraction, purchased it from some shopkeeper. No. It is already there. Simply by combination it becomes aroused. That's all. Similarly, *kṛṣṇa-prema* is there.
>
> (Lecture on *Bhagavad-gītā* 2.22. Hyderabad, November 26, 1972)

This final quote below concludes the theme of Part Three of *Journey of the Soul*: the spirit souls in this world have yet to manifest their spiritual forms, which are now lying in seed.

> In further reference to your question about the form of the spirit soul of the conditioned living entity, there is a spiritual form always, but it develops fully only when the living entity goes back to Vaikuṇṭha. This form develops according to the desire of the living entity. Until this perfectional stage is reached, the form is lying dormant like the form of the tree is lying dormant in the seed.
>
> (Letter to Rūpānuga. Los Angeles, August 8, 1969)

The above-mentioned quotes establish that once we become pure devotees by taking shelter of Śrī Kṛṣṇa's associate, the bona fide self-realized spiritual master, and by following the process of *bhakti-yoga*, we develop our spiritual forms. Then we, like all the other residents of Vaikuṇṭha and Goloka Vṛndāvana, reside there for eternity in unlimited happiness.

We can have faith in that realm, as stated by Śrīla Prabhupāda's *paratpara-guru*, Śrīla Bhaktivinoda Ṭhākura, in his *Jaiva-dharma* (Chapter Sixteen): "Inasmuch as they reside in the spiritual world, *māyā* stays far from them and does not affect them at all. Always absorbed in the bliss of serving their worshipable Lord, they are eternally liberated and completely unaware of material happiness and distress. Their life is love alone, and they are not even conscious of misery, death or fear."

Part Four

OVERVIEW

Overview

An End Note from the Editors

There are two categories of *vibhinnāṁśa jīvas*, not three. The *jīvas* who are manifest in the spiritual world are eternally liberated (*nitya-mukta*) *vibhinnāṁśa jīvas*; and the *jīvas* who manifest in the *taṭasthā* region and who look from there towards the spiritual world are also eternally liberated (*nitya-mukta*) *vibhinnāṁśa jīvas*. The *jīvas* who look towards the material world from the *taṭasthā* region are called conditioned souls, *nitya-baddha* (or *nitya-saṁsāra*) *vibhinnāṁśa jīvas*.

Although the *jīvas* manifested by Baladeva and His expansions in the spiritual worlds are eternal associates (*nitya-pārṣadas*), they are technically *vibhinnāṁśa-tattva*, or *vibhinnāṁśa jīvas*. *Jaiva-dharma* states, "When He (Kṛṣṇa) is situated in the *jīva-śakti*, He manifests His *svarūpa* as Baladeva." It also states, "Innumerable *nitya-pārṣada jīvas* manifest from Śrī Baladeva Prabhu to serve Vṛndāvana-vihārī Śrī Kṛṣṇa as His eternal associates in Goloka Vṛndāvana, and others manifest from Śrī Saṅkarṣaṇa to serve the Lord of Vaikuṇṭha, Śrī Nārāyaṇa, in the spiritual world."

Evidence that there are two kinds of *jīva* is given in the discourse entitled "Origin of the Living Entity" (Part One, Chapter Three) as follows:

sei vibhinnāṁśa jīva – dui ta' prakāra
eka – 'nitya-mukta', eka – 'nitya-saṁsāra'

'nitya-mukta' nitya kṛṣṇa-carane unmukha
'kṛṣṇa-pāriṣada' nāma, bhuñje sevā-sukha

(*Śrī Caitanya-caritāmṛta, Madhya-līlā* 22.10–11)

The living entities [*jīvas*] are divided into two categories. Some are eternally liberated and others are eternally conditioned. Those who are eternally liberated are always awake to Kṛṣṇa consciousness, and they render transcendental loving service at the feet of Kṛṣṇa. They are eternal associates of Kṛṣṇa, and eternally enjoy the transcendental bliss of serving Him.

"Origin of the Living Entity" also quotes Śrīla Jīva Gosvāmī:

tad evam anantā eva jīvākhyās taṭasthāḥ śaktayaḥ
tatra tāsāṁ varga-dvayam eko vargo' nādita eva bhagavad-
unmukhaḥ anyas tv anādita eva bhagavat-parāṅmukhaḥ
svabhāvatas tadīya-jñāna-bhāvāt tadīya-jñānābhāvāt ca

(*Paramātma-sandarbha, Anuccheda* 47, Text 1)

Thus the Lord's marginal potency is comprised of individual spirit souls. Although these individual spirit souls are limitless in number, they may be divided into two groups: (1) the souls who from time immemorial are favorable to the Supreme Lord; and (2) the rebellious souls who from time immemorial are averse to the Supreme Lord. One group is aware of the Lord's glories and the other group is not aware of them.

Śrīla Jīva Gosvāmī continues:

tatra prathamo 'ntaraṅgā-śakti-vilāsānugṛhīto / nitya-bhagavat-parikara-rūpo garuḍādikaḥ / thoktaṁ pādmottara-khaṇḍe tri-pad-vibhūter / lokas tu ity adau bhagavat-sandarbhodāhṛte
asya ca taṭasthatvaṁ jīvatva-prasiddher īśvaratva-koṭāv apraveśāt

(*Paramātma-sandarbha, Anuccheda* 47, Text 2)

The first group consists of Garuḍa and the other eternal associates of the Lord. These devotees take shelter of the Lord's internal potency and enjoy pastimes with Him. They reside in the spiritual world, which will be described in the *Bhagavat-*

> *sandarbha* (*Anuccheda* 78). They are termed as '*taṭasthā*' because they are famous as *jīvas* and they do not enter the category of Īśvara (God).

When the word '*taṭasthā*' is used to refer to the eternal associates, as mentioned in the verse above, it does not mean that such souls have a tendency to look towards either the spiritual world or the material world. They are too far away from *māyā* to see it. In this connection it means that they are very close to being God in the sense that they have qualities like God's – but they are not God. They are qualitatively one with Him as confirmed in all the Vedic scriptures (*sākṣād-dharitvena samasta-śāstraih*), and at the same time they are His most confidential servants (*kintu prabhor yaḥ priya eva tasya*).

They are close to being God in quality, but they are not God because (1) He is *vibhu* (unlimited) and they are *aṇu* (infinitesimal), and (2) He is the energetic source of all energies and they are always His energy. They are not God and they are not made of *māyā-śakti*; they are pure, transcendental, and free from material qualities. Thus they are called *taṭasthā*, or situated in the marginal category.

A problem in harmonizing the various references of the word *taṭasthā* in its different contexts arises from daily usage and emotional connotations associated with it. Many of us may not be familiar with *taṭasthā* in reference to Kṛṣṇa's eternal associates, and therefore we see the word as minimizing their greatness and making them somewhat equal to us *nitya-baddhas*. We tend to think like this when we read Śrīla Bhakivinoda Ṭhākura's beautiful explanation in *Jaiva-dharma*, Chapter Sixteen, stating that the *jīvas* manifest by Baladeva in the spiritual world and the *jīvas* manifest by Mahā-Viṣṇu in the *taṭasthā* region are essentially the same in quality. Chapter Sixteen states:

> These *nitya-pārṣadās* are eternally engaged in serving their object of worship, the Supreme Godhead, who is absorbed in *rasa* ... They are forever extremely spiritually potent, being imbued with the *cit-śakti* of the Lord. They have no connection with *māyā* – they are even unmindful of her existence ... *Prema* being their life and soul, they do not even know that lamentation, death, or fear actually exist.
>
> Also, countless, infinitesimal *jīvas* emanate from Kāraṇodakaśāyī Mahā-Viṣṇu, lying within the Causal Ocean, whose glance impregnates the *māyā-śakti*. As these *jīvas* are the neighbours of *māyā*, they

> witness her variegatedness. **The symptoms of the *jīvas* as discussed earlier are also present in these *jīvas*.** However, because they are minuscule in size and situated at the margin, their constitutional nature is to look at both the material world and the spiritual sky. Their marginal condition makes them vulnerable because – up to this point of time – they have not been reinforced with *cit-bala*, the strength of spiritual potency, by the mercy of the Supreme Lord, their worshipable object.

A necessity therefore arises to consider the alternative interpretation of *taṭasthā* mentioned by Śrīla Jīva Gosvāmī, which glorifies the qualitative oneness of the *nitya-pārṣada jīvas* with God, and their intimate, confidential relationship with Him. We need not be limited to the understanding of *taṭasthā* which refers to a provisional concept of the geographical location of origin. The Sanskrit language is extremely deep and no one word has only one meaning. The understanding associated with *taṭasthā* as a 'place' does not preclude the way in which it has been used by Śrīla Jīva Gosvāmī and Śrīla Kṛṣṇadāsa Kavirāja Gosvāmī.

When we hear or read, "Garuḍa, the great bird-carrier of Lord Viṣṇu, the *nitya-siddha pārṣada* of the Lord, is a *taṭasthā-śakti jīva*," we may say, "That is absurd *apasiddhānta*." This may be because we feel we are being told to believe that Garuḍa emanated from Mahā-Viṣṇu in the region between the spiritual and material worlds. On the basis of that interpretation of the word, it is of course absurd *apasiddhānta*.

As mentioned above, Śrīla Bhaktivinoda Ṭhākura explains in *Jaiva-dharma* that the *nitya-pārṣada jīvas* manifested from Baladeva and the *jīvas* manifest in the *taṭasthā* region from Kāraṇodakaśāyī Viṣṇu are essentially the same in quality: "Although they have all the qualities of the [*nitya-pārṣada*] *jīvas* I have already described, because of their minute and marginal nature, they sometimes look to the spiritual world, and sometimes to the material world."

Of course, to respect the eternal associates as being far superior to us in every respect is healthy, advantageous, and positive. Still, on a theoretical level, to say the associates of the Lord are not technically *vibhinnāṁśa jīvas* creates the necessity of making another special category for them in addition to the standard two types of expansions, namely *svaṁśa* and *vibhinnāṁśa*. With the exception of *kāyavyūha-rūpa* (direct expansions of Śrī Rādhā), there is no extra category mentioned in the writings of our Gosvāmīs.

Thus, the *vibhinnāṁśa* categorization here applies to those who are *nitya-mukta* (i.e. never conditioned [*baddha*] at any time) and *nitya-baddha* (having never been in the spiritual world at any time). The *nitya-mukta* category will therefore include *nitya-pārṣada jīvas* (eternal associates), who come from Baladeva, and also the *jīvas* who came from Kāraṇodakaśāyī Viṣṇu, who fortunately looked toward *yogamāyā* rather than *mahāmāyā*, and then became associates. According to their sphere of action they are differently termed as '*nitya-siddha*' ['*nitya-mukta*'] and '*sādhana-siddha*' when they are situated in the spiritual realm, and '*sādhaka*' and '*nitya-baddha*' when situated in the material realm.

It is stated in *Jaiva-dharma*, Chapter Fifteen:

> Kṛṣṇa establishes Himself in each of His *śaktis*, and manifests His *svarūpa* according to the nature of that *śakti*. When He is situated in the *cit-svarūpa*, He manifests His essential *svarūpa*, both as Śrī Kṛṣṇa Himself, and also as Nārāyaṇa, the Lord of Vaikuṇṭha; when He is situated in the *jīva-śakti*, He manifests His *svarūpa* as His *vilāsa-mūrti* of Vraja, Baladeva; and when He situates Himself in the *māyā-śakti*, He manifests the three Viṣṇu forms: Kāraṇodakaśāyī, Garbhodakaśāyī, and Kṣīrodakaśāyī.
>
> In His Kṛṣṇa form He manifests **all the spiritual affairs to the superlative degree**. In His Baladeva *svarūpa* as *śeṣa-tattva*[1], He manifests *nitya-mukta-pārṣada-jīvas* who render eight types of service to Kṛṣṇa Himself, the origin of *śeṣa-tattva*. Again, as *śeṣa-rūpa* Saṅkarṣaṇa in Vaikuṇṭha, He manifests eight types of servants to render eight kinds of services as eternally liberated associates of *śeṣī-rūpa* Nārāyaṇa.
>
> Mahā-Viṣṇu, who is an expansion of Saṅkarṣaṇa, situates Himself in the heart of the *jīva-śakti*, and as Paramātmā manifests the *jīvas* in the material world. These *jīvas* are susceptible to the influence of *māyā*, and unless they attain the shelter of the *hlādinī-śakti* by Bhagavān's mercy, it is possible that they will be defeated by *māyā*. The countless conditioned *jīvas* who have been illusioned by *māyā* are under the control of the three modes of material nature.

As stated above, Baladeva is the predominating Deity of *jīva-śakti*. He is also the predominating Deity of *sandhinī-śakti*, which maintains

1 Baladeva is *śeṣa-tattva*. This means that He assumes varieties of forms to serve Kṛṣṇa, and also He manifests as Lord Śeṣa, who also manifests in various forms for service. For more information, kindly refer to *Śrī Caitanya-caritāmṛta*, *Ādi-līlā* 5.8–11 and 5.123–124.

and manifests all the variegatedness of the spiritual world. He is both. As stated in Śrīla Nārāyaṇa Gosvāmī Mahārāja's *Śrī Prabandhāvalī*, Chapter Eight:

> **Kṛṣṇa's** first extension is Baladeva. **Kṛṣṇa's stick, the peacock feather in Kṛṣṇa's crown, all of Kṛṣṇa's paraphernalia, the** *gopīs'* **paraphernalia, Vṛndāvana-dhāma** – all of these are manifest by *sandhinī-śakti*, and the embodiment of that potency is Baladeva Prabhu. The embodiment of *hlādinī-śakti* is Rādhikā, and Kṛṣṇa is the possessor of *cit-śakti*. These three together are *sac-cid-ānanda*, the complete form of Kṛṣṇa (eternity, knowledge, and bliss). Neither Rādhikā nor Baladeva are separate from Him; together They are one. From Baladeva Prabhu alone, all the eternally perfected devotees of Kṛṣṇa are manifest.

While the *jīva* is a manifestation of *jīva-tattva*, the *sandhinī-vṛtti* [*vṛtti* means 'function' or 'activity'] of *svarūpa-śakti* is present in him. Like Kṛṣṇa Himself, the pure form of the *jīva* is by constitution *sac-cid-ānanda* (*Bhagavad-gītā* 15.7). It is stated in *Jaiva-dharma*, Chapter Fourteen:

> **Bābājī**: *Jīva-śakti* is the atomic (*anu*) potency of *svarūpa-śakti*, and all three aspects of *svarūpa-śakti* are present in it to a minute (*anu*) degree. Thus, the *hlādinī-vṛtti* is always present in the *jīva* in the form of spiritual bliss; *saṁvit-vṛtti* is present in the form of transcendental knowledge; and *sandhinī-vṛtti* is always present in the *jīva's* minute form (as *anu-caitanya*).

In addition to being the predominating Deity of *jīva-śakti* and *sandhinī-śakti*, Baladeva Prabhu is also the *akhaṇḍa-guru-tattva*, meaning the undivided, original principle of *guru*. Many merciful *ācāryas* in *guru-paramparā* come to this world and teach us the truths of the inconceivable *jīva*.

Śrīla Nārāyaṇa Gosvāmī Mahārāja's writes in his *Veṇu-gīta*, *Ānanda-varddhinī* commentary:

> These *gopīs* are of three types: Śrīmatī Rādhikā's *kāya-vyūha*, the *nitya-siddha*, and the *sādhana-siddha gopīs*. Those who directly appear from Śrīmatī Rādhikā are called *kāya-vyūha*. Śrīmatī Rādhikā expands Herself in many forms to enrich the flavors of Kṛṣṇa's pastimes. *Nitya-siddha* (eternally perfect) *gopīs* are *jīva-tattva* appearing from Baladeva Prabhu. They are never bound by *māyā*.

Regarding the *gopīs* and other consorts who are not *jīvas*, as mentioned in the reference above they are plenary expansions of *svarūpa-śakti* Śrīmatī Rādhikā. We find the following in *Śrī Caitanya-caritāmṛta*, *Ādi-līlā* 4.76–81:

> Just as the fountainhead, Lord Kṛṣṇa, is the cause of all incarnations [*svaṁśa*], so Śrī Rādhā is the cause of all these consorts. The goddesses of fortune are partial manifestations of Śrīmatī Rādhikā, and the queens are reflections of Her image. The goddesses of fortune are Her plenary portions, and they display the forms of *vaibhava-vilāsa*. The queens are of the nature of Her *vaibhava-prakāśa*. The *vraja-devīs* have diverse bodily features. They are Her expansions [*kāya-vyūha rūpa*] and are the instruments for expanding *rasa*. Without many consorts, there is not such exultation in *rasa*. Therefore there are many manifestations of Śrīmatī Rādhārāṇī to assist in the Lord's pastimes. Among them are various groups of consorts in Vraja who have varieties of sentiments and mellows. They help Lord Kṛṣṇa taste all the sweetness of the *rāsa* dance and other pastimes.

Śrīla Nārāyaṇa Gosvāmī Mahārāja has elaborately explained in his *Pinnacle of Devotion*, in the chapter entitled "Supreme Chastity," that we conditioned *jīvas* of this world can attain the position of *sādhana-siddha* as one of the five kinds of *sakhīs* of Śrīmatī Rādhikā, namely Her maidservant (*nitya-sakhī*), under the guidance of Śrī Rūpa Mañjarī and her followers.

References:

Śrī Caitanya-caritāmṛta, Ādi līlā 4.76–81, *Ādi-līlā* 5.8–11, *Ādi-līlā* 5.123–124, *Madhya-līlā* 8.164, *Madhya-līlā* 22.9–13
Śrī Caitanya Mahāprabhu kī Śikṣā (Hindi), 6th *Paricched* (*Jīva-tattva*), p 77–78
Paramātma-sandarbha, Anuccheda 47, 1–2
Veṇu-gīta, Verses 3–4, *Ananda-varddhinī Vyākhyā*
Pinnacle of Devotion, Supreme Chastity
Jaiva-dharma, Chapter 14–17
Bhakti-rasāmṛta-sindhu 3.2.56 (*Dāsya-parikāras*)
Bhakti-rasāmṛta-sindhu 3.3.53 (*Sakhya-parikāras*)

Part Five

ABOUT THE AUTHORS

Śrīla Bhaktivinoda Ṭhākura

The following is an excerpt from Śrīla Bhakti Prajñāna Keśava Gosvāmī Mahārāja's introduction to Jaiva-dharma.

Śrīla Bhaktivinoda Ṭhākura has broadcast the transcendental instructions of Śrī Caitanya Mahāprabhu in many different languages. He has written approximately one hundred books in Sanskrit, Bengali, Oriya, Hindi, Urdu, and English. When one sees the list of his books, one can easily infer that the author was a vastly learned scholar of many different languages.

I think it necessary at this point to shed some light on a special feature of the author's life. Although he was a pre-eminent scholar of Western thought, he was completely free from Western influences. Western educators say, "Don't follow me; follow my words." In other words, "Don't do as I do; do as I say." The life of Śrīla Bhaktivinoda Ṭhākura refutes this principle, for he personally applied and demonstrated all the instructions of his books in his own life. Therefore, his instructions and manner of *bhajana* are known as *bhaktivinoda-dhārā* (the line of Bhaktivinoda).

There is not a single instruction in his books that he did not personally follow. There is no disparity between his writings and his life, between his actions and his words. They are one in all respects.

It is natural for readers to be curious to learn about a great personality who possesses such extraordinary character. Modern readers in particular, who seek to know about any subject, cannot have faith in an author's writings without being acquainted with the author himself. Therefore, I am submitting a few words about Śrīla Bhaktivinoda Ṭhākura.

When it comes to discussing the life of great, self-realized personalities who are transcendental to mortal existence, it would be a mistake to consider their birth, life span, and departure from the vision of this world to be similar to that of mere mortals. They are beyond birth and death, they are situated in eternal existence, and their coming and going from this world is strictly a matter of their own appearance and disappearance.

Śrīla Bhaktivinoda Ṭhākura appeared on September 2, 1838, and thus illuminated the sky of Gauḍīya Vaiṣṇavism. He took birth in a high-class family in a village named Vīra-nagara, which is located within the Nadiyā district of West Bengal, not far from Śrīdhāma Māyāpura, the appearance place of Śrī Gaurāṅga. He disappeared from this world on June 23, 1914, in the city of Calcutta, at which time he entered the midday pastimes of Śrī Śrī Gāndharvikā-Giridhārī (Rādhā-Kṛṣṇa), who are the supreme objects of worship for the Gauḍīya Vaiṣṇavas.

In his brief lifespan of seventy-six years, he instructed the world by personally carrying out the duties of the four stages of spiritual life: *brahmacārya* (celibate student-life), *gṛhastha* (religious householder-life), *vānaprastha* (withdrawal from worldly duties), and *sannyāsa* (formal renunciation). He first underwent *brahmacārya* and obtained various elevated instructions. After that, he entered *gṛhastha* life and set an ideal example of how to maintain family members through honest and noble means. All householders should follow this example.

During his householder life, he travelled all over India as a highly placed officer in the administration and justice department of the British government of India. By his exacting discrimination and expert administrative skills, this great personality managed to regulate and bring to order even those places that were infamous as lawless states. In the midst of family duties, he astonished all his contemporaries by the religious ideal he displayed. Although engaged in pressing responsibilities, he wrote many books in different languages. If the reader studies the list of his books, he can clearly deduce Bhaktivinoda's incredible creative power.

After retiring from his government responsibilities, Śrīla Bhaktivinoda Ṭhākura adopted the stage of *vānaprastha* and intensified his spiritual practice. At that time, he established an *āśrama* at Surabhi-kuñja in Godrumadvīpa, one of the nine districts of Navadvīpa. He remained there and performed *bhajana* for a considerable time.

Later he accepted the life of an ascetic and resided at Svānanda-sukhada-kuñja, which was nearby. While residing there, he established the appearance place of Śrī Caitanya Mahāprabhu and many other places of *gaura-līlā*. In this, he followed the example of Mahāprabhu and His followers, the Six Gosvāmīs, who had discovered the birthplace and other pastime places of Śrī Kṛṣṇa.

If Śrīla Ṭhākura Bhaktivinoda had not appeared in this world, the pastime places and instructions of Śrī Gaurāṅga Mahāprabhu would have disappeared from the world. The entire world of Gauḍīya Vaiṣṇavas will therefore remain indebted to him forever. It is for this reason that he has been awarded the highest honor in the Vaiṣṇava community by being addressed as the Seventh Gosvāmī.

Śrī Śrīmad Bhaktivedānta Nārāyaṇa Gosvāmī Mahārāja

Śrī Śrīmad Bhaktivedānta Nārāyaṇa Gosvāmī Mahārāja is the glorious disciple of *oṁ viṣṇupāda* Śrī Śrīmad Bhakti Prajñāna Keśava Gosvāmī Mahārāja, who is one of the foremost leading disciples of *oṁ viṣṇupāda* Śrī Śrīmad Bhaktisiddhānta Sarasvatī Prabhupāda.

On February 7, 1921, in order to bless the entire world, Śrīla Nārāyaṇa Gosvāmī Mahārāja took his divine birth in the village of Tewaripur, near the sacred Ganges River in Bihar, India. It was here that Lord Rāmacandra killed the Taraka demon.

Śrīla Mahārāja appeared in this world on the *amāvasyā* (new moon) day, and his birth name was Śrīman Nārāyaṇa Tiwari. He was born in a very religious Trivedi *brāhmaṇa* family, and throughout his childhood he had many opportunities to regularly accompany his father to *kīrtanas* and lecture assemblies.

In February of 1946, he had his first meeting with his Gurudeva, in Śrī Navadvīpa Dhāma, West Bengal. He had traveled there from his village after meeting a disciple of Śrīla Bhaktisiddhānta Sarasvatī Ṭhākura named Śrīla Narottamānanda Brahmacārī, who had been touring in his area to preach the message of Śrī Caitanya Mahāprabhu. After some discussions with him, Śrīla Mahārāja had become convinced of the paramount position of the philosophy disseminated by the *ācāryas* in the line of Śrīla Rūpa Gosvāmī. Within days, he had left home to join the mission of his spiritual master and surrender his life to him.

Arriving in Śrī Navadvīpa Dhāma, Śrīla Mahārāja enthusiastically joined the annual *parikramā*. At the end of the *parikramā*, on Gaura-pūrṇimā, he was given both *harināma* and *dīkṣā mantras* by Śrīla Bhakti Prajñāna Keśava Gosvāmī Mahārāja, receiving the name Śrī Gaura Nārāyaṇa Brahmacārī. Soon afterward, his Gurudeva also awarded him the title 'Bhakta-bāndhava,' which means 'friend of the devotees,' as he was always serving the Vaiṣṇavas in a very pleasing manner.

Over the next seven years he traveled extensively with his Gurudeva on preaching tours throughout India. In 1952, again on Gaura-pūrṇimā, his beloved Gurudeva awarded him initiation into the sacred order of *sannyāsa*. In 1954, his Gurudeva gave him charge of the newly opened temple in Mathurā, Śrī Keśavajī Gauḍīya Maṭha. Śrīla Mahārāja then began to spend part of the year in Mathurā and the other part in Bengal, serving extensively in both areas. This continued for the next fourteen years.

His responsibility further increased when Śrīla Bhakti Prajñāna Keśava Gosvāmī Mahārāja appointed him vice-president of his institution, the Śrī Gauḍīya Vedānta Samiti, as well as editor-in-chief of its Hindi publications and monthly magazine, *Śrī Bhāgavat Patrikā*.

In 1968, his Gurudeva departed from this world and Śrīla Mahārāja personally performed all the necessary ceremonial rituals for his *samādhi*. During this time period, as a humble servitor of the Śrī Gauḍīya Vedānta Samiti, he began to organize the annual Kārtika Vraja-maṇḍala *parikramā*, which continues to take place up to this present day.

Śrīla Mahārāja was requested by his Gurudeva to translate the books of Śrīla Bhaktivinoda Ṭhākura from Bengali into his native language, Hindi. He has carried out this request by translating some of the Ṭhākura's most prominent books, such as *Jaiva-dharma*, *Caitanya-śikṣāmṛta*, *Bhakti-tattva-viveka*, *Vaiṣṇava-siddhānta-mālā*, to name only a few. All these books, as well as his translations and commentaries of other prominent *ācāryas* of the *guru-paramparā*, are presently being translated into English and other languages by his followers. Śrīla

Mahārāja has translated and published over eighty books in Hindi, and over sixty books in English. In addition, many of his English books have now been translated into other languages, including Spanish, French, German, Italian, Russian, Portuguese, Chinese, and several Indian languages.

Śrīla Mahārāja also lectured incessantly in Hindi, Bengali, and English throughout India and internationally, and all of his discourses were recorded. Several Hindi lectures have been transcribed, as well as translated into English and other languages for publication. Additionally, thousands of his English lectures have been recorded and filmed, and they are also being sent as transcriptions, audios, and videos over the internet to reach hundreds of thousands of fortunate souls.

A significant relationship in the life of Śrīla Nārāyaṇa Gosvāmī Mahārāja is his association with Śrīla Bhaktivedānta Svāmī Mahārāja, known throughout the world as Śrīla Prabhupāda, the famous preacher of Gauḍīya Vaiṣṇavism and Founder-Ācārya of ISKCON, the International Society for Kṛṣṇa Consciousness. They first met in Calcutta, in 1946, on the occasion of the inauguration of a new branch of the Gauḍīya Vedānta Samiti when they had both come to render their services. Along with Śrīla Mahārāja's Gurudeva, Śrīla Prabhupāda Bhaktivedānta Svāmī Mahārāja is one of the founding members of the Gauḍīya Vedānta Samiti.

Śrīla Nārāyaṇa Gosvāmī Mahārāja accompanied his Gurudeva to Jhansi, where Śrīla Prabhupāda, or Abhaya Caraṇāravinda Prabhu as he was formerly known, had been trying to start a Vaiṣṇava society named The League of Devotees. A few years later, in the early fifties, Abhaya Caraṇāravinda Prabhu came to reside in Mathurā at Śrī Keśavajī Gauḍīya Maṭha, on the invitation of his god-brother, Śrīla Bhakti Prajñāna Keśava Gosvāmī Mahārāja, and he remained there for some months. Sharing regular devotional exchanges and deep discussions of Vaiṣṇava *siddhānta* with him, Śrīla Nārāyaṇa Gosvāmī Mahārāja developed a still further intimate relationship with him during this time period, regarding him both as his *śikṣā-guru* and bosom friend.

In 1959 Śrīla Bhakti Prajñāna Keśava Gosvāmī Mahārāja initiated Abhaya Caraṇāravinda Prabhu into the sacred *sannyāsa* order, giving him the *sannyāsī* name and title Śrī Śrīmad Bhaktivedānta Svāmī Mahārāja, and the ceremony of Vedic fire *yajña* and all the rituals were personally performed by Śrīla Nārāyaṇa Gosvāmī Mahārāja. Śrīla Prabhupāda Bhaktivedānta Svāmī Mahārāja was already residing in

Vṛndāvana during this period, first at the Vaṁśī Gopāla Mandira and a few years later at the Śrī Śrī Rādhā-Dāmodara Mandira, and Śrīla Nārāyaṇa Gosvāmī Mahārāja would often go there to visit him. He would cook for him and honor *prasādam* with him, and they would exchange intimate discussions on Vaiṣṇava philosophy.

When Śrīla Prabhupāda went to preach in the West and succeeded in starting the first Rādhā-Kṛṣṇa temple in America, Śrīla Nārāyaṇa Gosvāmī Mahārāja sent him the first *mṛdaṅga* drums and *karatālas* that he would be using for *saṅkīrtana*. Śrīla Bhaktivedānta Svāmī Mahārāja maintained regular correspondence every month or two with Śrīla Bhakti Prajñāna Keśava Gosvāmī Mahārāja and Śrīla Nārāyaṇa Gosvāmī Mahārāja up until 1968, when Śrīla Keśava Gosvāmī Mahārāja entered *nitya-līlā*. After that, he continued to write Śrīla Nārāyaṇa Gosvāmī Mahārāja, until his own divine departure in 1977.

Toward the end of his manifest stay in this world, he requested Śrīla Nārāyaṇa Gosvāmī Mahārāja several times to kindly give his association to his western disciples and help them to understand the deep truths of the Vaiṣṇava philosophy in the line of Śrīla Rūpa Gosvāmī. Śrīla Nārāyaṇa Gosvāmī Mahārāja humbly agreed to honor his request, considering him to be one of his worshipable *śikṣā-gurus*. Śrīla Prabhupāda also requested Śrīla Mahārāja to take complete charge of performing all the rituals for his *samādhi* after his departure. Both of these requests clearly demonstrated his firm and utter confidence in Śrīla Mahārāja.

For three decades since Śrīla Prabhupāda's departure from the vision of this world in November 1977, Śrīla Mahārāja unwaveringly carried out this final request, by providing insightful guidance and loving shelter to all who would come to him seeking it. Through the medium of his English books and extensive world touring, he gave his association and divine realizations to Śrīla Prabhupāda's followers and all other sincere searchers throughout the globe. Until he was ninety years of age, he would regularly travel throughout India and abroad, preaching the glories of Śrī Caitanya Mahāprabhu and Śrī Śrī Rādhā-Kṛṣṇa, and the true glory of ISKCON's Founder-Ācārya Śrīla Prabhupāda and his entire *guru-paramparā*.

Śrīla Nārāyaṇa Gosvāmī Mahārāja completed thirty-one world preaching tours. In many countries he was invited to prominent Hindu temples to give lectures on India's Vedic *sanātana-dharma*, and in India dignitaries would regularly invite him to speak at their spiritual programs. A prominent member of the Brahma-Madhva-Gauḍīya disciplic succession, he is highly acclaimed throughout India as a spiritual scholar and teacher, and as a pure devotee of Lord Śrī Kṛṣṇa in the line of Śrī Caitanya Mahāprabhu. He is recognized as a strict follower of Vedic culture, Hindu *sanātana-dharma*, Vaiṣṇava etiquette, *daivī-varṇāśrama*, and *bhāgavat-bhajana*. Most of the notable spiritual scholars of Mathurā and Vṛndāvana would invite him to speak at their assemblies, and he would also invite them to attend programs at his Maṭha.

Many Indian government officials, like the DCP (Deputy Commissioner of Police) and also many court judges, in Delhi, Bombay, Calcutta, Mathurā, and elsewhere are his disciples. Many renowned industrialists and businessmen used to regularly come to him to inquire about spiritual life and receive his blessings.

Many head *pūjārīs* throughout Vraja-maṇḍala would visit him. The head *pūjārī* of the well-known Rādhā-Govinda Mandira in Jaipur regularly arranged to bring garlands and *mahā-prasādam* from the Deities, especially on the occasions of Śrīla Mahārāja's commencement of another world tour. This is also true of the *pūjārī* of Śrī Jagannātha Mandira in Purī. The leader of all Lord Jagannātha's servants, the Dayitā-pati of Purī, also used to attend Śrīla Mahārāja's classes when he was in Purī.

For over fifty years Śrīla Nārāyaṇa Gosvāmī Mahārāja conducted Vraja-maṇḍala *parikramā*, and during that time, the heads of all the villages would come to him and pay their respects. He also engaged in organizing the renovation of many holy places in Vṛndāvana, such as Bhāṇḍīravaṭa in Bhāṇḍīravana, Kadamba-kyārī near Nandagrāma, Brahma-kuṇḍa and Surabhi-kuṇḍa in Govardhana, and Kāliya-ghāṭa in Vṛndāvana. His work in this regard is recognized by the public, the government and the press. For this and his other spiritual achievements, he was awarded the title Yuga-Ācārya by the heads of the various villages throughout Vraja-maṇḍala.

Śrīla Mahārāja also lead a Navadvīpa-dhāma *parikramā* every year at the time of Gaura-pūrṇimā. At that time he and his *sannyāsīs* were followed by over 20,000 pilgrims from Bengal, and over 2,000 other Indian and Western pilgrims. Because most of the devotees from Bengal are poor village people, they were given free facilities and *prasādam* throughout the week-long festival.

At the age of ninety years, on December 29, 2010, Śrīla Nārāyaṇa Gosvāmī Mahārāja concluded his pastimes in this world at Cakratīrtha, in Śrī Jagannātha Purī-dhāma. The following day, in Śrī Navadvīpa-dhāma, Śrī Gaurasundara's fully empowered emissary, the very embodiment of His unique compassion, was given *samādhi*. Śrīla Mahārāja has demonstrated and exemplified the unadulterated life of utter dedication and pure loving service to his Gurudeva, his *guru-paramparā*, Śrī Caitanya Mahāprabhu, and the Divine Couple, Śrī Śrī Rādhā-Kṛṣṇa. As Their intimate servitor, he illuminated the path for those who wish to discover and dive deeply into the ecstatic ocean of *rādhā-dāsyam*, service to the radiantly beautiful lotus feet of Śrī Kṛṣṇa's dearly beloved, Śrīmatī Rādhikā. He will never cease to reside in his divine instructions and in the hearts of those who are devoted to him. From his *samādhi*, he will guide the world forever.

GLOSSARY

GLOSSARY

ācārya – preceptor, one who teaches by example. One who accepts the confidential meanings of the scriptures and engages others in proper behavior, personally following that behavior himself.

anartha – *an-artha* means 'non-value;' unwanted desires, activities or habits that impede one's advancement in *bhakti*, or pure devotion for the Supreme Lord Śrī Kṛṣṇa.

antaraṅga-śakti – Śrī Kṛṣṇa's internal potency (*antaraṅga* – internal; *śakti* – potency), also known as *cit-śakti* and *svarūpa-śakti* (see *svarūpa-śakti*).

aṣṭāṅga-yoga – the eightfold *yoga* process; the *yoga* system consisting of eight parts: *yama* (control of the senses), *niyama* (control of the mind), *āsana* (bodily postures), *prāṇāyāma* (breath control), *pratyāhāra* (withdrawal of the mind from sensory perception), *dhāraṇā* (steadying the mind), *dhyāna* (meditation), and *samādhi* (deep and unbroken absorption on the Lord in the heart).

ātmā – the soul; it may also refer to the body, mind, intellect, or the Supreme Self. It usually refers to the *jīva* soul.

bābājī – a person who is absorbed in meditation, penance, and austerity; a renounced.

bahiraṅgā-śakti – the external or material potency of the Supreme Lord, also known as *māyā-śakti*. This potency is responsible for the creation of the material world and all affairs pertaining to the material world. Because the Lord never directly contacts the material energy, this potency is known as *bahiraṅgā*, external.

Baladeva or **Balarāma** – Baladeva Prabhu is the first *vaibhava-prakāśa* expansion of Śrī Kṛṣṇa. *Vaibhava-prakāśa* means that there is no difference between Them except for a difference in color: Kṛṣṇa is black and Baladeva is white.

Baladeva prabhu continuously renders service to Śrī Kṛṣṇa. This service is His all in all, whether it is in Vṛndāvana, Mathurā, or Dvārakā. Baladeva Prabhu has six kinds of expansions: From His original form as Baladeva in Vṛndāvana comes Mūla-Saṅkarṣaṇa, or root-Saṅkarṣaṇa, in Mathurā and Dvārakā. He then expands into Mahā-Saṅkarṣaṇa in Vaikuṇṭha, and next into Kāraṇodakaśāyī Viṣṇu, Garbhodakaśāyī Viṣṇu, and Kṣīrodakaśāyī Viṣṇu. Finally He expands as Śeṣa. As Śeṣa He has millions upon millions of heads (hoods), and He is holding millions upon millions of universes on his heads as if they were mustard seeds, while also taking the form of the beds on which all three *puruṣa-avatāras* (Kāraṇodakaśāyī Viṣṇu, Garbhodakaśāyī Viṣṇu, and Kṣīrodakaśāyī Viṣṇu) lie.

When Śrī Kṛṣṇa comes to this world in any of His forms, Baladeva prabhu always comes first in the form of the *dhāma*. He also comes as Kṛṣṇa's eternal associates, who manifest from Baladeva prabhu (or one of His expansions), and who accompany Him to this world for the sake of performing His pastimes. Baladeva personally comes as well, and joins into the pastimes. When Śrī Rāmacandra descends, Baladeva comes as Lakṣmaṇa, in the pastimes of Kṛṣṇa He comes as Baladeva, and in the pastimes of Mahāprabhu He comes as Nityānanda Prabhu.

Bhagavān – the Supreme Lord; the Supreme Personality of Godhead, Śrī Kṛṣṇa. The *Viṣṇu Purāṇa* (6.5.72–4) defines Bhagavān as follows: "The word *bhagavat* is used to describe the Supreme Spirit Whole, who possesses all opulence, who is completely pure and who is the cause of all causes. In the word *bhagavat*, the syllable *bha* has two meanings: one who maintains all living entities and one who is the support of all living entities. Similarly the syllable *ga* has two meanings: the creator and one who causes all living entities to obtain the results of *karma* and *jñāna*. Complete opulence, religiosity, fame, beauty, knowledge, and renunciation are known as *bhaga*, fortune." The suffix vat means possessing. Thus, one who possesses these six fortunes is known as Bhagavān.

bhakti – the primary meaning of the word *bhakti* is 'rendering service.' The performance of activities which are meant to satisfy or please the Supreme Lord Śrī Kṛṣṇa, which are performed in a favorable spirit saturated with love, which are devoid of all desires other than the desire for His benefit and pleasure, and which are not covered by *karma* and *jñāna*.

bhakti-yoga – the path of spiritual realization through devotional service to Lord Kṛṣṇa.

Bharata Mahārāja – a king of ancient India and a great devotee of the Lord. At an early age, he renounced his kingdom and family and went to a remote forest to absorb in the worship of God. He became very advanced in spiritual practice, but in the last part of his life he developed affection for a little deer. At the time of death he remembered the deer and then took birth as a deer.

Due to his previous spiritual practices, and out of Kṛṣṇa's great mercy upon him, he could remember his previous life and understand how he had fallen from his advanced position. Even as a deer he therefore remained separate from the association of family and friends, and spent his time in the hermitages of the sages, hearing topics of the Lord. In his next life, he took birth as Jaḍa Bharata in the house of a religiously devoted *brāhmaṇa*. Having achieved the human form of life again, he was very careful this time not to spoil his energy, and thus he achieved perfection.

bhāva-bhakti – the initial stage of perfection in devotion. A stage of *bhakti* in which *śuddha-sattva*, the essence of the Lord's internal potency consisting of spiritual knowledge and bliss, is transmitted into the heart of the practising devotee from the heart of the Lord's eternal associates.

It is like a ray of the sun of *prema* and it softens the heart by various tastes. It is the first sprout of pure love of God (*prema*) and is also known as *rati*. In *bhāva-bhakti*, a soul can somewhat realize love for Kṛṣṇa as well as the way in which he can serve Him. Then, after some time, divine absorption and love for Him manifests, and thus the soul attains the final stage called *prema*.

brahma – the impersonal, all-pervading feature of the Lord, which is devoid of attributes and qualities. It is also sometimes known as *brahman*.

Brahmā – the first created being in the universe. Directed by Śrī Viṣṇu, he creates all life forms in the universe and rules the mode of passion.

brāhmaṇa – the highest of the four *varṇas* (castes) in the Vedic social system called *varṇāśrama*; one who is a member of this *varṇa*, such as a priest or teacher of divine knowledge.

cit – consciousness; pure thought; knowledge; spirit; spiritual cognition or perception.

cit-śakti – the Lord's internal potency by which His transcendental pastimes are accomplished (also see *svarūpa-śakti*).

darśana – seeing, meeting, visiting or beholding, especially in regard to the Deity, a sacred place, or an exalted Vaiṣṇava.

Dvārakā – the lower part of Goloka, which is the highest realm of the spiritual world (see Goloka). Dvārakādhīśa Kṛṣṇa, the Kṛṣṇa who resides in Dvārakā, is a plenary expansion of the supremely complete Śrī Kṛṣṇa who resides in Vṛndāvana. In Dvārakā, Śrī Kṛṣṇa appears as a prince of the Yadu-dynasty and He performs many loving pastimes with His queens, who are all full expansions of His supremely complete pleasure potencies, the *gopīs*.

Ekādaśī – the eleventh day of the waxing or waning moon; the day on which devotees fast from grains and beans and certain other foodstuffs, and increase their remembrance of Śrī Kṛṣṇa and His associates.

Garbhodakaśāyī Viṣṇu – the second of three *puruṣa-avatāras* (see also *puruṣa-avatāras*). He enters each and every universe, where He lies down on the Garbha Ocean, which emanated from the perspiration of His own body. Thus, He is the Supersoul within each individual universe.

From His navel springs the stem of a lotus, and on the flower petals of that lotus Lord Brahmā, the first living entity within the universe, is born. He puts Lord Brahmā in charge of creating all the material objects and all the forms of living beings within that Universe.

Goloka – the highest realm of the spiritual world. It is divided into three sections according to the stage of *prema* of the devotees who reside there. The lower part of Goloka is called Dvārakā. Devotees in this part have some knowledge of Śrī Kṛṣṇa's opulence as Śrī Bhagavān, the Supreme Lord. In the middle part, called Mathurā, this mood of opulence, awe and reverence is still present but it is less than in Dvārakā. In the upper part of Goloka, called Vraja, Vṛndāvana, or Gokula, no one knows that Śrī Kṛṣṇa is God Himself, and the mood of sweetness (*mādhurya*) fully covers the mood of opulence (*aiśvarya*).

Goloka Vṛndāvana – the upper part of the highest realm of the spiritual world; the abode of Śrī Kṛṣṇa, where He is manifest in His original and topmost feature as a cowherd boy.

gopīs – the young cowherd maidens of Vraja, headed by Śrīmatī Rādhikā, who serve Śrī Kṛṣṇa in the mood of amorous love.

hari-kathā – narrations of the holy name, form, qualities, and pastimes of Śrī Hari (Kṛṣṇa) and His associates.

hari-nāma – the chanting of Śrī Kṛṣṇa's holy names.

Hiraṇyakaśipu – the demoniac father of a great devotee named Prahlāda Mahārāja. To protect Prahlāda, who was being severely oppressed by his father, Śrī Kṛṣṇa appeared in His half-man, half-lion *avatāra* known as Nṛsiṁhadeva, and in a ferocious mood killed the demoniac father.

In his previous life, Hiraṇyakaśipu was one of the two doorkeepers of Lord Nārāyaṇa (Jaya and Vijaya) who were cursed by the four Kumāra-brothers to take birth on Earth as demons (also see Jaya and Vijaya).

hlādinī, hlādinī-śakti – the potency relating to the bliss aspect of the Supreme Lord (also see *svarūpa-śakti*).

Janmāṣṭamī – the appearance day of Lord Śrī Kṛṣṇa, which occurs on the eighth day of the dark lunar fortnight of the month of Bhādra (August-September).

Jaya and Vijaya – two gatekeepers of the Lord in Vaikuṇṭha. Externally they were cursed by the four Kumāras for mistaking them for children and refusing them entrance. Factually this was an arrangement of the Lord to send Jaya and Vijaya to fight with Him in the material world. They became Hiraṇyākṣa and Hiraṇyakaśipu in Satya-yuga, Rāvaṇa and Kumbhakarṇa in Tretā-yuga, and Śiśupāla and Dantavakra in Dvāpara-yuga. After finishing their mock fighting, both the devotees and the Lord are again associated in the spiritual planets. No one falls from the spiritual world, or Vaikuṇṭha planet, for it is the eternal abode. But sometimes, as the Lord desires, to fulfill His purposes devotees come into this material world as preachers or as atheists. While expansions of Jaya and Vijaya came to the material world, in their original forms they never left Vaikuṇṭha.

jīva – the eternal, individual living entity, who in the conditioned state of material existence assumes material bodies of the innumerable species of life.

jīva-śakti – the potency comprised of the living entities.

jñāna – (1) knowledge in general; (2) knowledge which leads to impersonal liberation; (3) transcendental knowledge of one's relationship with Śrī Kṛṣṇa.

Kaṁsa – the demoniac ruler of Mathurā, who came to power by dethroning and imprisoning his own father, King Ugrasena. He is the brother of Devakī, and thus he is Śrī Kṛṣṇa's maternal uncle. Kaṁsa also imprisoned Devakī and her husband Vasudeva, as an aerial voice had announced that their eighth son would be the cause of Kaṁsa's death. Although Kaṁsa killed the first six sons of Devakī at birth, by the arrangement of the *yogamāyā* potency he was not able to touch Baladeva and Kṛṣṇa, who appeared as Devakī's seventh and eighth sons. Both Boys escaped the danger of child-slaughter because They were transferred to the house of Nanda Mahārāja in Vraja.

When Kaṁsa understood what had happened he started sending his demoniac companions to Vraja to kill Kṛṣṇa, but all their attempts failed: instead of Kṛṣṇa being killed by the demons, it was the demons who were killed by Kṛṣṇa and Balarāma. Finally, on the pretext of a wrestling match, Kaṁsa invited Kṛṣṇa and Balarāma to Mathurā, conspiring to kill them there. But again all the demons were defeated and killed instead. At last, Śrī Kṛṣṇa leapt onto the platform of the wrestling arena where Kaṁsa was sitting, and catching hold of his hair, threw him to the ground. Kṛṣṇa then jumped on his chest, causing his life-air to leave him. Śrī Kṛṣṇa thus wonderfully slew Kaṁsa and his associates without any effort. Kaṁsa was thus liberated by Śrī Kṛṣṇa's mercy.

Kāraṇodakaśāyī Viṣṇu – also called Mahā-Viṣṇu; the first of the three *puruṣa-avatāras* (also see *puruṣa-avatāras*), who lies on the Kāraṇa (Causal) Ocean and is the creator of the total material energy. As He breathes, innumerable universes emanate from the pores of His body. He glances over the material nature, impregnating it with the living entities. He is the original Supersoul of the entire material creation, which is the aggregate of material universes.

karma – (1) any activity performed in the course of material existence; (2) reward-seeking activities; pious activities leading to material gain in this world or in the heavenly planets after death; (3) fate; previous actions which lead to inevitable reactions.

Kṣīrodakaśāyī Viṣṇu – the third of the three *puruṣa-avatāras* (also see *puruṣa-avatāras*). Within each Universe, He enters into each and every atom of the material creation, and also into the hearts of all living entities. Thus He is known as the Supersoul of all the individual living beings and the Supersoul in all material objects.

Kumāras (Four) – the four Kumāras are named Sanaka, Sanātana, Sanandana, and Sanat. Brahmā created them in the beginning of creation, from his mind (*manaḥ*). That is why they are called Brahmā's *mānasa-putra* (sons born of his mind). Because of their profound knowledge, they were completely detached from worldly attraction, and they did not give any assistance in their father's task of creation.

Brahmā was extremely displeased with this, and he prayed to Bhagavān Śrī Hari for the welfare of his sons. Śrī Bhagavān was pleased by Brahmā's prayers, and in His Haṁsa (swan) *avatāra*, He attracted their minds away from dry impersonal knowledge to the knowledge of pure devotional service on the absolute platform. Because of this, Śanaka Ṛṣi and his brothers are known as *jñānī-bhaktas*. They are the originators of the Nimbāditya disciplic succession.

mahāmāyā – there are two kinds of *māyā* – *yogamāyā* and *mahāmāyā*. *Mahāmāyā* is a shadow expansion of *yogamāyā*. *Yogamāyā* manages the spiritual worlds, causing its residents to consider themselves in various human-like relationships with Lord Kṛṣṇa; whereas *mahāmāyā* manages the material world and bewilders the conditioned souls.

Mahā-Saṅkarṣaṇa – an expansion of Baladeva. From this expansion the eternally liberated souls who reside in Vaikuṇṭha, as well as the three Viṣṇu *puruṣa-avatāras*, are manifested (also see Mūla-Saṅkarṣana and *puruṣa-avatāras*).

Mahā-Viṣṇu – see Kāraṇodakaśāyī Viṣṇu.

māyā, māyā-śakti – the illusion-generating potency that is responsible for the manifestation of the material world, time, and material activities.

Māyāvāda – the doctrine of illusion and impersonalism; a theory advocated by the impersonalist followers of Śaṅkarācārya, which holds that the Lord's form, this material world, and the individual existence of the living entities are *māyā*, or false.

Mīmāṁsā – a philosophical doctrine which has two divisions: (1) *pūrva* or *karma-mīmāṁsā* founded by Jaiminī, which advocates that by carrying out the ritualistic *karma* of the Vedas, one can attain the celestial planets; and (2) *uttara-mīmāṁsā* founded by Bādarāyaṇa Vyāsadeva, which deals with the nature of *brahman*.

Mohinī – an incarnation of the Supreme Personality of Godhead. During the churning of the Ocean of Milk, nectar was extracted. The demons and the demigods argued over who would get it. The demigods took shelter of the Lord, and He thus appeared in the beautiful feminine form of Mohinī to bewilder the demons. Lord Śiva once asked the Lord to reveal to him His form as Mohinī-Mūrti.

Mūla-Saṅkarṣana – *mūla* means 'root;' the Saṅkarṣaṇa from whom all the other Saṅkarṣaṇa forms come. Baladeva is the original Saṅkarṣaṇa, manifest in Dvārakā as Mūla-Saṅkarṣaṇa. From Him comes Nārāyaṇa, from whom comes Maha-Saṅkarṣaṇa, from whom the three Viṣṇu *puruṣa-avatāras* manifest. In the form of Mūla-Saṅkarṣaṇa, Baladeva also manifests the eternally liberated souls who reside in Dvārakā and Mathurā.

Nārada Ṛṣi – a great sage among the *devas*; he is thus known as Devarṣi. He was born from the mind of Brahmā. He is a liberated associate of Śrī Kṛṣṇa, who travels throughout the material and spiritual worlds broadcasting His glories. In *caitanya-līlā* he appears as Śrīvāsa Paṇḍita.

Nārāyaṇa – *nāra* means 'mankind' and *ayana* means 'the shelter of' Nārāyaṇa thus means 'the shelter for mankind.' He is the opulent, four-armed expansion of the Supreme Lord Śrī Kṛṣṇa, who eternally resides in Vaikuṇṭha.

nitya-baddha – souls who have been bound by material nature since time immemorial (*nitya* – perpetually; *baddha* – bound).

nitya-mukta – eternally liberated souls (*nitya* – eternally; *mukta* – liberated).

nitya-saṁsāra – the repetition of birth, death, old age and disease.

nitya-siddha – eternally perfected devotees (*nitya* – eternally; *siddha* – perfected).

Nṛsiṁhadeva – the half-man, half-lion incarnation of Śrī Kṛṣṇa. He appeared in a ferocious mood to protect His beloved *bhakta*, Prahlāda Mahārāja, when Prahlāda was being severely oppressed by his demoniac father, Hiraṇyakaśipu.

nyāya-śāstra – the *śāstras* dealing with a logical analysis of reality. The precepts of *nyāya* are mostly explained through analogies drawn from an analysis of common objects such as a clay pot (*ghaṭa*) and a piece of cloth (*paṭa*). Thus, these words are repeatedly encountered in discussions of *nyāya*.

parama-guru – grand-spiritual master; the *guru* of one's *guru*.

Paramātmā – the Supersoul situated in the hearts of all living entities as the witness and source of remembrance, knowledge, and forgetfulness.

paramparā – the system of transmission of divine knowledge from *śrī-guru* to disciple through an unbroken chain of pure spiritual masters.

parā-śakti – Śrī Kṛṣṇa's superior, or transcendental, potency (*parā* – supreme; *śakti* – potency) (see *svarūpa-śakti*).

paratpara-guru – great-grand-spiritual master; the *guru* of one's *guru's guru*.

prema – love for Śrī Kṛṣṇa, which is extremely concentrated, which completely melts the heart, and which gives rise to a deep sense of possessiveness in relation to Him.

prema-bhakti – pure love of Lord Kṛṣṇa, the highest perfectional stage in the progressive development of pure devotional service.

puruṣa-avatāras – three plenary portion of Śrī Kṛṣṇa, known as Kāraṇodakaśāyī Viṣṇu (or Mahā-Viṣṇu), Garbhodakaśāyī Viṣṇu, and Kṣīrodakaśāyī Viṣṇu. They are the Lords of the universal creation – They are responsible for generating, maintaining, and destroying the entire material cosmos, and They are the Supersoul of everything that exists. (The word *viṣṇu* indicates 'He who is all-pervading, omnipresent.')

Rāma – a *līlā-avatāra* or pastime *avatāra* of Śrī Kṛṣṇa; He is the famous hero of the *Rāmāyaṇa*. He is also known as Rāmacandra, Raghunātha, Dāśarathi-Rāma, and Rāghava-Rāma. His father is Mahārāja Daśaratha, His mother is Kausalyā, and His wife is Sītā. He had three brothers, named Lakṣmaṇa, Bharata, and Śatrughna. The celebrated monkey Hanumān was His beloved servant and devotee. After killing the pernicious demon, Rāvaṇa, and rescuing Sītārānī with the help of the monkey army, Rāma returned to Ayodhyā and was crowned king.

rāsa-līlā – Śrī Kṛṣṇa's dance-pastime with the *vraja-gopīs*, which is a pure exchange of spiritual love between Kṛṣṇa and the *gopīs*, His most confidential servitors.

rasika – one who is expert at relishing *rasa*; a connoisseur of *rasa*.

Rāvaṇa – the ten-headed demoniac king of Laṅkā, who kidnapped Lord Rāmacandra's wife, Sītā-devī. Śrī Rāmacandra thus came to Laṅkā and killed Rāvaṇa, along with all of Rāvaṇas demon followers.

sādhana-bhakti – the practicing stage of devotion; the various spiritual disciplines performed for the satisfaction of Śrī Kṛṣṇa are undertaken through the medium of the senses for the purpose of bringing about the manifestation of *bhava-bhakti*.

sādhu – a highly realized soul, who knows life's aim.

sādhu-saṅga – the association of advanced devotees.

śākhā-candra-nyāya – the logic of showing the moon by first pointing to a tree branch where the moon is visible.

sakhī – a female friend, companion, or attendant; a *gopī* friend.

śakti – (1) power; potency; energy; (2) the Lord's potencies, which are innumerable. They are generally grouped into three categories: *antaraṅga-śakti*, the internal potency; *taṭasthā-śakti*, the marginal potency; and *bahiraṅgā-śakti*, the external potency; (3) the wife of Lord Śiva, also known as Durgā, who presides over the material energy.

sampradāya – a particular school of religious teaching; an established doctrine transmitted from one teacher to another; a line of disciplic succession.

saṁvit, saṁvit-śakti – the potency by which the Supreme Lord knows Himself and causes others to know Him (also see *svarūpa-śakti*).

sandhinī, sandhinī-śakti – the potency that maintains the spiritual existence of the Supreme Lord and His associates (also see *svarūpa-śakti*).

Saṅkarṣaṇa – see Mūla-Saṅkarṣaṇa.

sāṅkhya-yoga – that *yoga* which gives analytical knowledge about *ātmā-tattva* and *anātmā-tattva* (scientific knowledge of the soul, the Supersoul, and inert objects); the path of knowledge involving an analysis of spirit and matter.

sannyāsa – the renounced order; the fourth *āśrama*, or stage of life, in the Vedic social system called *varṇāśrama-dharma*, which organizes society into four occupational divisions (*varṇas*) and four stages of life (*āśramas*); renounced ascetic life.

śāstra – Vedic scripture.

śuddha-bhakti – pure devotion or pure devotional service; devotion which is unmixed with fruitive action or monistic knowledge, and which is devoid of all desires other than the exclusive pleasure of Kṛṣṇa; it is also known as *uttama-bhakti*.

Svarga – the celestial planets within this material universe.

svarūpa – constitutional nature; the eternal constitutional nature and identity of the self.

svarūpa-śakti – Lord Kṛṣṇa's complete, internal potency. It is called *svarūpa-śakti* because it is situated in His form, or *svarūpa*. This potency is *cinmaya*, fully conscious, and thus it is the antithesis of matter. Consequently it is also known as *cit-śakti*, potency, which embodies the principle of consciousness. Because this potency is intimately connected with the Lord, being situated in His form, it is further known as *antaraṅga-śakti*, the internal potency. Because it is superior to His marginal and external potencies both in form and glory, it is known as *parā-śakti*, the superior potency. Thus, by its qualities, this potency is known by different names – *svarūpa-śakti*, *cit-śakti*, *antaraṅga-śakti*, and *parā-śakti*.

The *svarūpa-śakti* has three divisions: (1) *sandhinī*, the potency which accommodates the spiritual existence of Kṛṣṇa and all of His associates; (2) *saṁvit*, the potency which bestows transcendental knowledge of Him; and (3) *hlādinī*, the potency by which Kṛṣṇa enjoys transcendental bliss and bestows such bliss upon His devotees (see *sandhinī*, *saṁvit*, and *hlādinī*).

taṭasthā – marginal. When there is a point on the bank of a river which is exactly on the boundary between land and water, it is called the marginal position. It may sometimes be submerged beneath the water and may sometimes be exposed to the air.

This same adjective is applied to the living entity, who is the marginal potency of Śrī Kṛṣṇa, and who may be submerged in the darkness of the material energy or may remain forever under the shelter of Kṛṣṇa's personal energy. The living entity can never remain in the marginal position, but must take shelter of the spiritual energy or be subjected to the material energy.

taṭasthā-śakti – literally: the *taṭa* (marginally) - *stha* (situated) - *śakti* (energy); the marginal energy of the Supreme Lord Śrī Kṛṣṇa in which the *jīvas* are situated. Although the *jīvas* are part and parcel of the internal energy (*cit-śakti*) of the Lord, they are subject to be overcome by the Lord's external energy, *māyā*, and be covered over. Thus they are known as *taṭasthā*, or marginal.

tattva – truth, reality, philosophical principle; the essence or substance of anything.

Tulasī – the sacred plant whose leaves and blossoms are used by Vaiṣṇavas in the worship of Śrī Kṛṣṇa; a partial expansion of Vṛndā-devī; the wood is also used for making chanting beads and neck beads.

Upaniṣads – 108 philosopical treatises that appear within the Vedic literatures.

Vaikuṇṭha – the eternal planets of the spiritual world. The majestic realm of the spiritual world, which is predominated by Lord Nārāyaṇa and His various expansions. All the residents of Vaikuṇṭha have eternal, spiritual bodies. They possess four arms and a darkish complexion like that of Bhagavān and are fully engaged in His service in pure devotional love. Their sense of intimacy with Śrī Bhagavān is somewhat hampered, however, due to their *aiśvarya-bhāva* (mood of awe and reverence). Superior to this is Goloka Vṛndāvana, the topmost planet of Śrī Kṛṣṇa, which is characterised by *mādhurya* (sweetness) and intimacy.

Vaiṣṇava – literally means one whose nature is 'of Viṣṇu', in other words, one in whose heart and mind only Viṣṇu or Kṛṣṇa resides. A devotee of Śrī Kṛṣṇa or Viṣṇu.

Vedānta – 'the conclusion of Vedic knowledge.' The Upaniṣads are the latter portion of the Vedas and the *Vedānta-sūtra* summarises the philosophy of the Upaniṣads in concise statements. Therefore Vedānta especially refers to the *Vedānta-sūtra* (see *Vedānta-sūtra*). *Śrīmad-Bhāgavatam* is considered to be the natural commentary on *Vedānta-sūtra* by the same author, Vyāsadeva. Therefore, in the opinion of the Vaiṣṇavas, *Śrīmad-Bhāgavatam* is the culmination or ripened fruit of the tree of all Vedic literature.

Vedānta-sūtra – the philosophy established by Śrīla Vyāsadeva dealing with the latter division of the Vedas. After thorough analysis of the

Upaniṣads, which comprise the latter portion of the Vedas, and the *smṛti-śāstras* which are supplements to the Upaniṣads, Vyāsadeva summarised the philosophical conclusions of those treatises in the *Vedānta-sūtra*, which is also known as *Brahma-sūtra*, *Vedānta-darśana*, and *Uttara-mīmāṁsā*.

Veṇu-gita – *veṇu* literally means 'bamboo;' it also is the name of Śrī Kṛṣṇa's bamboo flute. *Gita* means 'song.' Thus *veṇu-gita* can be translated as 'the song of the flute.' *Veṇu-gita* is the name of the Twenty-first Chapter of the Tenth Canto of *Śrīmad-Bhāgavatam*, in which the *gopīs* glorify the song of Śrī Kṛṣṇa's flute.

viṣṇu-tattva – categorical knowledge of the unlimited expansions of Viṣṇu.

Vraja – the eighty-four square mile track of land where Śrī Kṛṣṇa enacted His childhood and youthful pastimes with His cowherd friends, girl-friends, parents and well-wishers.

Vṛndāvana – 'the forest of Vṛndā;' the famous place where Śrī Kṛṣṇa enacted unlimited enchanting pastimes (see Goloka Vṛndāvana).

yajña – (1) a sacrifice in which a deity is propitiated by the chanting of prayers and *mantras* and the offering of ghee into the sacred fire; (2) any kind of intense endeavour which is directed at achieving a particular goal.

yogamāyā – the internal spiritual mystic potency of the Lord which engages in arranging and enhancing the Lord's pastimes.

BIBLIOGRAPHY

BOOKS BY ŚRĪLA BHAKTIVEDĀNTA SVĀMĪ MAHĀRĀJA

Brahma-saṁhitā
Kṛṣṇa, The Supreme Personality of Godhead
Nectar of Devotion
Nectar of Instruction
Śrī Caitanya-caritāmṛta
Śrī Īśopaniṣad
Śrīmad-Bhāgavatam

LECTURES BY ŚRĪLA BHAKTIVEDĀNTA SVĀMĪ MAHĀRĀJA

Bhagavad-gītā 2.55–58. New York, April 15, 1966
Bhagavad-gītā 4.1. Montreal, August 24, 1968
Bhagavad-gītā 2.62–72. Los Angeles, December 16, 1968
Bhagavad-gītā 2.6. London, August 6, 1973
Bhagavad-gītā 4.5. Bombay, March 25, 1974
Śrīmad-Bhāgavatam 6.1.34–39. Surat, December 19, 1970
Śrīmad-Bhāgavatam 6.1.11. New York, July 25, 1971
Śrīmad-Bhāgavatam 1.10.5. Māyāpur, June 20, 1973
Śrīmad-Bhāgavatam 7.9.30. Māyāpur, March 8, 1976
Śrīmad-Bhāgavatam 5.5.6. Vṛndāvana, October 28, 1976
Śrī Caitanya-caritāmṛta, Madhya-līlā 22.6. New York, January 8, 1967
Śrī Caitanya-caritāmṛta, Madhya-līlā 22.11–15. New York, January 9, 1967
Śrī Caitanya-caritāmṛta, Madhya-līlā 20.255–281. New York, December 17, 1966
Śrī Caitanya-caritāmṛta, Madhya-līlā 20.124–125. New York, November 26, 1966
Śrī Caitanya-caritāmṛta, Madhya-līlā 22.6. New York, January 8, 1967
Śrī Caitanya-caritāmṛta, Ādi-līlā 7.108. Francisco, February 18, 1967
What is a Guru? London, August 22, 1973
Lecture at Conway Hall. London, October 6, 1969
Lecture at St. Pascal's Franciscan Seminary. Melbourne, June 28, 1974

CONVERSATIONS WITH ŚRĪLA BHAKTIVEDĀNTA SVĀMĪ MAHĀRĀJA

Morning Walk. Toronto, June 21, 1971
Morning Walk. Los Angeles, December 6, 1973
Morning Walk. Melbourne, April 24, 1976
Room Conversation. Boston, April 27, 1969
Room Conversation. New York, April 11, 1969
Room Conversation. Bombay, January 7, 1977

LETTERS BY ŚRĪLA BHAKTIVEDĀNTA SVĀMĪ MAHĀRĀJA

Letter to Jagadīśa. Los Angeles, March 25, 1970
Letter to Rūpānuga. Los Angeles, August 8, 1969
Letter to Upendra. Tittenhurst, October 27, 1969
Letter to Upendra. Los Angeles, July 15, 1970

BOOKS BY ŚRĪLA BHAKTIVEDĀNTA NĀRĀYAṆA GOSVĀMĪ MAHĀRĀJA

Bhakti Prajñāna Keśava Gosvāmī – His Life and Precepts
Bhakti-rasāyana
Going Beyond Vaikuṇṭha
Jaiva-dharma
Secret Truths of the Bhāgavatam
Śrī Bhakti-rasāmṛta-sindhu-bindu
Śrī Śikṣāṣṭaka
Veṇu-gīta

LECTURES BY ŚRĪLA BHAKTIVEDĀNTA NĀRĀYAṆA GOSVĀMĪ MAHĀRĀJA

Inconceivable Jīva-tattva. March 29, 1993.
Whom Can You Trust? Perth, December 27, 1998.
The Origin of the Living Entity. Badger, June 2, 2000.
Lecture on *Jaiva-dharma*. Paderborn, December 12, 2001
Moon on the Branch. Paderborn, December 15, 2001.
No One Falls From the Eternal Abode. Murwillumbah, February 16, 2002.
A Map of the Worlds. Badger, June 14, 2005
The Truth of the Soul. Badger, June 15, 2005.
Defeating Māyāvāda. Houston, May 14, 2006

CONVERSATIONS WITH ŚRĪLA BHAKTIVEDĀNTA NĀRĀYAṆA GOSVĀMĪ MAHĀRĀJA

Darśana. Vṛndāvana, June, 1992.
Morning walk. Badger, June 14, 2008.
Morning walk. Venice, June 9, 2009.

BOOKS BY OTHER VAISNAVAS

Paramātma Sandharba, by Śrīla Jīva Gosvāmī
Śrī Bṛhad-bhāgavatāmṛta, by Śrīla Sanātana Gosvāmī
Vraja-vilāsa-stava, by Śrīla Raghunātha dāsa Gosvāmī

English titles published by Śrīla Bhaktivedānta Nārāyaṇa Gosvāmī Mahārāja

Arcana-dīpikā
Beyond Nīrvāṇa
Bhagavad-gītā
Bhajana-rahasya
Bhakti-rasāmṛta-sindu-bindu
Bhakti-rasāyana
Bhakti-tattva-viveka
Brahma-saṁhitā
Bṛhad-bhāgavatāmṛta (Vol. 2.1)
Butter Thief
Caitanya Mahāprabhu – The Original Form of Godhead
Camatkāra-candrikā – A Moonbeam of Complete Astonishment
Controlled by Love
Dāmodara-līlā-mādhurī
Dāmodarāṣṭakam
Discerning the True Sentiments of the Soul
Distinctive Contribution of Śrī Rūpa Gosvāmī
Essence of All Advice
Essence of Bhagavad-gītā
Eternal Function of the Soul
Fearless Prince
Five Essential Essays
Gauḍīya Gīti-guccha
Gauḍīya Vaiṣṇavism versus Sahajiyāism
Gaura-vāṇī-pracāriṇe
Gift of Śrī Caitanya Mahāprabhu
Gīta-govinda
Going Beyond Vaikuṇṭha
Gopī-gīta
Guru-devatātmā
Happiness in a Fool's Paradise
Harināma Mahā-mantra
Harmony
Hidden Path of Devotion
Impressions of Bhakti
Jaiva-dharma
Journey of the Soul
Letters From America
Maharṣi Durvāsā and Śrī Durvāsā-āśrama
Manaḥ-śikṣa
My Śikṣā-guru and Priya-bandhu
Navadvīpa-dhāma Māhātmya
Navadvīpa-dhāma Parikramā
Nectar of Govinda-līlā
Origin of Ratha-yātrā
Our Eternal Nature
Our Gurus: One in Siddhanta, One at Heart
Ours Lasting Relationship
Pinnacle of Devotion
Prabandhāvalī
Prema-sampuṭa
Rādhā-kṛṣṇa-gaṇoddeśa-dīpikā
Rāga-vartma-candrikā
Rāya Rāmānanda Saṁvāda
Saṅkalpa-kalpadrumaḥ
Secrets of the Undiscovered Self
Secret Truths of the Bhāgavatam
Shower of Love
Śikṣāṣṭaka
Śiva-tattva
Ślokāmṛtam
Ślokāmṛtam-bindu
Soul of Book Distribution
Śrī Śrīmad Bhakti Prajñāna Keśava Gosvāmī – His Life and Teachings
To Be Controlled by Love
True Conception of Guru-tattva
Ujjvala-nīlamaṇi-kiraṇa
Upadeśāmṛta
Utkalikā-vallarī
Vaiṣṇava-siddhānta-mālā
Veṇu-gīta
Śrī Vraja-maṇḍala Parikramā
Walking with a Saint (2007, 2008, 2009, 2010)
Way of Love
Rays of the Harmonist (periodical)

Worldwide Centers & Contacts

Please contact us at the address stamped or written on the first page of this book, or at the listings below:

WORLD WIDE

www.purebhakti.com/contact-us/centers-mainmenu-60.html

INDIA

Mathura: *Shri Keshavaji Gaudiya Math* – Jawahar Hata, U.P. 281001 (Opp. Dist. Hospital), Email: mathuramath@gmail.com • **New Delhi**: *Shri Raman-vihari Gaudiya Math* – Block B-3, Janakpuri, New Delhi 110058 (Near musical fountain park), Tel: 9810192540; *Karol Bagh Centre*: Rohini-nandana dasa, 9A/39 Channa Market, WEA, Karol Bagh, Tel: 9810398406, 9810636370, Email: purebhakti.kb@gmail.com • **Vrindavan**: *Shri Rupa-Sanatana Gaudiya Math* – Dan Gali, U.P. Tel: 09760952435; *Gopinath Bhavan* – Parikrama Marga (next to Imli-tala), Seva Kunja, Vrindavan 281121, U.P., Email: vasantidasi@gmail.com • **Puri**: *Jay Shri Damodar Gaudiya Math* – Sea Palace, Chakratirtha Road. Tel: 06752-223375 • **Bangalore**: *Shri Madan Mohan Gaudiya Math* – 245/1 29th Cross, Kaggadasa pura Balaji layout, Bangalore-93, Tel: 08904427754, Email: bvvaikhanas@gmail.com; *Shri Ranganath Gaudiya Math* – Hesaraghatta, Bangalore, Tel: 09379447895, 07829378386 • **Faridabad**: *Shri Radha Madhav Gaudiya Math* – 293, Sector-14, Hariyana, Tel: 09911283869 • **Navadvipa**: *Shri Shri Keshavaji Gaudiya Math* – Kolerdanga Lane, Nadiya, Bengal, Tel: 09153125442

AUSTRALIA

Garden Ashram – Akhileshvari dasi, Tel: 612 66795916, Email: akhileshvari.dasi@gmail.com • *Shri Gaura Narayan Gaudiya Math* – Brisbane, Queensland, Tel: +61 403 993 746, Email: bhaktibrisbane2010@gmail.com

CHINA / HONG KONG

15A, Hillview Court, 30 Hillwood Road, Tsim Sha Tsui, Kowloon, Tel: +85223774603

UNITED KINGDOM & IRELAND

Birmingham: *Shri Gour Govinda Gaudiya Math* – 9 Clarence Road, Handsworth, Birmingham, B21 0ED, U. K., Tel: (44) 121551-7729, Email: bvashram108@gmail.com • **London**: *Shri Gangamata Gaudiya Math* – 631 Forest Road, E17 4NE London, Tel: 02080578406, Email: gangamatas@hotmail.com • **Galway**: *Family Centre* – Tel: 353 85-1548200, Email: jagannathchild@gmail.com

USA

Gaudiya Vedanta Publications Offices – Tel: (800) 681-3040 ext. 108, Email: orders@bhaktiprojects.org • **Alachua:** *Shri Shri Radha-Govinda Mandir* – Tel: (1) 386-462-2682. Email: yourbvgi@gmail.com, Website: www.bvgi.org • **Houston:** *Shri Govindaji Gaudiya Math* – Tel: (1) 281-650-8689. Email: info@sggm.org, Website: www.sggm.org

For further information, please visit our websites

www.purebhakti.com
for news, updates, and free downloads of books and lectures

www.harikatha.com
to receive, by email, the lectures and videos of Śrīla Bhaktivedānta Nārāyaṇa Gosvāmī Mahārāja on his world tours

www.purebhakti.tv
to watch and hear, or to download, classes online

Or write our correspondence secretary at:

connectwithussoon@gmail.com

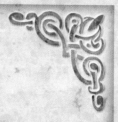

Tattva-siddhānta
(Conclusive Truth)

kṛṣṇa bhuli' sei jīva anādi-bahirmukha
ataeva māyā tāre deya saṁsāra-duḥkha
(*Śrī Caitanya-caritāmṛta, Madhya-līlā* 20.117)

The *jīva* who has forgotten Kṛṣṇa has been preoccupied with the external potency since a time without beginning. Consequently, Kṛṣṇa's illusory potency, *māyā*, gives him misery in the form of material existence.

The words *kṛṣṇa bhuli* in the above-mentioned verse apparently mean 'forgetting Kṛṣṇa,' but what is the deeper understanding? Does it mean that the *jīva* was once engaged in Kṛṣṇa's service in His spiritual abode, and has now forgotten that service? The intended meaning is very different.

What is the harm in believing that this verse confirms the *jīva's* previous residence in Goloka and his falldown from there to the material world? The harm is this: If it is possible to fall from the spiritual world, if one were vulnerable there, then what use would it be to engage in spiritual practices (*sādhana*) and devotional absorption (*bhajana*) for attainment of that abode? If, by the performance of *bhajana* one attains the spiritual world and later falls back to the material world, what would be the use of endeavoring with great determination to reach there? There would be no use; it would be better to stay here in the material world.

Moreover, the idea of the *jīvas'* fall-down from Goloka Vṛndāvana suggests that the deluding material potency also exists there.

The idea that *māyā* is present in Goloka implies that even Śrī Kṛṣṇa's cowherd friends like Sudāmā, Śrīdāmā, and Madhumaṅgala, His parents Mother Yaśodā and Nanda Bābā, and all the *gopīs* including Śrīmatī Rādhikā may also forget Kṛṣṇa and fall down from there. But it is not possible for them to forget Kṛṣṇa.

Here, by the influence of the material energy, we have a certain vocabulary and we use certain words like *kṛṣṇa bhuli*, meaning 'forgetting Kṛṣṇa.' We can purify our understanding of those words by performing *sādhana-bhajana*. We cannot understand spiritual topics through words alone because, as mentioned above, mundane language does not extend beyond matter. Nevertheless language is our tool for expression, and therefore we require the help of pure devotees to assist us in comprehending it.

(Quoted from Chapters Four and Five of *Journey of the Soul*)

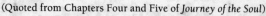